The Hidden
Professoriate

The Hidden Professoriate

CREDENTIALISM, PROFESSIONALISM, AND THE TENURE CRISIS

edited by ARTHUR S. WILKE

CONTRIBUTIONS IN SOCIOLOGY, NUMBER 29

GREENWOOD PRESS
WESTPORT, CONNECTICUT • LONDON, ENGLAND

Library of Congress Cataloging in Publication Data
Main entry under title:
The Hidden professoriate.

(Contributions in sociology; no. 29 ISSN 0084-9278)
Bibliography: p.
Includes index.
1. College teachers—Tenure—United States.
2. Higher education and state—United States.
3. Sociologists—United States. I. Wilke, Arthur S.
II. Title.
LB2335.7.H5 378.1′22 77-84774
ISBN 0-8371-9886-0

Library of Congress Catalog Card Number: 77-84774
ISBN: 0-8371-9886-0
ISSN: 0084-9278

First published in 1979

Greenwood Press, Inc.
51 Riverside Avenue, Westport, Connecticut 06880

Printed in the United States of America

10 9 8 7 6 5 4 3 2 1

For Arthur and Kate Wilke
and Ewald Fust

Contents

Tables

Preface

In the 1960s, higher education was, in the language of economics, a growth industry. Degree enrollments more than doubled, and the number of higher education facilities increased by one-fifth. Capturing the spirit of the decade was an editorial note in the Fall 1964 issue of *Daedalus* entitled "The Contemporary University: USA." It read: "This issue of *Daedalus* appears when the American university is being treated with ever increasing seriousness as a vital national resource." A decade later, the same journal devoted two issues, Fall 1974 and Winter 1975, to the less than optimistic theme, "American Higher Education: Toward an Uncertain Future."

Part of the optimism of the 1960s flowed from the great Western idea that education should be an instrument for social justice. But as controversies over such issues as war and human rights became dramatized, the resources of higher education were found to be meager. A counter-cultural movement highlighted the vulnerabilities, and the economic recession of the 1970s revealed an even more precarious set of circumstances. As a result, this great idea has had some negative consequences. Among them are:

1. The crowding of individuals, including women and minorities, into institutions of higher learning at a time when jobs for them are evaporating. This could create an educated lumpenproletariat.
2. The abuse of graduate students under the conflicting pressures of credentialism, professionalism, and genuine education.
3. The conflicting pressures of teaching and professionalism on the younger staff members.

4. The massive assault on the tenure system and the tendency to create a stratum of educational untouchables at the bottom of the heap condemned to do the dirty work of teaching but largely denied the awards of respectable salary and tenure.

5. The pressures to publish or perish.

In the process, we are witnessing a dramatic but relatively unnoticed structural transformation of higher education: the emergence of a quasi-closed elite at the top and a permanent underprivileged stratum of untouchables at the bottom.

This work addresses some of the predicaments that graduate students and young or minority status (e.g., female) professors are experiencing as a result of these circumstances. Like nontenured, probationary faculty, graduate or advanced-standing students can serve as a barometer of academic life. Changes in the academic environment are mirrored in shifts in the conditions for their success or failure, in the kinds of salient professional roles they can emulate profitably, and even, in some instances, in the dominant intellectual emphases they find are being forwarded. In addition, many advanced students may discover that the imperatives of bureaucratic education, such as the demand for the growth and survival of a specific academic program, are antithetical to the realization of their personal ambitions. Despite academic success, the individual may be plunged into unemployment or underemployment, or if an academic position is secured, the person may face intense competition as he or she tries to escape the stratum of academic untouchables who have temporary and probationary positions in the academic hierarchy.

The Introduction presents a general discussion of the state of higher education in the 1970s. It also covers, through case studies, the peculiar situation of graduate students. Part I contains case studies focusing on faculty and the growing tenure crisis; and Part II discusses the consequences of the tenure crisis.

All of the case studies in this volume are true. Pseudonyms are used for all principals and the institutions involved. These case studies draw attention to the ambiguities and conflicts associated with the changing face of higher education in the 1970s. The studies deal principally with the policies and procedures affecting graduate students and nontenured faculty. Often those who are affected by these policies and procedures find they do not know what the policies are, how to find out about them, or how they are changed or administered. In some instances, the policies and procedures are deployed in a Humpty-Dumpty fashion, by those in power positions. In other instances, they are forged in the midst of controversy surrounding a particular student or faculty member.

The developments portrayed here are endemic to large segments of American academic life; they do not simply affect those singled out in these pages or persons with similar career experiences. For any time a policy or procedure is enunciated or deployed, expectations arise which affect the assessment of all students and faculty, although among the faculty the nontenured will feel the most immediate effects. Increasingly, expectations take on formalized characteristics. As contentions deepen in an academic environment, these formalized expectations are instituted, in order to reduce ambiguity and facilitate administrative decisions regarding academic personnel.

The significance of this growing formalization in higher education is hotly debated. The adherents of formalization argue that it should create a healthier competitive climate, one in which merit is the guiding principle. The detractors suggest that formalization can have chilling effects. Rather than promoting merit, it can create mediocrity, forcing attention to be directed less to outcomes than to whether a particular policy is easiy administered. Harried administrators, this side argues, will select personnel who will easily accede to new, often cumbersome rules. Such persons, it is suggested, will be docile, accepting the rewards of academic life as grateful servants and suffering disappointments in quiet despair.

The case studies in this volume represent the actual experiences of some individuals who have been directly involved in the convulsions shaking higher education today. Their experience does not imbue them with more or, necessarily, less merit than the multitude of graduate students and faculty who never have to live through such events. However, because of the growth of such controversies and because of the changing nature of procedures and laws affecting higher education, these case studies serve, in Max Weber's terms, as ideal types. They are conditions that can be taken as crucial barometers measuring the organizational climate of higher education.

Further, if a dispassionate view is given to these case studies, the circumstances and people portrayed suggest, as Albert Camus has, that in many problematic encounters, the determination of victims and executioners may be difficult. Many of the principals are neither exclusively victims nor exclusively executioners, but are rather inextricably tied together as both victims and executioners. But in defense of those immediate victims, the graduate students and faculty members whose experiences are dealt with at some length, their circumstances and often their actions resulted in the uncovering of abuses that would otherwise have remained hidden.

The cases presented here are not intended to be representative of all categories of persons experiencing conflicts in higher education. They are centered principally in the social sciences. The social sciences, in particular sociology, are well suited as exemplars inasmuch as a significant proportion of people with post-bachelor degrees in these fields are employed in the academic community. Their identity and survival are intertwined with the fate of higher education. Furthermore, more politicization is expected in the social sciences, in part because of their close relationship to the ideological dimensions of education. Not only have the social sciences often been in the forefront in promoting higher education as a vehicle of social justice in the United States, but also they have been among the first to politicize their resistance to numerous national, local, and institutional policies. In the Vietnam conflict, local segregation practices, and retrenchment efforts, for example, academic social scientists and their students have been viewed as an enclave of dissidence. This does not mean that such concerns and questions are critical to most social scientists, only that there is a greater likelihood of politicized expression in these ranks. Neither does this mean that social scientists are necessarily more altruistic. Many who have resorted to political resistance in the current challenges facing higher education were mute when similar disasters affected the humanities and engineering in the past.

Nor are the cases representative of all segments of graduate students and nontenured faculty. Conspicuously absent are situations in which major theoretical and ideological disputes have been critical. While such cases are important, in many ways they are more difficult to explore. They often combine the mobilization of adversary positions derived not only from the immediate conflict, but from intellectual and ideological positions as well. Hence, they have not been included. This work also excludes cases involving traditional conflicts such as matters of academic freedom and cases hinging on some of the unique issues surrounding affirmative action, the development of special academic programs, and similar circumstances. Each of these could constitute independent volumes.

Acknowledgments

Many people contributed to the completion of this project. Among them are Todd Hanson, Virginia Norman, R. Joseph Rude, and Thomas J. O'Leary. Each provided me with insights into various facets of academic organization and life that either confirmed previous views or extended my understanding. Their contributions have aided me in gaining confidence regarding the importance of telling the story of some of the current struggles engaged in by embattled academics. Among my congenial colleagues and former colleagues, four are recognized as providing support and encouragement for undertaking and continuing with this project: Alfredo Mirandé, Aqueil Ahmad, Fran French, and Raj P. Mohan. Each has shown me some of the rich and various facets of professional life that make both teaching and research especially worthwhile endeavors.

A special thanks is owed Don Martindale for his enthusiasm and active encouragement of this project in its early stages. Also, the assistance of Amelia Johnson and T. Tilson is acknowledged. Their clerical assistance, along with their taking over many other burdensome chores, made working on this project much easier.

There are few words to express the debt of gratitude owed to Barbara, my wife, and to Erik and James, my sons. Barbara's active encouragement and flashing insights, Erik's continual testimony to causes of social justice, and James' testimony on the effects of public life on the individual have sustained this project, giving me an intense, and quite personal, commitment to the issues addressed in this volume.

The Nation magazine is acknowledged for its publication of an earlier version of Chapter 2 by Paul Blumberg: "Lockouts, Layoffs, and the New Academic Proletariat." Published originally as "Status Is Not Power: The New Academic Proletariat," it appeared in *The Nation*, August 14-21, 1976. Also acknowledged is the *International Journal of Contemporary Sociology*, Raj P. Mohan, editor, for permission to reprint Don Martindale's, "Sociology's Students and Teachers," which appeared in Volume 13, Nos. 3-4 (July/October 1976), pp. 183-208.

Finally, the editors of Greenwood Press are thanked for their painstaking efforts in editing the manuscript and making numerous suggestions. The final responsibilities for the manuscript, however, remain with me and the contributors.

The Hidden Professoriate

Introduction

The emergence of higher education as a commonplace in American life is a recent development. Prior to World War II, for example, higher education was of limited significance. Few individuals viewed it as a necessity, and fewer regularly planned for higher education for themselves or their children. It was not within the realm of general social expectations and thus was not as universal as it is today.[1] Furthermore, those who held command posts in business and government were less likely to view higher education as a weapon deployed from an arsenal committed to advancing peaceful social change.

The close of World War II was a watershed in the history of American higher education. With the GI Bill, enacted at the end of the war, American higher education was transformed from a particularistic, elite-oriented system to a universalistic, mass-oriented one. When the GI Bill was passed, higher education was enlisted on a national scale in the cause of social justice. Those who were regarded as having sacrificed themselves in the national interest were awarded the benefits of subsidized higher education without consideration of social origins. If persons met academic requirements and had been in military service, they were entitled to financial support.

The effects of the GI Bill were dramatic. Higher educational institutions grew significantly, and the character of many changed. An older, more socially experienced, and more diverse student body came to dominate many campuses. And most important, numerous individuals for whom higher education had once been only a dream obtained degrees and, with degrees in hand, launched upon very successful careers.

The success of many ex-GIs both in higher education and in their careers gave support to the sociological truism that economic and educational success are related. For years social scientists had shown that education and occupational status are highly correlated and that education and occupational status seem to account for the kinds of beliefs people hold, their life expectancies, and the success or failure of their children.[2] Not only did the GI Bill provide a test of this general idea, but more important, it reflected a social-engineering mentality that had been cultivated over several generations. The correlation between education and occupational status was seen increasingly, both within and outside sociological ranks, as a causal relationship: the more education a person has, the greater that person's economic success. In order to increase the number of successful people in a community, it was believed, opportunities for greater participation in education, particularly higher education, had to be provided. This argument was particularly compelling to the postwar leadership of the United States. Larger and larger sums of money were earmarked for higher education. By the mid-1970s, with annual enrollments hovering around 10 million, the national outlay for higher education surpassed $35 billion annually.

The assumed connection between education and occupational status and, in particular, the effort to translate the correlational relationship into programs that are relevant to individual people are suspect. They reflect the common confusion between statistical correlations and causal relationships along with the unwarranted view that categorical relationships can be translated into personal strategies. In the aftermath of World War II little attention, however, was given to these suspicious claims. Analysts and policy makers seemed content to maintain uncritically that there *was* a direct relationship between increased educational opportunities and increased occupational success, and the commitment to upward mobility, or what one pundit has described as "upward skidding," was reinforced.

Increasing opportunities for higher education in order to increase upward mobility resulted in a puzzling concept of social justice, however. Social justice was tied to expanded opportunities for upward social mobility, but for such a program to be effective there still had to be a lower stratum. Otherwise, the measure of personal and programmatic success would flounder. This aspect of the situation would be stressed only much later, however, during the 1960s and 1970s. For the period immediately after World War II, higher education was established as a template for change and social justice.

Only with the convulsive experiences of the 1960s, such as the demonstrations against the Vietnam conflict, and the depression-inflation of the 1970s, has there been some rethinking about the relationship between education and occupation. Why has it taken more than a decade to question some of the presuppositions regarding the role higher education can play in individual and community affairs? Several reasons can be suggested. First, those with a higher education were highly successful in the years immediately following the war because American economic life was booming. American business enjoyed both domestic and international superiority. The war-ravaged economies of Western Europe and Japan had major rebuilding to do before they could return to their competitive, prewar positions. Second, business sought trained personnel from the nation's campuses, as had both government and business before the war, particularly from the professional schools such as the law, medical, and engineering schools. Inspired by the success of the professional schools, numerous other disciplines began to copy them, simultaneously promoting a demand for their services while beginning to forge some idea of controlling credentials. The growth of the Ph.D. as a prerequisite for teaching positions in higher education was fostered in many fields. As a result, an already growing educational establishment was inflated. More graduate degrees had to be turned out to meet the growing demand, and such efforts involved the expanding of graduate programs, particularly at the Ph.D. level.

Third, as the need for higher education increased, growing numbers of people came to include a higher education in their general expectations. Less than a generation after the GI bills of World War II and the Korean War had paved the way for this cultural transformation, an explosive ingredient was added: the coming of age of those born during the postwar baby boom. by the early 1960s an unprecedented number of young adults sought a college education.

Fourth, accompanying the increase in the proportion of youth was a transformation of American economic life. The traditional economic opportunities found in industry no longer dominated economic life after the war. From 1950 to 1975 those employed in manufacturing industries decreased from one-third to one-fifth of the nation's labor force. Although employment in wholesale and retail trade and contract construction showed moderate gains in that period, employment in transportation exhibited little gain, and mining not only lost its rank in the proportion of the labor force it employed but also lost its rank in absolute numbers. Simultaneously, employment in the service and government sectors increased dramatically. In 1950, these sectors provided opportunities for less than one-fourth of the labor force in nonagricultural establishments; in 1975, they accounted for nearly 37 percent.[3] Universities and colleges facilitated these transformations, and their growth assisted in expanding employment in the public sector.

Fifth, it was not until the 1960s that organized support of the civil rights and antiwar movements began to make its presence felt on the nation's campuses. Colleges and universities began to embrace the expansion of educational opportunity for minorities, sometimes reluctantly and simply as a response to mounting political pressures from both local communities and the federal government.

By the early 1970s, the glow that had been lighted in the cause of social justice began to dim. Higher education's efforts to expand educational opportunity seemed more fragmented, and community life was in disarray. Not only did a war-weary nation become less interested in many of the programs for social justice, both within higher education and without, but the financial capacities of the economy were eroded. The Vietnam conflict had extracted a heavy toll. So too did the resurgence of the foreign business community, which challenged American business both domestically and internationally. As the 1970s unfolded, the role of education in community affairs was beginning to be doubted. Going to college did not guarantee a job for a graduate. Obtaining a Ph.D. did not lead to numerous job opportunities. And too there emerged the distinct possibility that the upper limit of college enrollment was or would be soon reached. For the first time in nearly a generation, higher education had to compete aggressively for public service dollars.

Meanwhile, extramural sources of support in the forms of special programs and grants became more difficult to obtain while the competition for them increased. The strain on higher education's administrations, as they faced high overhead, competition for needed dollars, and inflation, became intense.

One area in which this strain is particularly acute is that of staffing. To appreciate this problem, we need to pay some attention to the nature of higher education personnel. Professors are not only ranked according to a general system of merit as professors, associate professors, and assistant professors, but they are also ranked as tenured and nontenured. In most instances, tenure is awarded professors who (1) have taught successfully for seven years, three at the institution where they are seeking tenure, (2) have the highest academic degree recognized in their field, and (3) are recommended by tenured colleagues with the concurrence of specifically identified committees and persons within the college or university. Tenure does not provide an absolute job guarantee, but it does protect the faculty member from arbitrary dismissal. Tenured persons will not be dismissed unless there is a clear financial exigency or hardship requiring the dismantling of an academic program or there is some type of professional malfeasance and due process has been followed.

Tenure is principally a procedural right given to a faculty person. It provides an individual with some standing within both an institution and the courts. Tenure is not an automatic guarantee that all parties will adhere strictly to the provisions of the tenure system, but it has, with the assistance of faculty organizations such as the American Association of University Professors, provided some power that can be exercised in behalf of an individual professor.

The effect of tenure on administrators and faculty concerned with the staffing of colleges and universities is to reduce an area of flexible decision-making. This reduction is particularly acute today where there is intense pressure to obtain tenure. In recent years, the proportion of faculty having tenure (recently called "tenure density" in administrative circles) has increased. Meanwhile, the pool of persons with credentials for teaching positions has increased. There is growing concern over awarding tenure, not only because of the long-term financial commitments implied if large numbers of faculty are tenured, but because many academic programs may, it is argued, appreciably suffer if newly trained talent does not come to infuse a department or program. Furthermore, in some areas of basic research, such as chemistry and physics, there is growing concern that if talented young Ph.D.'s cannot find suitable employment, the source of new and innovative ideas may shrink. It is not uncommon in such fields to find significant theoretical breakthroughs made by people under thirty.

American higher education is not monolithic. There are, as noted in Chapter 1, different types of institutions, and they respond somewhat differently to the current crises in higher education. These differential responses are manifested in the treatment of nontenured faculty, of whom many become recruits to a ragtag type of academic Coxey's Army identified as "the hidden professoriate."

The idea of a hidden professoriate provides a conceptual means for examining recent developments in higher education. Although the majority in higher education (frequently these are the tenured faculty in most colleges and universities), never become part of the hidden professoriate, the concept directs attention to the changing policies and procedures in higher education. Furthermore, it lays the basis for treating the cases in this and the following section in terms of deviant case analysis.[4]

Deviant case analysis, as the term indicates, is the examination of nonconforming conditions or circumstances. Such conditions or circumstances are critical because they are often the arena for intense controversy, controversy that may result in changes in, and development of, critical rules of procedure and assessment. The deviant case is not to be considered in opposition to the "normal" case. The "normal" case does not, for practical purposes, exist, although many faculty members do not find themselves in conflict with their administrations, at least not overtly.

In the wake of the strains in higher education, however, numerous institutions have instituted new policies and procedures for awarding tenure. Most schools now appoint new faculty to either probationary, tenure-track positions or temporary, nontenure-track positions. Indefinite appointments, wherein a faculty member can serve with commendation for many years and still be denied tenure, are increasingly rare. Under these new conditions, however, many new appointees are chagrined to find that what they thought was a tenure-track appointment is, in reality, a temporary appointment. Meanwhile the professional accomplishments of those with a probationary status are increasingly measured by such indices as the quantity and quality (as indicated by appearance in prestige journals) of publications and scores on students' evaluations of teaching. There is still much latitude in the weighting of research, teaching, and public service, and the vulnerable faculty member should try to be above average on these evaluation schema, though such a rating is not, in itself, a guarantee that tenure will be awarded. Many colleges and universities have increased their efforts to communicate expectations and revised the tenure-review process, making it more formal and instituting formal, annual reviews. Those appointed to reviewing committees are more representative of the faculty at large, and in some instances due-process procedures, as well as appeal and grievance procedures, have been extended to probationary faculty. Though there are wide variations among institutions and informal systems of evaluation do remain, formal systems of procedures are expanding.

These new systems constitute changes in the salient norms or rules in particular colleges and universities, and as a result expectations are changing. Although these changes may not result in dramatic modifications in the day-to-day behavior of many professors, new systems of accountability can introduce new strains in an already stressful environment. Questions of merit, as well as the conditions for merit, may undergo rapid change. One year faculty teaching may be emphasized, the next, research, and the next, public service. While faculty are not solidly behind each administrative change, the structure of higher education is, nevertheless, undergoing transformation on a regular basis.

Deviant case analysis highlights the way some of the structural transformations in higher education proceed. The procedure is more informative than polling a random sample of faculty who find themselves struggling in a world of competing and changing demands. In many instances, faculty members may be unaware of the significance that the issues involving recruits for the hidden professoriate have, over the long term, for higher education.

Centralized administration has grown in higher education since the close of World War II, a situation that has intensified in recent years. Although individual departments still have a great deal of autonomy in setting up curriculums, increased administrative attention and expertise is needed for personnel, legal, financial, and maintenance concerns. The overall character of an institution's personnel is more critical to the administration than to individual departments. The various rules regarding personnel, funding, and research procedures, for example, are handled by the administration, as are the continuing efforts to sustain adequate levels of funding and to maintain the physical plant and administrative organizations. When controversies requiring the formulation of new procedures arise, the administration often expends resources to be in compliance with various public laws or at least to be in a position where they will not be vulnerable to outside challenge.

The growth of centralized administration has resulted in intense internal competition for funds between faculty and administrators. Furthermore, given the depressed market for academic personnel, combined with the decline in the growth rate of academic institutions, many faculty members experience a degree of relative deprivation. That is, compared to the many professional opportunities and high salary expectations of just a few years ago, some find the prospects of less professional mobility and lower salaries depriving. When this relative deprivation is combined with structural changes resulting from changes in personnel policies, a broad-based dissatisfaction is frequently detected. In some instances, as at the City University of New York (noted in Chapter 2), there is far more than dissatisfaction; there can be loss of jobs. These circumstances may lead, suggests David Riesman, to the distinct possibility that, in at least the public sector of higher education, the union movement will find a hospitable audience.[5] Whether such developments foretell new opportunities or disasters is not our immediate concern. It is sufficient to note that they do constitute historic changes that translate into changes in the organization of higher education. Concomitant with these changes are alterations in the ideas and ideals associated with higher education, changes that can be witnessed in the expectations and hopes not only of faculty but also of students, parents, and citizens.

In Chapter 2, Paul Blumberg describes some of the developments that are giving rise not only to the growth of discontent among some college and university faculty but also to the growth of the hidden professoriate. He details how the storm signals regarding staffing requirements were apparent over a decade ago, yet nothing was done to respond to these signals. The failure to respond is traced partly to organizational features of higher education, features not unique to this sector of American life. When a continual imperative for growth exists in a highly competitive context, it is difficult to rein in the various contending forces. Moreover, higher education is intricately tied to other features of community life, as Blumberg's discussion of the fate of CUNY reveals. By the mid-1970s, the CUNY system not only faced the strains of over a decade of unbridled expansion, but it also suffered from its link to the financial fortunes of New York City. Once the city's financial house of cards was exposed and austerity programs were introduced, the university was a vulnerable target. Except for the response of the faculty, the students and some of the laid-off personnel, the response when CUNY closed because it could not meet its payroll was not remarkable. When an institution the size of CUNY can terminate business without a significant public outcry, there emerges concern as to how legitimate such an educational system is. For defenders of higher education, there is seldom a question of legitimacy. However, once the fate of higher education can be treated like any other commodity in a boom or bust economy, its value is significantly lessened.

Blumberg graphically describes the careers of people who have ended up in the hidden professoriate or are valiantly attempting to stave off this fate. Their efforts, combined with the general devaluation of higher education, foretell the creation of different intellectual strategies in which obtaining knowledge and pursuing truth are easily sacrificed to the imperatives of personal survival. The emergence of an entrepreneurial, opportunistic approach to the intellectual life on the part of many academics can change the role of higher education in American culture.

Among the disciplines serving as barometers of the fortunes and misfortunes of post-World War II higher education are the social sciences, particularly sociology. Sociology is an academic bellwether, a point amplified in Chapter 3 by Don Martindale. Martindale's essay examines the changing circumstances of academic sociology—a discipline he describes as one in search of itself—and also provides a foundation for considering many of the case studies in sociology and other social science departments. He highlights the cultural contradictions of a discipline which, on the one hand, is wedded to students for survival but on the other hand, in the growth of the large bureaucratic educational system, is increasingly dedicating itself to research. As is characteristic of Martindale's work,[6] his understanding of bureaucratic affairs is wedded to a continued awareness of, and sensitivity to, biography.

The changing political milieu of academic life, especially in the social sciences, is depicted by Sil Dong Kim in Chapter 4. During the 1960s, when the nation's higher educational system was rocked by numerous social movements, and the possibility arose that the period of unbridled growth, discussed by Blumberg, might end, there were convulsive responses to this imminent decline in many departments.

One of the classic confrontations of the period was revealed in the Department of Political Science at Midwest University. In this confrontation the political issues gravitated around two different orientations towards the study of human affairs, the qualitative and the quantitative. The hapless graduate student Kim describes, Ri Sing Moon, was caught up in numerous departmental conflicts. A Korean, Moon had to struggle with a new culture as well as with the crucial conflicts involving his major professor and an ex-chairperson. Because he remained loyal to his traditional value orientations, he was not responsive to the various efforts to radically transform the department's orientation and discredit his advisor. In a sense, he became a "marked man," and an easy target for those who were systematically attempting to transform the political science program at Midwest. Moon was able to garner some support, and as his story unfolds, a trail of questionable practices and procedures emerges.

Moon's case indicates the existence of intellectual "fads and foibles," as the late sociologist Pitirim A. Sorokin labeled them, and the abrupt and devastating changes they can lead to. Academics live within sections of the educational institution, and their responses are governed by individual concerns, as Martindale notes, as well as by the unfolding opportunities for career development.

At Midwest, for example, the quantitative approach to political science emerged as the dominant intellectual orientation at the expense of the more reflective, value-sensitive approach that had initially interested Moon and prompted him to enroll at Midwest. Quantitative emphases in the social sciences have long been adjuncts to bureaucratic organizations. In the public sector quantitative approaches have harmonized with and underwritten growing administrative concerns expressed in such key words as "accountability," "performance testing," and "evaluation research." Midwest University was not immune to this growing interest in the quantitative, both within and outside of the university, and the Department of Political Science adjusted accordingly. Sacrificed in the process were the idea of the university as an intellectual citadel and a belief in the promotion of knowledge through argumentation and disputation.

The administration of Midwest, however, did not execute the program changes, nor did it direct people to treat students in the fashion Ri Sing Moon was treated. Rather, a segment of the faculty was responsible. Thus, any portrait of higher education must continually be mindful that the competing interests of faculty too can set in motion conditions for the hidden professoriate. Meanwhile, students who benefited under the new program, who may even have enlisted to discredit the emphasis of the old program and its staff, have come to learn some lessons of academic survival that may ill-equip them for confronting the general challenges to higher education that Blumberg outlines in Chapter 2. Their first responses to academic crisis may well be to initiate self-aggrandizing strategies and seek favor from those believed to have power. Perhaps such self-serving attitudes account for the lack of a developed political base representing faculty interests in the nation's colleges and universities. In any case, such strategies may have less and less salience in the coming decade as opportunities for program redevelopment decrease, and even the most opportunistic may find themselves threatened by membership in the hidden professoriate.

Another deviant case analysis, Chapter 5, "Due Process," focuses on some structural features of a law school. This case details the attempts of one student, Dennis Russell, to mount an appeal for reentry into law school after he was dismissed for poor academic performance. The case focuses on a struggle between two contesting principles of legal-bureaucratic processes: due process versus social control.[7] Russell, fired by the raging controversies of the 1960s, embraced a due process approach to his case, challenging the very procedures under which he was to be judged. The faculty, however, responded with a control model that stressed very narrow grounds for review; these grounds upheld the original negative judgment of Russell.

Russell's case and the controversy it provoked can be taken as symptomatic of the times. During the 1970s, there has been a general shift away from due process concerns. Russell's treatment at North Mountain State and the attitudes of the faculty involved in the case, eventually the entire law faculty, mirror this trend. Though distressed, the faculty did not ponder the challenges Russell posed; nor did they consider the challenges to be critical, in any substantial way, of the underlying philosophic concerns of law and legal training. Instead, it appears, the faculty drifted with the times and events of the day. The faculty at North Mountain State was not necessarily wrong in dismissing Dennis Russell, but its handling of the situation was uncritical.

This criticism may not be serious in and of itself, but if uncritical, unreflective practices come to predominate the study of law, then law can become reduced to little more than base opportunism: law is whatever one can get away with at the moment. Thus, the value of the law as a means of adjudicating disputes between competing social realities is significantly diminished.

Dennis Russell was clearly in a vulnerable position. The same was not true of Frank Herndon (Chapter 6, "Vendetta"). Herndon's case reveals the damage that occurs when habitual modes of behavior are steadfastly adhered to while negative preconceptions or stereotypes are entertained. More so than in Russell's case, Herndon's institution had no reasonable procedural concerns. Even common courtesies were not observed. Circumstances which could have and should have been handled with dispatch became the bases for personally agonizing encounters.

Herndon's case reveals the need for open procedures; such procedures protect all parties. Students in environments such as the one Herndon found himself in are denied standing in administrative affairs. For the casual observer familiar with the controversy, a frightening vision of academic affairs is being transmitted: the strong prey on the weak. Indeed, this may have been the experiences of many of Herndon's mentors.

Those faculty members who are not concerned about fair and equitable procedures for students are often less than enthusiastic about fair and equitable procedures for embattled academics. In some instances, these very same persons are less than forthright toward their colleagues, thereby setting the stage for the negative appraisals of their competitive counterparts. Frequently this negative competition is not detected. For example, when a hapless professor joins the ranks of the hidden professoriate, the claim is made—sometimes erroneously—that a particular college or university administration had a hand in the professor's undoing. It may very well be the professor's *colleagues* who prefer to embrace hearsay, innuendo, and preconceptions. As we shall see in the following section, many of these covert professionals are motivated by well-honed commitments to self-interest and survival, while those who demand open and direct confrontation on issues and procedures are threatened with, and often meet, the fate of the hidden professoriate.

NOTES

1. Martin Trow, "Reflections on the Transition from Mass to Universal Higher Education," *Daedalus* (1970), and Martin Trow, "Admissions and the Crisis in American Higher Education," in W. Todd Furniss, ed., *Higher Education for Everybody* (Washingon, D.C.: American Council on Education, 1970).

2. This is a commonplace finding.

3. U.S. Bureau of the Census, *Statistical Abstract of the United States: 1974* (96th ed.) (Washington, D.C., 1975), p. 353.

4. Cf. Seymour Martin Lipset, Martin Trow, and James Coleman, *Union Democracy* (Garden City, N.Y.: Anchor Books, 1956), pp. 12-13.

5. David Riesman, "Commentary and Epilogue," in David Riesman and Verne A. Stadtman, eds., *Academic Transformation* (New York: McGraw-Hill, 1973), pp. 409-74.

6. Cf. Don Martindale, *The Romance of a Profession* (St. Paul, Minn.: Windflower Publishing Co., 1976) and Don Martindale and Edith Martindale, *Psychiatry and the Law* (St. Paul, Minn.: Windflower Publishing Co., 1973).

7. The distinction is developed at length in Herbert L. Packer, *The Limits of the Criminal Sanction* (Stanford, Calif.: Stanford University Press, 1968).

1 ARTHUR S. WILKE AND B. EUGENE GRIESSMAN

The Hidden Professoriate: A Challenge in the Emerging Tenure Crisis

The tenure system, especially in times of financial crisis, diminishes the institution's opportunity to recruit and retain younger faculty. In this respect, the system operates to the disadvantage of new entrants into the profession and makes it especially difficult to expand the representation of women and members of minority groups in faculties.[1]

There are two national professoriates in academic life: one is well-organized and vocal in sustaining professional-disciplinary competence; the other is a loose aggregate of disparate individuals who can be observed on most campuses. The first, the elite professoriate, includes active participants in major fields of study, voting members of what de Solla Price has termed the *invisible colleges*.[2] Shuttling between major universities and research centers and regularly communicating with each other, they are prominent members of regional and national associations, editors of prestigious journals, board members or fellows of foundations, and consultants to government agencies. In these capacities, they exercise gatekeeping functions. In the ranks of the elite professoriate is found the largest concentration of recipients of academic honor and acclaim.

The second professoriate does not form such a tight-knit community. Its members also shuttle across the country, but most frequently from campus to campus in pursuit of work. These are contemporary counterparts to the Goliards—defrocked monks and priests who roamed across Europe during the Middle Ages sharing their learning through poems and songs. Today's Goliards are, by contrast, less mirthful. Denied access to academic sacraments, such as tenure, they doggedly pursue academic careers, filling in temporary, often nontenured positions.

Who are these modern-day Goliards? They are those who have received terminal notices from academic institutions for a variety of reasons: flaws of character or of professional life; conflicts in ideological orientation; financial difficulties at the host institution; the phasing out of projects funded on "soft money"; policy changes in the hiring institution, and the like. In addition, they are those who have just entered the labor force, frequently with newly earned doctorates. They find that they are part of that growing supply of academic personnel which, in many fields, has outstripped the demand. These individuals comprise the *hidden professoriate*.

The hidden professoriate, despite its obscurity, is growing, and its growth suggests changes in the academic climate. The status of educational institutions and their faculty has become more unpredictable. The requirements for radical structural realignments press down upon administrators and faculty, as Paul Blumberg suggests in Chapter 2. Euphemisms such as "tenure density" indicate that the assault on the tenure system, the structural provision for intellectual independence, is gaining momentum. Meanwhile, as the conditions of a buyer's market continue, short-term adjustments such as postdoctoral study become less attractive, forcing talented men and women who may have seriously considered an academic career to consider alternative careers. Sometimes well-liked, competent faculty are dismissed simply because of retrenchment. In some fields, where competition is intense, such a dismissal constitutes a kind of academic death which friends and colleagues witness in a helpless fashion, not unlike many of the characters in Chekhov's *The Cherry Orchard*, who go through rituals no longer convincing to those around them or, possibly, to themselves.

Frequently administrators and faculty, the survivors and the threatened, seek educational gimmicks in terms of attractive courses. Such strategies are sought to make institution competitive with institution, department with department, faculty with faculty. As competitive forces proliferate, resources get diluted, and instead of a sharing environment, so necessary for free inquiry, the reverse obtains. Departments and colleges, particularly in the major universities, begin to take on characteristics of mini-colleges and universities.

With the proliferation of survival strategies, administrators find themselves making highly unpopular decisions. Weak programs and departments can be cut back, although such action must be undertaken judiciously. The less painful approach is to shift the criteria for operations, alternately stressing good teaching, productive research, community service, and, in some instances, grantsmanship. If conditions of growth obtain, these strategies are sound. When retrenchment is necessary, however, the conditions for intensified competition for some and general demoralization for others appear more likely. The extremes may constitute a volatile mix that cannot be comprehended by students, faculty, administrators, or the public. As some of the case studies in this volume reveal, the mercurial forces converge in dramatic fashion. Here one sees recruitment, albeit involuntary, for the hidden professoriate.

Not all academics or all academic institutions are similarly affected by the current problems facing higher education and the variety of educational settings makes it difficult to establish perspective. It may be possible, however, to discern some general themes, and the hidden professoriate is one such theme. The growth of the hidden professoriate signals not only the ascendency of these problems, but the possibility that a watershed in the history of higher education is being reached.

The challenge that the hidden professoriate poses for higher education needs attention. The hidden professoriate has not been critically explored or accorded the detailed attention that other facets of academic affairs have. To redress this imbalance, the remainder of this chapter explores the hidden professoriate in terms of (1) its lack of recognition; (2) its institutional relationships; and (3) major trends in the national educational establishment and the accompanying changes in the local administrative organization of institutions of higher education.

LACK OF RECOGNITION

The hidden professoriate exists at the margins of academic life. The precarious position of this large number of individuals has

remained virtually undiscussed for two reasons—economic vulnerabilities and political realities. The hidden professoriate is neither
an effective nor a well-organized countervailing economic power.

The hidden professoriate's lack of economic power contributes to
its lack of visibility, a condition endemic to all academics as well as
to much of the rest of the labor force. Academics possess no effective
checks in the marketplace and have little voice in the formation of
national educational policy. National educational policy is generally
beyond the scope or immediate interest of the day-to-day world of
academics. Yet, the formation of such policies and the ideas that
inform them contribute significantly to the economic vulnerability
of academics, causing many to lower their expectations and others
to join the hidden professoriate in search of a job.

Economists have never reached a consensus on national educational policy. On one side have been those who maintain that an
investment in education creates a form of capital, human capital,
similar to the investment in nonhuman capital (e.g., plant, machines,
and raw materials).[3] On the other side are those who claim that
only nonhuman capital is critical in economic affairs.[4] Human
capital advocates are appealed to during times of boom, and nonhuman capital advocates at other times. Both groups, however,
have focused attention on the product of education, the educated
individual, and not the academic personnel.

The visible component of educational policy which dictates the
economic need for academic personnel centers on the current market for educated individuals and the anticipated market for would-
be students. To determine the appropriate policy, aggregated individual cost-benefit ratios are computed. Potential costs in the
acquisition of a college degree (i.e., tuition, loss of income) are
compared to the potential benefits (i.e., increase in potential earnings) of a college degree. In the 1960s, the benefits were estimated
to be at least $500,000 to $750,000 higher than those the high school
graduate could expect, with costs viewed as negligible. By the 1970s,
a declining job market, the requirement for large amounts of capital
simply to keep the scale of educational operations going, and the
threat of a declining pool of possible students in the post baby boom
generation combined with unprecedented inflationary pressures to
give substance to the watchword of the 1970s, "accountability."

Discussions began shifting away from an emphasis on growth and toward one emphasizing a "steady state."

Because academic personnel constitute a cost in the equation of producing the educated product, they have borne some of the transitional costs in higher education's move from a growth to a steady-state condition. This has resulted in inconspicuous economies in the form of less than cost-of-living salary increases for many faculties and, in some instances, demands for increased productivity (e.g., higher student-faculty ratios). Meanwhile, nontenured, low-ranking faculty have been removed or circulated, thereby adding to the ranks of the hidden professoriate.

The hidden professoriate's lack of organization is the other major contributor to its lack of visibility. Generally, existing professional organizations have viewed the hidden professoriate as beyond their traditional interests and concerns. Organizations such as the American Association of University Professors may, at best, deal only occasionally with the candidate destined for membership in the hidden professoriate, most often the nontendured faculty member. Frequently, they become involved when a faculty member who has received a terminal appointment or been rejected for tenure seeks redress. Unfortunately, many faculty members do not know the procedures for seeking redress, as Constance Sullivan points out (see Chapter 12), and in some instances universities and colleges have been slow in developing appeal procedures. And even when procedures exist, time is against the faculty member, for delay in resolving a case may conflict with the task of finding a new position.

When no institutional procedures exist or a faculty member has exhausted existing procedures, he or she may appeal to the AAUP. But for the nontenured such an appeal does not automatically result in an ally. As with most administrative procedures in higher education, when a complaint is made to the AAUP, the burden of proof lies with the complaining faculty person. And occasionally the person has difficulty getting reasons, as the case of Richard Stewart (Chapter 9) demonstrates, although a faculty member who has, for instance, been turned down for tenure has the right to know why. Sometimes the reasons given are transparently inadequate, or the individual may be reluctant to pursue the matter, for the "real" reasons might damage future opportunities for obtaining other professional employment. Thus these difficulties, combined with the reluctance of professional academic organizations to respond to a request for assistance from nontenured individuals, assist in keeping the hidden professoriate in disarray.

Once a local chapter of a professional organization such as the AAUP gets involved, the concerned faculty member may find that, unless the case includes serious and gross misbehavior, his or her fate revolves around small technical, procedural details. The initial negative decision may have mobilized resistance to the faculty person. And there may be a protracted conflict which nets very little in terms of redress. Even when the local chapter notes a serious administrative error, that chapter may find that the national organization is reluctant to pursue the matter, as Fran French notes in Chapter 11. Thus, there is an unwitting complicity to support administrative actions.

Meanwhile the national professional organizations themselves face a variety of demands, including maintaining their own viability. Financial solvency is a major concern, as it is for the universities. With collective bargaining rights for higher education personnel a distinct possibility in the near future, conflicts betwen competing organizations (e.g., AAUP, AFT, NEA, or the Teamsters Union) have intensified. As the stakes in this battle are high, the hidden professoriate has been only a footnote to this unfolding drama.

INSTITUTIONAL RELATIONSHIPS

Four general types of higher education institutions can be identified: Core institutions, established schools on the periphery, new schools on the periphery, and the failing institutions. Each responds to the hidden professoriate.

Core institutions are the well-endowed private institutions and the major public universities. They have solid financial footing and extensive political leverage which is frequently regional and sometimes national or international in scope. In these centers prestige and recognized creativity are most likely to be found; by far the greatest amount of research is undertaken there. Many of the elite professoriate, members of the *invisible colleges*, belong to these institutions. During the 1960s, the combination of individual and institutional prestige helped produce, albeit indirectly, a blueprint for educational policy stressing professional disciplinary development, with specific emphases on research, publishing, and strong graduate programs. Although these academic leaders will continue to dominate in their respective disciplines, some of their influence over national educational policy has declined.

The established schools on the periphery consist of relatively stable institutions. The majority of students obtaining the B.A. degree attend these institutions which, for the most part, are primarily concerned with transmitting basic knowledge and providing career-specific programs.[5] These institutions contribute less to professional knowledge and have less impact on innovations in educational policy than do the core institutions. Because such institutions are readily accessible to students and because of their relative lack of prestige, most of these schools do not have the academic mystique that is associated with the core schools.[6]

Among the new schools on the periphery are the junior and community colleges which Jencks and Riesman[7] describe as anti-university colleges. In the past, these schools struggled hard to obtain funds, but in recent years their expansion has been phenomenal. With the support of the recently concluded Carnegie Commission on Higher Education, which urges the development of "230-280 new two-year community colleges to handle 35-45% of all undergraduates by 1980," and with the strong urging by the President's Task Force on Higher Education that such schools shift their attention from the liberal arts to occupational training,[8] the future of these schools appears rather bright.

Two types of institutions make up the failing schools: (1) those which were formed in the 1960s to capitalize on educational expansion but did not get fully established, and (2) the established small liberal arts and sectarian private schools. The second category has declined because of rising costs, poor investment portfolio performance, decreasing contributions, and otherwise marginal academic operations. Financial countermeasures in the form of increased tuition have only produced an exodus of students, especially students from the small liberal arts colleges whose families are of modest means. According to the Association of American Colleges

(AAC), the threat to these schools still exists. In its study of 100 private colleges and universities, the AAC noted that "(s)mall liberal arts colleges are having the hardest time of it, both in terms of enrollments and finances."[9] They make up a significant proportion of the 27 out of 100 institutions studied which, according to the AAC, are in "serious trouble." Also in this category are a large number of schools that are solvent financially but have questionable academic histories. Certain categories of institutions, such as a predominant number of black-oriented colleges, are, in Jencks and Riesman's controversial terms, "academic disaster areas."[10]

Core institutions have long contributed to potential membership in the hidden professoriate. High performance standards (e.g., "publish or perish") and an institutionalized system of temporary appointments (e.g., lectureships) have regularly set people loose from these schools.

Most colleges and universities on the established periphery employ some of the same practices as core institutions and thus also contribute to the hidden professoriate. Because these institutions are politically more vulnerable to both internal and external pressures, do not have established faculty traditions, and frequently have greater centralized control, they are more likely to engage in major shake-ups of the faculty which can cast faculty adrift. National professional organizations have only recently begun to respond to this situation. Even in cases where such organizations could side with the contesting faculty member in litigation, the limited financial and emotional resources of the affected faculty member may blunt the effect, virtually guaranteeing membership in the hidden professoriate.[11]

Numerous established schools on the periphery frequently experience periods of great expectations and dismal results. Their efforts to emulate trends in core institutions are hazardous because of their lack of resources and established academic traditions. Their response to the innovative, creative, and upwardly mobile aspirants in their ranks, those who model careers after leading members of the elite professoriate and aspire to become members of core institutions, is ambivalent. Such persons are often found in the nontenured ranks. Though their recruitment is often heralded, their desirability as tenured faculty is limited. During affluent times, these persons have been the disloyal ones who have abandoned these periphery schools for higher status. During times of recession their presence may be considered troublesome. When such persons are terminated, they may resist with uncommon determination. If a peripheral school has experienced particularly contentious conflicts over dismissal of such persons, the administration may, in its search for future personnel, select only those who are likely to follow the career patterns of the school's established personnel.[12] Or the school may select marginal employees, who have shown themselves to be less than effective in academic settings,[13] but who can be easily dominated and can be dismissed in the near future without difficulty. Thus, two types of recruits to the hidden professoriate emerge: highly talented individuals who cannot find suitable employment in a depressed market and a less talented army of persons whose duty is limited to short-term engagements at a number of institutions. Although these two types may create a very uneven teaching and learning environment, the long-run prospects are that an equilibrium near the lowest common denominator of talent will prevail in peripheral institutions.

Schools that have historically served minorities and have persisted at the periphery may provide some respite for the hidden professoriate, particularly the talented members. These schools, because of their segregated identities, their lack of integration into the national prestige system of higher education, and their meager salaries and resources, have often been bypassed by those aspiring to careers in higher education. Undoubtedly they have also been found to be unattractive by those who view minorities with less than charitable eyes. However, the recent growth in their revenues may provide a few new opportunities and a potentially invigorating environment for professional development. As the AAC survey indicates, "the 10 predominantly Negro institutions in the sample (n = 100) have made most rapid progress in revenues because of increased government aid."[14] These institutions might enable some to escape life in the hidden professoriate.

The new schools on the periphery, the community and junior colleges, have also helped relieve some of the strain on the hidden professoriate. This effect will be lessened once they reach their growth limits or are staffed by a highly qualified faculty. Since an increasing number of these schools operate under collective bargaining agreements rather than the tenure system, they will probably not suffer the same kind of upheavals as other schools. Obviously, a fuller assessment of this matter will have to be made at a later date. Viewed by some as academic disaster areas, they have been a haven for marginal academics; for some they have been the only escape from the hidden professoriate or the only alternative to switching occupations. Whether the growing pool of talent found in the ranks of the hidden professoriate will provide a significant challenge to these institutions is unknown. Because of the long established history of insecurity and marginality of many personnel in these schools, the responses to the talented members of the hidden professoriate may be similar to those found in the established schools on the periphery.

Finally, there are the failing institutions. Their contribution to the hidden professoriate is most direct. Some faculty of defunct institutions may, because of age or training, never be able to obtain another academic appointment, and others will find themselves trapped in an endless cycle of one temporary position after another. While the few "stars" undoubtedly will find no difficulty in getting further employment, most will have a more difficult time remaining in academic life. To date, however, the problem as regards failing schools has been minor. As the AAC reports, between 1969-1970 and 1973-1974, only 16 of 868 private schools closed their doors. This may, however, herald only the beginning.

MAJOR TRENDS IN THE NATIONAL EDUCATIONAL ESTABLISHMENT

Three developments have accompanied the growth of the hidden professoriate: the decline of pluralistic centers for cultural and intellectual expression, greater centralization in the nation's educational establishment, and the move away from trans-local academic forces shaping the organization of colleges.

American higher education has been remarkably pluralistic, as is reflected not only in the different sizes of colleges and universities, but also in their different missions. If current trends continue, however, public schools, particularly large national public universities, will constitute the norm, while small private liberal arts and sectarian colleges will find it difficult to battle for necessary students and funds. As federal funds are sought and survival strategies come to predominate, the variety and idiosyncrasies in administrative and academic affairs may very well decline. Diversity may be limited to a few schools in the core which have the necessary resources to be experimental and innovative.

The role of new peripheral schools, such as community and junior colleges, is unknown, but established schools on the periphery—while generally stable—appear headed for further reorganization. Because their scale is such that certain economies cannot be practiced, severe program evaluation is mandated in an effort to maximize marginal resources, a process observed in numerous states. In some instances, certain programs are being suspended or eliminated. Under these circumstances, competition between various segments of the institutions involved can become intense and bitter. One example of this competition is that for the undergraduate student, since a substantial undergraduate clientele can provide accountable assets to be used in the academic decision-making process. In some instances, this situation can lead to the continued use of undergraduate students in teaching capacities. In a midwestern university, a once innovative program was staffed primarily by undergraduate preceptors whose pay was calculated in terms of none too costly credit hours. The program continued even though the university was dismissing faculty. The value of this program to the administration was expressed by the chairperson who volunteered that "they" (referring to his superiors) were happy as long as he kept making "$50,000 a year profit."

As debate over this issue becomes more contentious, a critical eye will focus upon another large number of marginal teaching personnel: the graduate teaching assistants. Some critics are already saying that faculty welfare should precede financial assistance for students. Quite clearly, for some programs the removal of graduate teaching assistants would severely constrict, if not curtail, most of the teaching done or redistribute it. This could be an inducement, where the opportunity exists, to turn some positions over to the hidden professoriate.

Because of the scale of their personnel and other resources, core institutions are less mercurial in their operations than other sectors of American higher education. In fact, during the 1970s these schools have grown as private schools failed or became unattractive. Despite their apparent success, however, these large schools face problems common to all large-scale systems. Often there is no clear connection or communication between decision-making centers, where personnel policies for academic staff are formulated and administered, and the classroom, the arena where critical activities take place. In such settings, the various participants tend to seek advice and counsel from others in positions similar to their own; that is, administrators consult with administrators, faculty with faculty, and students with students. As administrators from different institutions share experiences with each other, their policies become increasingly specific and often more legalistic.

A scenario for the future may already be present in some schools. It may take the form suggested recently by Pierre van den Berghe:

Keen resource competition leads to the development of either territoriality, or hierarchy, or both to prevent a constant war of all against all; but, at the same time, the more hierarchy and territoriality there are, the more numerous the occasions for the aggressive challenge and defense of monopoly and privilege.[15]

For the faculty keen competition for scarce resources means mobilizing countervailing forces, and the result can be an increase in the standardization of policies and procedures, and the specification of rights and responsibilities. If, however, the conflict is orchestrated by the higher command posts of organized interests (i.e., the faculty of institutions), the isolated faculty person may confront the Herculean task of deciphering what the policies and procedures are and whether certain ideas, activities, and proposals fall within the compass of current policies. The task of deciphering can create personal insecurity and an ethos of personal discontent. Such environments become fertile grounds for self-fulfilling prophecies. Relatively easy to establish, the hidden professoriate can easily be sustained in such circumstances—assessed and simply dismissed as being comprised of inadequate persons.

As faculty and especially those anticipating teaching careers confront a changing organizational and intellectual milieu, pressures to succeed intensify. Some may pursue conventional activities:

teaching and publication. Others may hope for special opportunities for research, postdoctoral work, government service, or for the development of a new governmental agency (e.g., NASA), and others may simply give up the dream of an academic career and seek other employment.

With the documentation of the change in national professoriates, from the dominance of the elite professoriate to the growth of the hidden professoriate, a barometer of organizational life in higher education emerges. In the 1950s and especially in the 1960s, the *invisible colleges* dominated by the elite professoriate constituted a dominant force in educational affairs. Though their members were frequently associated with core institutions, their familiar relationships with each other crossed institutional and even regional lines. They were the spokespersons for professionalization. Their stress on professional socialization[16] had a trans-local referent. Local colleges and universities adapted their organizations to the expanding standards of professional disciplines. The authority and legitimacy for these actions came from professionals, often professionals whose contacts were with not only other professionals, but also governmental agencies and businesses. The administrative problem for a local school was to negotiate among the various status groupings represented by the different professions and disciplines. Often the bargaining among various departmental representatives was based on prestige claims as well as which of the competing groups could best serve the vague agenda of institutional prestige.

In the 1970s, the individual academic disciplines were no longer viable social strata within local academic environments, for the *invisible colleges* had lost their degree of influence over the organizational directives of local environments. The collective problem now facing the local institutions was not socialization but social control, i.e., simply maintaining schools as viable entities. How, it was now asked, might the existing order of human affairs found in colleges and universities be sustained? As a result, a new administrative strategy emerged. Instead of the faculty serving as a dominant force capable of appealing to the leadership examples of the *invisible colleges*, administrators moved to maintain or salvage what many have rightfully recognized was a sinking ship. Administrators adopted more political and legal approaches, and the prestige claims of numerous professionals were no longer considered critical. One of the costs of this shift in organizational emphasis was the emergence of the hidden professoriate.

DISCUSSION

Higher education in the United States has undergone rapid change in the past decade. The shifts witnessed in the nation's colleges and universities in the 1970s after the unprecedented growth of the 1960s highlight such change. Current efforts to retrench and construct a "steady state" in higher education are significant reversals from the 1960s when growth seemed limitless.[17]

The dramatic reversal in the fortunes of higher education is particularly acute where institutional commitments in the 1960s were made without critically assessing possible changes in demographic and economic conditions. Thus, with the confluence of fewer youth, inflation, and a depressed market for college graduates, the effects were devastating. For institutions previously committed to indebtedness and postponement of critical policy-making, the results have been very costly.

One prominent area of contention in the 1970s involves academic personnel. As the market for college teachers continues to decline, efforts to formalize personnel policies, such as tenure quotas, are very likely. Efforts to develop such policies are already under way, and the immediate outlook is bleak. A generally unrecognized consequence of such efforts has been the expansion of detached academics, the hidden professoriate.

More and more are becoming aware of the hidden professoriate. This category has long been invisible because of its lack of organization and its obscure but symbiotic relationship to the dynamics of higher education policy. Hence, the most frequent sources of information on this group have been personal testimony and rumor. This has been most unfortunate, for it hints only of a threat of this unknown, seeming horde of detached professionals.

If educational policy in the coming decades is to be informed, farsighted, and sensitive to the unspoken threats rampant in academic affairs, the critical identification and analysis of the hidden professoriate are as vital as the conditions contributing to their rise. Although this identification may legitimize the hidden professoriate and create new challenges, the alternative—to remain oblivious—is unacceptable. Out of such disregard are sustained the age-old nemeses of intellectual and academic life: fear and ignorance.

Today, the idea of the hidden professoriate is a distant but emerging formulation. It is like the cadence of the distant drummer Thoreau identified in *Walden*. Like that distant sound, the hidden professoriate may be an idea whose season is still in its springtime, but one which if permitted to mature may provide a clearer picture of the challenges facing higher education during its winter of discontent. First, it is necessary to examine the current conditions.

NOTES

1. William R. Keast and John W. Macy, Jr., *The Tenure Debate*, Report on the Commission of Academic Tenure in Higher Education (San Francisco: Jossey-Bass, 1973), p. 3.

2. Derek J. de Solla Price, *Little Science, Big Science* (New York: Columbia University Press, 1963).

3. T. W. Schultz, "Investment in Human Capital," *American Economic Review* (1961): 1-17.

4. H. G. Schaffer, "Investment in Human Capital Comment," *American Economic Review* (1961): 1026-35.

5. Talcott Parsons and Gerald M. Platt, *The American University* (Cambridge, Mass.: Harvard University Press, 1973).

6. Neil J. Smelser, "Epilogue: Social-Structural Dimensions of Higher Education," in Parsons and Platt, op cit., pp. 389-422.

7. Christopher Jencks and David Riesman, *The Academic Revolution* (Garden City, N.Y.: Doubleday-Anchor Books, 1969), pp. 480ff.

8. "Great American Dream Freeze: Corporate Plans for Colleges," *Dollars & Sense* (March 1975): 5.

9. "Private Colleges Holding Their Own," *Science* (December 26, 1975): 1277.

10. Jencks and Riesman, *The Academic Revolution*, p. 433.

11. An associate professor not receiving tenure at a midwestern institution reports that instead of clarifying issues of rights, the dean of his college strongly indicated that in litigation the institution's resources would be far greater than that of the professor's. For even the strongest of heart, the effects of this type of message can be chilling.

12. Frequently, the standard of professional life tends to deviate from objective standards, with the personal interests of those in decision-making positions holding sway. Sometimes an indication of this can be gleaned from projections that suggest that personnel being terminated do not cater to "our kind of student."

13. The process of selecting marginal professionals was witnessed recently at a "hiring hall" organized in conjunction with a regional professional meeting. Again and again, a most pronounced demeanor was observed. Numerous candidates appeared humble and visibly emotional, and attempted to cater to what they perceived to be the demands of potential employers. This seemed to be a likely characteristic of at least one component of the hidden professoriate.

14. "Private Colleges Holding Their Own," p. 1277.

15. Pierre L. van den Berghe, "Bringing Beasts Back In: Toward a Biosocial Theory of Aggression," *American Sociological Review* (1974): 778.

16. Don Martindale suggests that any community must solve three problems for the individual as well as for a plurality of persons: socialization, social control, and the mastery of nature. To the degree that an academic setting is a community, these distinctions are valuable because they suggest that, under conditions of change, different problems may become highlighted. This is particularly true of academic affairs from the 1960s to the 1970s. Cf. Don Martindale, *Social Life and Cultural Change* (Princeton, N.J.: D. Van Nostrand Co., 1962).

17. Keast and Macy, *The Tenure Debate*, p. 224.

2 PAUL BLUMBERG

Lockouts, Layoffs, and the New Academic Proletariat

In early summer 1976, a distinguished group of New York intellectuals assembled in Manhattan. This important gathering was held
on West 90th Street, at the local office of the State Unemployment
Insurance Department where dazed faculty from the City University
of New York showed up to file claims for unemployment insurance.
Throughout the 1975-76 academic year, the university had limped
from crisis to crisis, a victim of New York City's financial debacle.
Budget cuts, layoffs, work load increases, the threat of payless
furloughs and other burdens which now seem as routine a part of
the college scene as textbooks and final exams were all heaped upon
the CUNY faculty. Then, late in May came the climax of a year of
chaos as Mayor Abraham Beame announced that CUNY had simply
run out of money and that faculty and staff would not receive their
May paychecks. The following day, Chancellor Robert E. Kibbee
announced the indefinite closing of the university. Thus began

SOURCE: Research for this article was supported (in part) by a grant from the City
University of New York Faculty Research Award Program. The description of the
unemployment office contained here was published in a slightly different version as
"Status Is Not Power: the New Academic Proletariat," *The Nation* 223 (August
14-21, 1976): 102-4. The helpful suggestions of Dean Savage, Robert E. Kapsis,
and James M. Murtha are also acknowledged.

what was the largest mass academic lockout in American history. As a consequence, this West Side unemployment office was adrift in Ph.D.'s, as hundreds of CUNY's locked-out faculty followed their union's advice and filed for unemployment insurance.

It was a strange but prophetic scene, this spectacle of middle-class professionals waiting in long lines to file their unemployment claims while reading the latest issue of the *New Yorker* or the *New York Review of Books* or a few pages in the esoteric paperbacks they carried with them. It would have been appropriate dramatic irony had they all worn their caps and gowns as they assembled obediently behind the notice that said all applicants should stand behind the white line until their turn came. It would have made a good Ingmar Bergman dream (or nightmare) sequence.

Perhaps out of bureaucratic convenience or perhaps out of social class consideration, unemployment officials set up a small segregated enclave for the academics on one side of the room. Fifty or so chairs were arranged for these middle-class supplicants to await their call for a short personal interview after completing the forms they had obtained in line. Thus arranged, the academics were neatly isolated from all the other applicants in the office, the *real* unemployed.

In their isolated enclave, some academics chatted, discussing the CUNY situation with as much sagacity as they could muster. Others sat quietly with their thoughts, their magazines, or their books, while still others milled about, directing newcomers to the proper lines and proper forms. The general mood seemed to be compounded of many elements: embarrassment and confusion (especially for those first entering the office); disbelief that "things have really come to this," as one woman said to a friend; subdued amusement at the whole preposterous affair; but finally, alarm and anxiety and the irrepressible feeling that this was the start of something big—and bad.

There was, in fact, a pathetic quality about this scene of professors herded together in the corner of this dreary unemployment office. Everything conspired to make everyone look bad: the social situation, the drabness of the office, the coldly efficient fluorescent lighting, even the way people were dressed. In this setting, the men looked like lower middle-class postal clerks, and the women as if they had slept in their clothes and had headed directly for the unemployment office without washing, brushing, or combing. Suddenly, the intellectual superstructure of their lives was reduced to this, as they were regimented and kept waiting for an hour to be called by a bureaucrat behind a desk. Forty years of unemployment insurance in the United States has not erased the stigma which still associates the whole thing with charity, begging, and weakness. Paylessness, regardless of cause or social class, tends to pull out the props from under one's self-respect. All the dignity associated with their professional presence on campus, with their degrees and titles, simply dissolved in the unemployment office. When called, everyone was addressed as Mr., Mrs., or Miss, no one as doctor or professor; unemployment has a strange leveling effect. Suddenly, the significance of their impressive academic training and their scholarly publications in respectable journals faded before the simple fact that they were utterly dependent upon men of wealth and power for their daily bread. Suddenly, in this scene of professors lined up for money, the fundamental powerlessness of the intelligentsia became transparent.

At first, most faculty thought that filing for unemployment insurance was only a formality; "do it just to cover yourself," colleagues urged. Most believed that they were just going through the motions, however. After the Board of Higher Education voted to impose tuition for the first time in CUNY's history, they were convinced that the state legislature would then settle the matter quickly and fund the bankrupt system, and that the university would reopen in a couple of days. Few realized that the board's acquiescence on tuition was just the beginning. Most underestimated the legislature's capacity to play cynical election year politics with tuition and the reopening of the university. They did not understand that while the university may be one of New York City's most prestigious institutions, it is also one of its "least important" and most powerful.

Although this historic lockout disrupted all activities at the university—final examinations, grading, graduation, summer school— in a sense *nothing* was disrupted because the public was completely unaffected. The closing of an institution of 270,000 students and 17,000 faculty and staff made barely a ripple in the ongoing life of

New Yorkers. No one was in any special hurry to reopen CUNY. Could any other institution of nearly 300,000 souls be shut down with such minuscule effect? Could such a casual attitude be taken toward the transit system, garbage collection, police and fire services, hospitals, or even the public schools? While a great university is certainly one of civilized society's highest achievements, in the short run it is also the least crucial for the functioning of that society. Herein lies the powerlessness of the university, the faculty, and the faculty union.

When the New York Transport Workers speak, everyone listens. When the Police Benevolent Association or the fire fighters or the sanitationmen's unions speak, everyone listens because they have real power and can do real damage. But who needs to listen to professors or even to their union? Nothing professors could do would bring the city to its knees. This point affirms the old Marxian dictum that it is still primarily the industrial working class that carries the clout in modern society, for it is the workers' labor that is uniquely indispensable for the operation of that society. Despite the flurry of faculty union activity following the lockout—the lobbying, meetings, rallies, vigils, and demonstrations—ultimately the union's major weapon was moral suasion and the status that comes from representing a rather classy constituency. But there is no power in mere status itself.

For the older, tenured faculty, this visit to the unemployment office was merely temporary middle-class slumming, a chance to get an inside view of the culture of the lower depths. For the younger faculty members, however, the visit was to be their first dip into the developing academic proletariat. Ironically, the problems of many younger faculty began in earnest, not there on the unemployment lines, but two and one-half weeks later when the university finally reopened. The euphoria produced when the state legislature finally "rescued" the university, permitting distribution of overdue paychecks and funding CUNY for the next year, dissipated quickly when the faculty realized what the legislature's rescue had cost. Not only had open admissions and the century-old tradition of free tuition been scrapped, but the university budget was cut to $471 million from $531 million the previous year and $585 million the year before that. The City University was thus caught in a double bind of sharply curtailed budgets in the midst of an inflationary economy. Worst of all, from the point of view of faculty jobs, the inevitable cuts demanded by this budget could come only through mass dismissals of full-time faculty. Previous budgets had already cut non-personnel expenses severely. Whatever amenities CUNY faculty had once enjoyed—and these were never very great—were long gone. At most campuses, one can no longer even count on the basics, such as stationery in the offices, chalk in the classrooms, or toilet paper in the bathrooms.

Moreover, the demands of this budget could not be met simply by firing the "dispensable" faculty—adjuncts and graduate assistants. The inevitable next step was to dismiss the regular faculty. And so in August 1976 nearly six hundred full-time teaching faculty and four hundred nonteaching faculty, many with tenure, were fired. Thus, America's greatest mass academic lockout was followed shortly thereafter by America's greatest mass academic layoff.[1]

Job scarcity did what scarcity always tends to do—bring out the best and the worst in those involved. In the 1976 crisis, valiant attempts were made to save jobs and to cut non-personnel expenses as much as possible in order to minimize the impact on faculty and students. At the same time, whatever cleavages existed in the university became the basis for conflict. Colleges began to compete with other colleges in the system for a larger slice of the remaining pie. Shifting alliances developed: senior colleges versus community colleges; "elite" colleges (City, Brooklyn, Queens, and Hunter) against the others. Departments vied with one another for survival. At some campuses, administrators, instead of making across-the-board cuts, made them selectively, imposing much greater sacrifices on vulnerable departments such as physical education, home economics, and education, decimating them and creating a pariah mentality among the survivors.

The division between younger, insecure faculty and older, secure faculty also became a basis for conflict. "If you'd retire, I'd still have a job," said one angry young man to a senior professor. The dynamics of faculty recruitment over the past decades has heightened the conflict between generations. Older faculty joined the university when it was still largely a teaching institution, without its present emphasis on scholarship and research. In recent years, however, because of their high salaries and the extraordinary buyers' market, the senior colleges at CUNY have been able to pick and choose among the best young Ph.D.'s in the country.

Consequently, many young faculty who were dismissed believe they are better scholars and teachers than the older faculty who were allowed to remain. How unfair, some say, that seniority should prevail over merit. In their view, tenure is not a priceless achievement of academic freedom, but rather a device used by other faculty to protect themselves from the competition of their younger colleagues. Younger faculty who worked hard teaching and who played the publish-or-perish game enthusiatically found that the rules had changed, and after they published, they proceeded to perish.

During the so-called golden age of higher education in this country, from the middle 1950s until about 1970, dismissal from one university merely meant that one pulled up stakes and put them down at another university. Academics have always been the migratory laborers of the professions. Today, however, the loss of an academic job means not simply a move to another university, but possibly a move to another occupation. Some of the professors fired at CUNY in 1976 may never teach again. Unemployment and underemployment rates for new Ph.D.'s in all disciplines have been mounting sharply in recent years. Between 1968 and 1974, for example, the proportion of new Ph.D.'s reporting no specific employment prospects at the time they received their degrees increased from 4 percent to 36 percent in English, 6 percent to 26 percent in psychology, 7 percent to 26 percent in engineering, 5 percent to 22 percent in chemistry, and 5 percent to 16 percent in economics.[2]

According to one report, of the 8,000 positions in philosophy departments nationwide in the early 1970s, 500 had been eliminated by 1975, and in 1976 there were seven applicants for every vacancy.[3] In history, less than one new historian in six found an academic job in 1973, and the situation is worse now.

In 1976, the Modern Language Association (MLA) surveyed a sample of *major* graduate departments in modern languages and found that of the Ph.D.'s and ABD's in English seeking academic jobs, only 21 percent had been placed in academic jobs by May 1 of that year.[4] In German and Slavic languages, only 27 percent had been placed, and in Romance languages (1975 data), only 26 percent of applicants had found jobs.

An employment guide for job candidates which the MLA published in 1975 strikes a very somber note indeed.[5] Of candidates seeking faculty positions in English and foreign language departments, the MLA states that "the search may well be one of the most difficult endeavors they have ever undertaken." It argues that the depression in the humanities generally, the enrollment declines, budget cutbacks, tenure quotas, and vacant positions left unfilled have "further shaken the confidence of our graduate students and younger faculty in their professional prospects." The MLA notes the "personal demoralization" and "waste of talent" resulting from the production of more qualified candidates for college teaching than there are positions to fill.

As discouraging as the present employment situation is, the next two decades will probably be even darker. The latest projections of the Bureau of Labor Statistics and the National Center for Education Statistics on the estimated supply and demand for Ph.D.'s in the next decade, although not as grim as their previous estimate,[6] nevertheless do not present a hopeful picture. Between 1974 and 1985, there will be some 200,000 Ph.D.-level job openings, but nearly 423,000 new doctorates will be competing for these jobs, or more than two qualified persons for every position (see Table 1).

Naturally, the outlook differs from discipline to discipline. The prospects for those in engineering and some natural sciences is not particularly alarming, for student enrollment in these areas is typically very responsive to changes in the job market.[7] The outlook in the social sciences, the arts and humanities, education, and business, however, is ominous indeed. In each of these fields, within the next decade and probably much beyond that, several new Ph.D.'s may be competing for each available position, and only a minority will be able to enter and work in their field of training.

Although the academic employment situation seems very bad now, we are merely on the outer edge of the crisis. As we move into the 1980s that crisis will deepen, for the most decisive depressing force on the profession, the demographic time bomb, has yet to hit. In 1945, the U.S. fertility rate (the number of children born

**Table 1.   PROJECTED OPENINGS FOR AND
NEW SUPPLY OF PH.D.'S, 1974-85**

FIELD	TOTAL OPENINGS 1974-85 (1)	PROJECTED NEW SUPPLY 1974-85 (2)	POTENTIAL NO. OF APPLICANTS PER JOB (3)*	PCT. POTENTIALLY UNABLE TO FIND EMPLOYMENT IN FIELD (4)*
All fields	201,900	422,900	2.1	52
Engineering & natural science	104,000	139,400	1.3	25
Engineering	30,300	29,100	.9	0
Physical science	34,200	38,300	1.1	10
Chemistry	14,200	18,000	1.3	21
Physics	6,600	12,000	1.8	45
Life science	33,600	59,500	1.8	44
Mathematics	5,900	12,400	2.1	50
Social science & psychology	48,400	88,800	1.8	45
Social science	20,900	50,700	2.4	59
Arts & humanities	9,100	52,600	5.8	83
Education	35,200	115,400	3.3	69
Business & commerce	1,600	13,300	8.3	88
Other fields	3,600	13,300	3.7	73

*Columns 3 and 4 were computed from columns 1 and 2.

SOURCE: U.S. Department of Labor, Bureau of Labor Statistics, *Occupational Projections and Training Data*, Bulletin 1918 (Washington, D.C., 1976), Table 13, p. 21.

per 1,000 women age fifteen to forty-four) was 85.9. During the postwar baby boom, the fertility rate increased until it peaked at 122.7 in 1957. It was this expansion in birth rates of the late 1940s and 1950s that gave us our burgeoning college enrollment of the 1960s and 1970s.

At the end of the 1950s, however, fertility rates resumed their historic downward course, falling steadily year by year, reaching 65.6 in 1976, the lowest rate in our history to that date. In that year, there were about 26 percent fewer births than in 1957. This dramatic decline in fertility will soon begin to affect college enrollments. The number of college-age persons (eighteen to twenty-one) is still increasing slightly, but that age group will peak in about 1980 and will thereafter decline until the mid-1990s. In 1980, there will be approximately 17 million young people of college age, but by 1994 this number will fall to about 12.75 million, a 25 percent reduction. This is not merely a projection that might later be modified, for those who will be eighteen to twenty-one in 1994 are already born, the survival rates are known, and, barring war, pestilence, or other unforeseen catastrophes, this is the demographic reality that confronts our profession.

Census projections in the mid-1970s forecast an increase in births and birth rates, and indeed the fertility rate in 1977 turned up slightly, the first time since the 1950s. Unless this rise is sustained over a long period, however, the increase of eighteen to twenty-one year olds after the mid-1990s will be minimal, and we may end the century with 18-20 percent fewer college-age persons than in 1980.

Unless college enrollment is supplemented either by a striking increase in the percentage of college-age youth attending college (not generally expected) or by a great infusion of new students over the traditional age in matriculated or non-matriculated programs (also fairly unlikely), the demographic shrinkage will have its inevitable effect upon college enrollment in the 1980s and 1990s. Allan Cartter, who over the years provided us with the most perceptive forecasts of future faculty needs, has estimated that full-time equivalent degree-credit enrollment may fall 13 to 20 percent between the early 1980s and the mid-1990s, with 15 percent the most likely reduction. This decline will only partly be offset by stabilized enrollment in graduate and professional programs and increased enrollment in nondegree studies.[8]

This expected decline in enrollment is only half the explosive mixture, for in "normal" times a decline of this magnitude would not be particularly serious. What is alarming, of course, is that these projected enrollment declines will come at a time when graduate departments are turning out more Ph.D.'s than ever before, many of whom will seek faculty positions in colleges and universities.

The number of persons earning doctorates has increased fivefold in the last generation. In 1950, American universities conferred only 6,600 Ph.D.'s; in 1960, this figure had grown to about 10,000 and to 16,500 in 1965. Only a decade later, in 1975, the number had doubled, with over 34,000 persons being awarded doctorates. The annual production of Ph.D.'s is expected to increase still further in the 1980s when there will be academic jobs for only a mere fraction of these young scholars (see Table 2).

Table 2. ACTUAL AND PROJECTED NUMBER OF DOCTORATES AWARDED AND NUMBER OF JUNIOR FACULTY OPENINGS, 1973-90 (in thousands)

YEAR	ESTIMATED NUMBER OF DOCTORATES		ESTIMATED NUMBER OF JUNIOR FACULTY OPENINGS
	NCES (1)	Cartter (2)	(3)
1973	34.4*	34.4*	13.3*
1974	33.7*	34.4	11.0
1975	34.1*	35.6	14.7
1976	34.1*	36.6	14.7
1977	37.0	37.4	15.1
1978	37.0	39.1	15.3
1979	36.0	40.6	17.3
1980	36.0	42.0	16.1
1981	37.0	42.8	10.8
1982	39.0	43.2	8.5
1983	40.0	43.1	3.1
1984	41.0	42.1	1.2
1985	42.0	40.2	−2.7
1986	42.0	38.0	−2.4
1987		34.8	3.7
1988		34.8	8.4
1989		35.5	10.1
1990		37.6	2.2

*Actual.
SOURCES: Column 1—advance data from the National Center for Education Statistics; columns 2 and 3—Allan M. Cartter, *Ph.D.'s and the Academic Labor Market* (New York: McGraw-Hill, 1976), p. 143.

While it is true that in recent years only about 50 percent of all those with doctorates enter college teaching, thus apparently reducing the surplus, at the same time only about 50 percent of those who enter college teaching have (or ever get) the doctorate. Even if the percentage of those new college teachers with Ph.D.'s rises to 75 percent of the total within the next decade, a figure Cartter believes to be the likely maximum, there will still be an enormous number of Ph.D.'s without a chance of entering the academic profession.

The figures in column 3 in Table 2 represent the expected number of junior faculty openings given the rates of faculty retirement and outmigration from the profession (negligible) that prevailed in the early 1970s. As the number of new Ph.D.'s builds up in the 1980s, however, more pressure may be expected on older faculty for early retirement, which would boost the number of junior faculty openings. (Pressures for early retirement, however, may be more than offset by state or federal legislation prohibiting mandatory retirement.) Also, if, as expected, salaries and conditions for faculty deteriorate further, there may be some outmigration from the profession, again creating openings for junior faculty. Cartter has estimated that as a result of both factors perhaps an additional 70,000 openings would be created during the 1980s, a number which would mitigate, but certainly not eliminate, the crisis.[9]

In any case, when one considers that in two boom years alone, 1964 and 1965, there were more than 75,000 new junior faculty openings, compared to a possible total of under 34,000 for the entire 1980s, and that annual Ph.D. production in the latter period will be two and one-half times what it was in the mid-1960s, one begins to appreciate the dimensions of the problem.

All disciplines will be hit, but some will be less devastated than others. As mentioned earlier, engineering and the natural sciences may be least affected, for graduate enrollment in these fields tends to fall off in periods of declining demand, and fewer Ph.D.'s in these fields enter college teaching (28 percent in engineering, 36 percent in chemistry, 39 percent in physics) than in other fields. The social sciences will be in an intermediate position. The humanities will suffer the most because, traditionally, graduate student enrollment in this field has not been responsive to job market conditions. (In the last year or two, first-year graduate student enrollment in the humanities finally began to decline.) Moreover, the vast majority of those with doctorates in the humanities enter college teaching (92 percent in English, 91 percent in foreign languages and literature, 86 percent in history).[10]

Although much has been written of the oversupply of Ph.D.'s in America, there is and will be a surplus of Ph.D.'s only in relation to the priorities of this society. If educational priorities were as great as defense priorities, for example, the growing number of Ph.D.'s would be regarded not as a disaster, but as an opportunity to enrich and enlarge higher education, to create a truly universal system of post-secondary education, to provide smaller classes and more individual attention, to expand continuing and adult education to all ages and social classes—to create, in short, what the Carnegie Commission has called "a learning society."[11] Marx argued that capitalism's major problem was not underproduction, but the overproduction of commodities. Similarly, the current problem in higher education is not one of a shortage of trained personnel but one of abundance. The question is not whether there are too many Ph.D.'s in an absolute sense, but whether American society as presently constituted can make rational and efficient use of the rich supply of trained manpower it has created.

A legitimate question to ask as we move toward the creation of a sizable academic proletariat is: how did we get into such a situation? By "we," I mean the over 400,000 intelligent men and women who make up the academic profession in the United States. How did we allow ourselves to travel the road to employment disaster without changing course before it was too late?

A number of factors are responsible. First, we must recognize that contemporary social science has an unerring *inability* to predict the future, the future often being defined as merely one year beyond the present. There are innumerable examples. The first that comes to mind is that of Harvard sociologist Daniel Bell, a well-known futurist, who in 1960, at the start of a decade of unprecedented ideological conflict, announced that America was a society at the end of ideology. Students of race relations were caught completely unawares by the civil rights movement of the 1960s. Sociologists were totally unprepared for the student movements of a decade ago, so accustomed were they to the campus quiescence of the 1950s. Because of the inevitable lag between social events and the interpretation of those events, it took some time for sociologists to dust off their theoretical apparatus to explain the student movement. By the time they had done so and written how and why the structural position of students predisposed them to political unrest, students confounded the social scientists again by their return to quiescence in the 1970s.

The record of economists is just as poor. Robert Heilbroner, for example, has argued that the main economic trends in the capitalist world since 1945 have been the emergence of the multinational corporation as the major international economic instrument; the development of chronic inflation; the weakening of America's economic position and the corresponding strengthening of Japan's; and the development of environmental constraints as a major economic problem. "What is remarkable," Heilbroner writes, "is that the economics profession did not foresee a single one of these major trends."[12]

Nor did many predict the employment crisis for college graduates or for college faculty that developed in the early 1970s. True, since about 1964, Allan Cartter's was a voice in the wilderness, calling attention to the falling birth rates, the increasing number of doctorates cranked out by graduate schools across the land, and the possible implications for faculty employment.

Earlier, over a quarter of a century ago (1951), C. Wright Mills himself foresaw the outlines of a crisis that might develop as a consequence of the overproduction of educated labor in American society. Almost as an aside in *White Collar*, he described a situation that captures the essence of our current dilemma. Taking a lead from sociologist W. Lloyd Warner, Mills wrote:

As demand for educated people falls behind supply, as educated occupations are divided and rationalized, as enrollments continue to rise, the income and prestige differences between the more-educated and the less-educated masses decrease. Among those who are not allowed to use the educated skills they have acquired, boredom increases, hope for success collapses into disappointment, and the sacrifices that don't pay off lead to disillusionment.[13]

One reason why no one listened to the few prophetic voices is that in the postwar euphoria, when education was viewed as a continuous growth industry, few academics had the foresight to imagine that things could ever be different. A generation of academics had grown up thinking that enrollment increases were inevitable and that the only possible shortage would be the shortage of faculty, not of jobs.

This was all part of what I call the *Time* magazine *Weltanschauung,* the endless but essentially deluded and shortsighted celebration through the 1950s and beyond of the affluent society, the good life, an increasingly educated society, of onward and upward in every socioeconomic dimension. Most academics shared the complacent view of educational expansion as the natural order of things. This selectively rosy perception blinded faculty, administrators, and government officials until the crisis was virtually upon us. As Allan Cartter wrote, "Right up until 1969, when the first signs of a weakening job market for college teachers began to emerge in a number of disciplines, it was difficult to get either educators or federal government officials to take seriously the likelihood of an oversupply of Ph.D.'s in the foreseeable future."[14] Throughout the 1960s, federal policy and funding was directed toward the expansion of graduate programs, and successive commissioners of education testified before Congress on the need for more college teachers at the doctoral level. Until about 1970 the National Science Foundation and the U.S. Office of Education were predicting shortages of doctorates for the 1970s. Cartter concludes:

Looking backward, it seems evident that this emerging problem could (and should) have been recognized by public-policy makers a decade ago [mid-1960s]. True, the magnitude of the decline in birthrates after 1965 was not then clear, but the mere likelihood of deceleration should have given sufficient advance warning. By 1969 or 1970 it had become quite clear that the 1980s were going to be years of contraction for higher education—yet it has only been in the last year or two that the message has finally sunk in for thoughtful educators.[15]

There is another explanation for our current problem, and this might be termed either faculty indifference or, more harshly, what

C. Wright Mills called in another context the "higher irresponsibility." Far too many professors have traditionally felt a responsibility only for the education of their graduate students and have had no concern for what happens afterwards. Especially in the humanities, there has always been a kind of otherworldly, academic snobbery about jobs. "Jobs?" These professors seem to say. "I am lecturing to you on John Donne and you speak to me about jobs?" Somehow students are supposed to be carried away by the aesthetics of it all and to rise above the crass considerations of jobs, career, and next month's rent.

Many languishing students resent their professors for this attitude, especially in the light of today's job market. One unemployed graduate student in English, pointing out the extraordinary sacrifices in time, effort, and money that students have to make in order to enter their chosen field, writes ". . . how irritating it is for a job seeker to be told that he or she is somehow sullying the purity of the Ph.D. by regarding it as connected with 'a job.' (This rebuke, I have found, often comes from established Ph.D.'s with tenure.)"[16]

Another doctoral candidate in English at Brandeis remarked bitterly:

When I began my graduate studies, I was told nothing about the difficulties of getting a job. The department had all the figures, the projections. Even if it refused to accept their accuracy, it was not ignorant of the problems its new Ph.D.'s were having. Certainly I'm bitter that not a word of this was passed on to me. If I had realized what the possibilities were for getting a job, I'd never have spent all the years, money, and hard work that I've plowed into my graduate education. Some members of the faculty spew a lot of rot about their functions as professors and not employment counsellors. Their failure to call attention to the glut is ruining lives, yet they just couldn't be bothered.[17]

Finally, an unemployed Ph.D. in French wrote that, despite the grim employment outlook, "graduate schools continue to churn out Ph.D.'s, senior professors refuse to acknowledge the situation, and, when forced to confront it, wring their limp knuckles in dismay. They seem to feel that their responsibility ends the day the degree is conferred."[18] Actually, professors who continue to train graduate students but who are not interested in what becomes of them once they leave the department are much like the rocket scientist satirized in a song by Tom Lehrer, not caring for its destination once it is launched.

Faculty indifference is not the only explanation for the problem, for academic departments have a certain vested interest in keeping enrollment high regardless of the employment prospects of graduates. For example, despite the great oversupply of school teachers in the United States, schools of education have not taken the lead in discouraging students from entering teacher training.[19] The decline in education enrollment has come largely as a result of information obtained on the outside: by word of mouth from student to student and from growing public awareness of the teacher surplus.

Indeed, the jobs, salaries, power, and prestige of faculty in the universities depend on maintaining the flow of raw material. Department budgets depend in part on the size of enrollment. The best way to ensure enrollment is to get majors, for a large part of each department's enrollment comes from its majors. The system thus encourages departments to entice majors regardless of job opportunities for graduates. Moreover, as both departments and professors derive more prestige from a large graduate program, pressures build up to increase the size of graduate departments.

In general, then, we can no more expect academic departments to discourage students than we can expect General Motors to advise its customers to buy bicycles. Arguing precisely this point, some members of the MLA claim that academic departments across the country are themselves partly responsible for the saturated faculty labor market:

Some of our colleagues argue that our profession as a whole is behaving irresponsibly and for highly questionable motives. They say that we continue to admit many more students than can be justified by anticipated needs in order to permit faculty members to continue to do what they are used to doing, or aspire to do; that large graduate programs are preserved because they provide prestige and power, both locally and nationally; and that graduate admissions are maintained at unreasonable levels in order to provide low-cost instruction for heavily-attended service courses.[20]

Unlike medicine, the academic profession has no tight central control over entrance into the occupation which might keep the number of new members in line with employment opportunities.

On the contrary, competition among departments and among colleges tends to increase the number of members in the profession beyond what the job market can absorb. All this helps to explain why between 1968 and 1974, when employment prospects for new doctorates were deteriorating in almost every field, the number of doctorates awarded increased by over 10,000 (46 percent), the number of first-year graduate students grew by 155,000 (34 percent), and forty additional universities began offering doctoral programs.[21]

There is also something inherently parochial and petty bourgeois about the outlook of academic departments which exacerbates the problem. Even when departments are aware of the employment crisis, they may continue their graduate program, or even expand it, reasoning that one small or even medium-sized department could not possibly alter the national supply/demand situation in an entire discipline. The collective effects of innumerable decisions such as this one are obvious.

The self-interested parochialism of academic departments is illustrated by one department at the City University of New York. There a graduate program is maintained which offers only a terminal M.A. in a discipline where there are very few jobs now for those with M.A.'s. The program continues simply because of tradition— the department has "always" had an M.A. program—*and* for the convenience of the faculty. An instructor teaching a three-credit graduate course meets it only once a week for an hour and forty minutes. If there were no graduate program, the same instructor would be required to teach in its place a three-credit undergraduate course which meets up to three times a week, fifty minutes per class. A prime (but obviously unofficial) reason this department clings to its graduate program is to cut the hourly teaching load of its faculty.

An additional peculiarity of higher education is aggravating the present job crisis. The university is the only factory in modern society that is not responsible for the disposition of its finished products.[22] An automobile manufacturer cannot assemble cars and then leave them unsold in the parking lot, but universities can turn out Ph.D.'s and then abandon them after they are produced. This obviously encourages unlimited production. If the prosperity of General Motors depended solely on how many cars they manufactured rather than on how many they were able to sell, 50 million more automobiles would be produced next year.

Of course, the most fundamental reason for the Ph.D. employment crisis is the absence of national economic and educational planning in the United States. Aside from fellowship and traineeship programs which have offered financial incentives for those entering fields where shortages exist, there is really very little overall coordination between higher education and the economy. Just as Marx spoke of the anarchy of production in the private economy, so we now have anarchy of production in the universities. In fact, with its rapid shifts in defense and aerospace spending in the last two decades, the federal government has actually been a destabilizing force on students' abilities to make long-range career plans.[23]

While planning may be an idea whose time is coming, until it comes, students have a right to expect, at the very least, widely publicized and state-of-the-art projections on the current and future job prospects in the field they are entering. In cases where such projections have been made by professional associations, as in physics and the engineering societies, the result has been informed students responsive to the market which in turn has helped to reduce dislocations stemming from an oversupply of trained persons.[24]

What will become of this new academic proletariat? How will they respond to the difficult market conditions of the 1980s and 1990s? Although little systematic research has been done, the few interviews and anecdotal accounts which exist, together with my own observations, suggest several themes which I will outline briefly.

Casualties of competition. The job search for many new Ph.D's will be a long and painful one. Because of the great number of qualified candidates for each academic position, standards will be continuously raised, competition will be tremendous, and life for many will be an endless process of selling themselves. One woman who received a Ph.D. in English from the Graduate Center of CUNY but could find only part-time teaching jobs around New York comments on the new competitive intensity in today's academic marketplace. "To get a position in your field now," she reports, "you have to be publishing not only very early but very extensively. You feel you can't breathe, that you don't have time to do any decent work, to think, to mature. You have to be a full-blown prodigy by the time you're 29."[25] One's whole life seems reduced to the dimensions of an academic vita.

The sheer volume and impersonality of rejection letters stands as a symbol of the competition for college teaching jobs these days. The unemployed French scholar mentioned earlier writes:

No matter how much self-confidence the candidate may have, he will eventually come to see his academic career as a stack of rejection letters. The job seeker is not treated as an individual; he is no more than one sheaf of papers in the department mail basket. I find it ironic that this kind of dehumanization is fostered by self-proclaimed humanists and that the victims are their would-be successors. . . . Despite my growing fear that I would not find a teaching position, I managed to convince myself that 1975 would not find me buying another file folder to hold my rejections. I was in one sense right; I bought not one, but four new folders.[26]

Eventually, the new Ph.D. may obtain a teaching position, but the insecurity of looking for a job is then merely replaced by the insecurity of holding onto a job. Many young Ph.D.'s will have to settle for part-time work where they will earn notoriously low wages, receive the worst teaching assignments, occupy a pariah status in the department, and, as their jobs depend on the term-to-term uncertainties of enrollment and the budget, have virtually no employment security.[27]

Competition and insecurity take another form for those young Ph.D.'s fortunate enough to secure full-time positions. Traditionally, those who landed jobs at elite institutions have been well suited for the rigors of academic competition. Now, however, the extraordinary buyers' market for instructors has created a situation where every mediocre college in the land can demand an exceptional record of research and publication from every assistant professor who desires tenure. Elite standards can be imposed upon the faculty of ordinary colleges only by the most ruthless survival-of-the-fittest tenure process.

What the long-term effects of this ubiquitous competitive atmosphere will be are unknown. Suffice it to say that many years ago Karen Horney identified competition, and its accompanying anxiety, envy, hostility, and fear of failure, as social structural features underlying much of the neurotic personality of our time.[28]

A crisis of legitimacy. Many of those excluded from academia or relegated to its margins will undoubtedly feel cheated by the system that made it impossible for them to fulfill their ambitions. As mentioned earlier, many young graduates feel that those who have made it are not really better qualified but simply got on the elevator before the doors were closed. Especially among those young instructors who are better trained than the older faculty who are now judging them, there is the sense that the system is based upon accident, not merit. As the young CUNY Ph.D. in English said, "You know that you're not getting jobs that your graduate professors, if they were applying now, would not be getting either, but they've got them. That is one of the most maddening things, because I'm no dumber than a lot of them."[29] The irony, then, is that older faculty are establishing standards for younger faculty which they themselves could not meet; if older faculty were to be judged by the criteria they are now using, many of them would have to be dismissed.

On the other hand, many older faculty who have managed to secure a scarce berth for themselves in the university have a vested psychological interest in believing that the system works well, that merit is rewarded, that the people who have the jobs have them by right, and that those outside somehow deserve to be there. In short, they tend to blame the academic victim for his troubles, which legitimizes the system and frees them from any sense of guilt they might have about their place within it.[30] At the same time, David Riesman has suggested that the less psychologically secure older faculty, confronted by a wave of highly qualified young Ph.D.'s, may secretly share the feelings of their younger colleagues—that they do not really deserve their positions and are able to hold onto them simply because of the good fortune of seniority and tenure.[31]

Failure. Most unemployed or underemployed Ph.D.'s realize that the cause of their woes is basically the inadequate demand for their skills, and many undoubtedly feel anger and bitterness toward "the system." It is difficult to avoid the feeling, however, that some people did get the jobs, that "I am not working, or just marginally working in the field for which I have spent years preparing, and in that sense I am a failure." The American class system, after all, points toward individual achievement, and it is the individual himself, not the system, who is held responsible for his own success or failure. "One of the major problems," says the CUNY Ph.D. in

English, "is your self-worth, not having a full-time job, not getting a decent position. Getting a decent job is only an accident, yet it affects your self-image and other people's judgments as though it had some objective validity." The first year this woman was in the job market, she hung all her form rejection letters on the wall and dismissed the whole thing as comic. Ultimately, they affected her: "The form letter makes you feel that if you're being treated like shit, you must be shit and so the ego problem was for a long time really, really major."[32] Those relegated to the limbo of part-time college teaching have their own stigma of failure to endure. A lecturer in English writing on the abuses of part-time faculty argues that many part-timers "seem to have internalized the unspoken prejudice against them . . ., that part-time teaching is . . . a badge of inferiority, [and] that only academic has-beens and hangers-on without professional ambition or ability would put up with it."[33]

What all this illustrates, of course, is that occupational failure and self-blame, long thought to be peculiar to the working and lower class, are now being played out in a middle-class setting. As we move into the 1980s and the academic job market continues to deteriorate, the sociology of middle-class failure may become a depressingly common research theme.

The sociology of the absurd. In the world of new Ph.D.'s, which is often a mix of Alice in Wonderland and Franz Kafka, nothing seems to make sense. Years of education and preparation for a career seem to be leading only to a bedroom wall papered with rejection letters. In such a situation, a kind of anomie develops that often expresses itself in gallows humor which highlights the absurdity of it all.

The unemployed French scholar mentioned earlier, who unsuccessfully looked for a teaching position for two years, finally secured a job—as part-time *secretary* in the department in which he had done his graduate work. One day, in the course of his secretarial duties, he found in the department files a mimeographed job announcement from "Kung Fu University" which "invited applications for an opening in French and martial arts, the successful candidate to be chosen through a series of Kung-Fu matches. . . ." What really unnerved him was that for a moment he thought the job announcement was genuine; he had become so used to job notices that made

the most outlandish demands of candidates that this one momen-
tarily seemed plausible.[34]

An unemployed doctoral student in English at an eastern university reports that posted on the English Department bulletin board
was a notice advertising a job at "Arsebeiten Community College"
located in Arsebeiten, Wyoming. The college was apparently looking for a medievalist who had published a novel or book of poetry,
who was also able to teach linguistics, seventeenth-century prose,
and could coach the girls' basketball team. Educational requirements for the job included a Ph.D. in medieval studies, an M.A. in
linguistics, a B.A. in physical education, and ten years teaching
experience (minimum). The announcement concluded:

Arsebeiten is an equal opportunity employer, and while we are looking for
a black woman to fill this position, we do not really believe the community
would stand for this, so we are looking either for a masculine woman or a
feminine man with a dark complexion. Some Spanish preferable. Due to
the number of applicants, we cannot respond to inquiries.[35]

Finally, a young scholar who managed to secure a position as
assistant professor of English (not at Arsebeiten Community College) offers his advice on the best way to get tenure. Strategy one:
never offend a tenured colleague: steer clear of all controversial
subjects. Strategy two: in relation to the administration, always
behave as an employee, not a colleague. Strategy three: acquire the
reputation of being a popular teacher by giving very high grades,
assuring students that their interpretations are as good as yours or
anyone else's, and letting students read as much popular literature
as possible. Strategy four: publish as much as possible regardless of
quality. Strategy five: learn to live with continuous insecurity.
In sum, ". . . modify St. Paul's advice to the Corinthians and use
the message as your guide: 'Give none offense, neither to the publishers, nor to the teachers, nor to the administration: Even as I
please all men in all things, seeking mine own profit that I may be
saved' (I Corinthians 10.32-33)."[36]

Politics and apolitics. The precise political response of the new
academic proletariat is difficult to anticipate. On the one hand, in
many countries, especially in the Third World, chronic underemployment of the college-educated intelligentsia is often associated

with political discontent and social reform movements.[37] In the French student upheaval of 1968 and in the current unrest sweeping French and Italian universities, an increasingly important dynamic seems to be the contradiction between a system of higher education which raises aspirations and an economy unable to fulfill them.[38] Moreover, the radicalization of the new academic proletariat has been anticipated by the theory of the new working class developed in recent years.

In contrast, there is no question that the scarcity of academic jobs in the United States has made graduate students and young faculty more docile than they were in the job-rich 1960s. Just as the blue-collar discontent of the 1960s was cooled by layoffs and rising unemployment in the 1970s, so discontent in the universities, which in the 1960s was supported and energized by graduate students and young faculty, has been tranquilized by the dimensions of the job crisis. Unfortunately, as suggested by the ironic guide to tenure mentioned earlier, the coming period will encourage opportunism, timidity, and blind conformity to established procedures.[39]

The question of whether the academic proletariat will move left or right ignores the likely possibility that politics will be irrelevant for them. Ph.D.'s unable to find full-time work in the university will be scattered about in various occupations and widely separated from one another, a condition ill suited to the development of class consciousness or political action. One study of advanced degree holders presently working in unskilled or dead-end manual jobs, for example, found that the disappointment many felt in being unable to use their academic training did not take a political or even broadly social direction at all, but was instead merely privatized.[40] Unless efforts are made in the next few years to expand opportunities for higher education to new constituencies, the employment crisis for college teachers, created by large socioeconomic forces, may very well play itself out—not politically, but in the personal tragedies of hundreds of thousands of young scholars.

Back at the unemployment office on the West Side, a young woman instructor who had brought a camera with her asked another woman to take her picture. Just when the pose was set up, a supervisor charged out from an inner office.

"Hey, what are you doing? You can't take pictures here," he shouted.

The woman, embarrassed by the sudden attention, replied, "I want to send this to my mother. She won't believe what's happening to me."

"I don't care; you can't take pictures in here without permission."

Flustered, all she could say was, "Hey, this is a free country."

"Not in here it's not!" snapped the bureaucrat, ending the discussion.

And that is precisely what the emerging academic proletariat is beginning to discover.

NOTES

1. The best and most detailed account of the massive layoffs at CUNY in 1976 can be found in "City University of New York: Mass Dismissals under Financial Exigency," *AAUP Bulletin* (April 1977): 60-81.

2. Richard B. Freeman, *The Overeducated American* (New York: Academic Press, 1976), p. 92. Cf. National Board on Graduate Education, *Outlook and Opportunities for Graduate Education* (Washington, D.C., 1975), p. 4.

3. Daniel C. Spitzer, "Ph.D.—The New Migrant," *The Progressive* 40 (September 1976): 25-8.

4. Neal Woodruff, "Only Connect . . . ," *ADE and ADFL Bulletins*, Special Joint Issue (September 1976): 73-7. Data for Romance languages in 1976 are unreliable; 1975 data are used in their place.

5. Modern Language Association of America, *A Guide for Job Candidates and Department Chairmen in English and Foreign Languages* (New York, 1975).

6. U.S. Department of Labor, Bureau of Labor Statistics, *Ph.D. Manpower: Employment Demand and Supply*, Bulletin 1860 (Washington, D.C., 1975).

7. Freeman, *The Overeducated American*, pp. 103-4, 112-17; Allan M. Cartter, *Ph.D.'s and the Academic Labor Market* (New York: McGraw-Hill, 1976), pp. 229-34.

8. Calculated from Cartter, *Ph.D.'s and the Academic Labor Market*, pp. 66-7.

9. Ibid., p. 239.

10. Ibid., p. 225.

11. Ibid., pp. 7-8.

12. Robert L. Heilbroner, "Balancing the World's Accounts," *The New York Review of Books* 20 (November 29, 1973): 31.

13. C. Wright Mills, *White Collar* (New York: Oxford University Press, 1951), pp. 271-2.

14. Cartter, *Ph.D.'s and the Academic Labor Market*, p. 20.

15. Ibid., p. 22.

16. George Karnezis, "A View from the Other Side," *ADE and ADFL Bulletins*, Special Joint Issue (September 1976): 8.

17. Spitzer, "Ph.D.—The New Migrant," p. 26.

18. Daniel Hawley, " 'No Race': The Candiate's View of the Job Market," *ADE and ADFL Bulletins*, Special Joint Issue (September 1976): 23.

19. Dwayne Ward, "Labor Market Adjustments in Elementary and Secondary Teaching: The Reaction to the 'Teacher Surplus'," *Teachers College Record* 77 (December 1975).

20. Modern Language Association of America, *A Guide for Job Candidates*, p. 4.

21. Cartter, *Ph.D.'s and the Academic Labor Market*, pp. 20-1.

22. Suggested by a remark in ibid., p. 240.

23. Freeman, *The Overeducated American*, p. 100.

24. Cartter, *Ph.D.'s and the Academic Labor Market*, pp. 229-34.

25. Susan O'Malley, "Nonworking or Speak Bitterness" (an interview with Toby Mortyssev), *The Radical Teacher* 1 (December 1975): 21.

26. Hawley, " 'No Race': The Candidate's View of the Job Market," p. 22.

27. See Jane Flanders, "The Uses and Abuses of Part-time Faculty," *ADE and ADFL Bulletins*, Special Joint Issue (September 1976): 49-52.

28. Paul Blumberg and James M. Murtha, "College Graduates and the American Dream," *Dissent* 24 (Winter 1977): 45-53.

29. O'Malley, "Nonworking or Speak Bitterness," p. 19.

30. Ibid., p. 25.

31. Freeman, *The Overeducated American*, p. 95.

32. O'Malley, "Nonworking or Speak Bitterness," p. 19.

33. Flanders, "The Uses and Abuses of Part-time Faculty," p. 50.

34. Hawley, " 'No Race': The Candidate's View of the Job Market," p. 23.

35. Karnezis, "A View from the Other Side," p. 6.

36. Henry Harris, " 'All Things to All Men'," *ADE and ADFL Bulletins*, Special Joint Issue (September 1976): 31. For an amusing account of how unemployed scholars in English might apply for jobs in the business world, see John T. Harwood, "From Genre Theory to the Want Ads," *ADE Bulletin*, no. 44 (February 1975): 21-4.

37. Seymour Martin Lipset and Philip G. Altbach, eds., *Students in Revolt* (Boston: Houghton Mifflin, 1969).

38. Michael Crozier, *The Stalled Society* (New York: Viking Press, 1973); Raymond Boudon, "Sources of Student Protest in France," in Philip G. Altbach and Robert S. Laufer (eds.), *The New Pilgrims: Youth Protest in Transition* (New York: David McKay, 1972); Michelle Patterson, "Governmental Policy and Equality in Higher Education: The Junior Collegization of the French University," *Social Problems* 24 (December 1976): 173-83.

39. Spitzer, "Ph.D.—The New Migrant," pp. 27-8.

40. Gregory Johnson, "The Underemployment of Advanced Degree Holders: Some Findings and Observations," Paper presented at the 71st Annual Meeting of the American Sociological Association, New York City, September 3, 1976.

3 DON MARTINDALE

Sociology's Students and Teachers

In a 1963 study for the Russell Sage Foundation, Elbridge Sibley estimated that about 3,500 persons in the United States held the Ph.D. degree in sociology; twice as many individuals held the M.A. degree. Between 150 and 200 new Ph.D. degrees were being conferred annually; between 50 and 100 Ph.D.'s were leaving the field yearly through death and retirement.[1] Three-fourths or about 2,000 of the Ph.D.'s in sociology were employed at universities and four-year colleges. A few were employed at junior colleges or lower schools. The rest were distributed in various health, welfare, correctional, and educational agencies, in business and industry, and in other miscellaneous employments.[2]

Sibley's was the most comprehensive study ever made of the problems and prospects of professional sociology. Coming as it did in the early 1960s, it was strategically timed to effect American sociology's final transformation from amateur to full professional standing.

The basic support of American sociology had always come from its status as an increasingly popular academic subject that was displacing the classical humanities as the discipline best able to orient contemporary man to his world. Moreover, not only were more American young people than ever before going to college, but children born in the post-World War II baby boom (eighteen year olds born after 1946) were about to swarm into the institutions of higher learning (see Table 1). Also in the 1960s ethnic minorities

Table 1.   BIRTH RATE PER 1,000 U.S. WOMEN,
            AGE 15-44, 1940-73

YEAR	BIRTH RATE
1940	79.9
1945	85.9
1950	106.2
1955	118.5
1960	118.0
1965	96.6
1970	87.9
1973	69.2

SOURCE: U.S. Bureau of the Census, *Statistical Abstract of the United States: 1975*, 96th ed. (Washington, D.C., 1975), p. 54.

(particularly the Blacks, Chicanos, and American Indians) hitherto underrepresented in higher education would begin coming into the colleges and universities in increasing numbers. These minorities were drawn to the social sciences. All of this meant that the 1960s would be a period of burgeoning demand for sociologists as teachers.

While undergraduate teaching had paid the bills, the focus of professionalism in sociology was its graduate education and research. The demand for sociology professors to meet the needs of college-age youth in the 1960s entailed an increase in the size of individual graduate programs and in the numbers of schools offering graduate training in sociology. Between 1958 and 1959, Sibley found that only seventy-eight institutions had active programs leading to graduate degrees in sociology. However, when the American Sociological Association sent out a questionnaire in 1975 to collect data for its *Guide to Graduate Departments in Sociology*, contact was made with all known graduate departments in the United States and Canada (282). Responses were received from 227—209 from the United States and 18 from Canada. Three out of every five reporting departments offered both the M.A. and the Ph.D. Even without considering the increasing expansion of individual graduate programs in terms of the sheer numbers of departments, in the decade following Sibley's study the graduate establishment in American sociology would double in size.

The 1960s were favorable to the development of professional sociology in still another respect. The Cold War had thawed somewhat, and the taboos had loosened on the study of areas previously forbidden to sociological research. The Kennedy and Johnson administrations were more receptive to the use of sociologists than previous federal administrations had been. The new national concern with health, education, and welfare, with civil rights, and with urban problems eventually centered on the War on Poverty, bringing an unprecedented increase in government and foundation grants to sociologists for research. Research grants freed sociologists who obtained them from the unrewarding activity of instructing undergraduates. At the same time, research projects supported graduate students, permitting a further buildup of graduate programs already expanded to meet the demand for sociologists as teachers.

Official sociology in the United States in the decade following the Sibley report seized the opportunity to achieve full professionalism. Sibley's study served as a basic handbook in the transformation. Ironically, responses to the burgeoning demand for sociologists as teachers and as research professionals were often at loggerheads. The drive toward professionalism at times appeared to be destroying the sociologist's effectiveness as a teacher, a fact which invites a review of the traditional role of the sociologist as teacher.

THE SOCIOLOGIST AS TEACHER

Auguste Comte (1798-1857), the founder of the discipline, envisioned sociology as the capstone of a pyramid of sciences rising on a foundation of mathematics. Lester F. Ward (1841-1913), America's pioneer sociologist, shared Comte's vision, describing the discipline as "the cap sheaf and crown of the sciences," occupying "the highest landing on the great staircase of education."[3] In the late 1950s Talcott Parsons (1902-   ) and C. Wright Mills (1916-62), despite their many differences, formulated positions essentially similar to those of Comte and Ward. In his article "Some Problems Confronting Sociology as a Profession," Parsons insisted that sociology is "coming increasingly to be a central symbol in the popular ideological preoccupations of our time."[4] And Mills maintained that "the social sciences are becoming the common denominator of our cultural period, and the sociological imagination our most needed quality of mind."[5] However, despite the fact that sociology has had more than 100 years to realize its pretensions,[6] it is still essentially an academic subject, with some anxiety about its standing as a science.

In the opening days of the twentieth century, Frank L. Tolman maintained that

> . . . sociology must define itself either as a body of doctrine, as a point of view, or as a method of research. It has tried to define itself as a body of doctrine, and it has failed in the attempt. . . . It has yet made no serious attempt to develop itself as a method of research, and must develop itself on these lines, and show its fruitfulness before it can demand consideration at the bar of science.[7]

Fourteen years later, Albion Small (1854-1926) undertook a review of the history of sociology in the United States. As of 1916, Small described sociology as a movement which reflected at least two major impulses: to improve the world and to improve ways of interpreting the world. Small argued that the people who called themselves and were called sociologists by others engaged in at least eight kinds of endeavor: improving the world (to aid the injured, to supply pure milk for babies, to abolish war); training persons for work in ameliorative agencies; developing technologies for social improvement (including vocational education); investigating and teaching abstract aspects of social conditions (ranging from physical anthropology to social geometry); investigating and teaching a comprehensive synthesis of human relationships; investigating and teaching group psychology; investigating and teaching methodology of the social sciences; investigating and teaching pure and applied ethics.[8]

Some of these enterprises, Small observed, were only tenuously connected with social science. The distribution of energy by individuals among the various elements loosely comprising sociology has by no means been uniform. "It is an absurdity to apply the name sociology to each and all of these divisions of labor, and at the same time to insist that the term is an instrument of scientific precision."[9]

In 1916, Small conceived sociology as having arrived at the threshold of scientific standing. It was at last, he thought, about to acquire a specific, distinctive subject matter.

In sociology, this reaction from omnibus interpretations to study of rather definitely bounded units of experience is a distinctive mark of our present stage of thinking. In and of itself this change is a scientific achievement. It is a result of much futile bombardment of the citadel of all reality. We are becoming aware of the relative superficiality of our knowledge of the most immediate and ordinary units of experience.[10]

Sociology was coming of age as a special science with a unique methodology and a distinctive body of abstract knowledge: the study of groups. "Sociology is that variety of study of the common subject matter of social science which trains attention primarily upon the forms and processes of groups."[11]

Writing in 1963, forty-seven years later, Sibley quotes observations by Leonard S. Cottrell, Jr., reflecting the view of some major contemporary social scientists that Small's optimism has not yet been realized and that Tolman's position, formulated at the turn of the century, still describes the predicament of sociology.

At present sociological theory is essentially a miscellaneous collection of descriptive formulations with little if any predictive power. . . . Ultimately, there will be no avoiding the disturbing question as to whether a science with no methods and no theory can become in fact a science. . . . Explicit theory applicable to most problems encountered does not exist, but training in sociology does develop a perspective and approach which sensitizes the sociologist to see problems in a context.[12]

The point has been repeatedly made: sociology remains predominantly a college and university subject. This is revealed, Howard Odum maintains, in the fact that since 1905, the presidents of sociology's national society, the American Sociological Association (originally the American Sociological Society), have been college and university professors. The presidents of the American Historical Association have included judges and representatives of the army and navy and public service. The presidents of the American Economic Association and the American Political Science Association have included many who were not university-related. The presidents of the National Council of Social Work include a large percentage of nonacademic persons. Moreover, the membership of the American Sociological Association is primarily institutional, while that of the American Political Science Association and American Economic Association is nearly 40 percent nonacademic.[13]

In her detailed study of the membership of the American Sociological Association during 1950-59, Matilda Riley confirmed Odum's finding that sociology is primarily a college and university discipline. From 1950 to 1959, the membership of the association increased from 3,522 to 6,345. Two-thirds of the members were located east of the Mississippi River, though the Pacific region's share grew from 9 to 13 percent during this period. In 1959, the membership was distributed as follows: 45 percent active, 24 percent associate, and 31 percent student. Teaching was the primary occupation of Association members (see Table 2). Sibley's study again confirmed the primacy of teaching among sociologists, but revealed some contrasts between the holders of the Ph.D. and the M.A. degrees. Ph.D.'s were far more likely than M.A.'s to be engaged in teaching and academic research (see Table 3).

Despite the megalomania peculiar to the discipline that has led sociologists from Comte to major contemporary figures to present sociology as the discipline in which the contemporary mind finds self-fulfillment, sociology has remained an academic discipline without a distinctive subject matter apart from materials designed especially for the consumption of undergraduates, graduate trainees, or other academic sociologists. In Sibley's study, sociology Ph.D.'s spent 73 percent of their time teaching, including teaching combined with research; 15 percent reported their principal activity to be research, including the administration of research; 7 percent consultation and administration; 1 percent social work; and 1 percent editing, writing, and lecturing as principal activities.[14] Meanwhile, the various nonacademic positions occupied by sociology Ph.D.'s lack any internally unifying principle.[15] Nonacademic sociology does not offer a stable target at which the creative sociologist can aim.

These facts present an ironic contrast to the claim from Comte and Ward to Parsons and Mills that sociology offers the decisive

Table 2.   OCCUPATIONAL AFFILIATION AND MEMBERSHIP CLASS OF THE AMERICAN SOCIOLOGICAL ASSOCIATION, 1959

CATEGORY	PERCENT IN CATEGORY	PERCENT ACTIVE MEMBERS AND FELLOWS	PERCENT ASSOCIATE MEMBERS
Liberal arts	59	67	40
Professional school	11	12	10
Federal government	5	4	7
Other	21	14	37
No information	4	3	6

SOURCE: Matilda White Riley, "Membership of the American Sociological Association, 1950-1959," *American Sociological Review* 20 (December 1960): 921-2.

Table 3.   DISTRIBUTION OF PERSONS WITH PH.D. AND M.A. DEGREES BY PRIMARY EMPLOYMENT

EMPLOYMENT	PERCENT WITH PH.D. DEGREES	PERCENT WITH M.A. DEGREES
Teaching and academic research	80	48
Nonacademic positions	12	7
Health, welfare, religious, and correctional work	2	20
Other: consultation and nonacademic	6	25

SOURCE: Elbridge Sibley, *The Education of Sociologists in the United States* (New York: Russell Sage Foundation, 1963), pp. 58, 60.

synthesis of the contemporary mind, for it is a discipline without a coherently defined subject matter apart from the activities of its own students, teachers, and researchers. The difficulties that sociology confronts in achieving a coherent self-definition must, therefore, be found in the conflicting claims of its various academic situations.

UNDERGRADUATE TEACHING

By the turn of the century, sociology was an established discipline in many universities and colleges. In Odum's estimate, expounded at midcentury, "the heart of American sociology is found in its place in the college and university curriculum as a subject, taken by thousands of students, taught by hundreds of instructors using a vast literature of texts and library readings."[16] From meager beginnings, sociology had grown by the midcentury to the status of an undergraduate subject taught by several thousand instructors to nearly 500,000 students in nearly all of the 1,810 (by 1974 there were 2,720) institutions of higher learning in the United States. In 1949-50, 7,887 B.A. degrees were earned in sociology, around one-eighth of all those earned in the social sciences. In 1973-74, 35,896 B.A. degrees were earned in sociology.

Much of the literature for the growing masses of sociology students has been supplied by their professors. Odum observed that the sale of college sociology texts is an index to the growth of undergraduate sociology courses. Already by the 1930s, a best seller sold ten times as many copies as all of the texts of American sociology's original Big Four: Ward, Sumner, Giddings, and Small. A former student of Small's reported sales of more than a million copies. By 1950, the sales of the books of E. A. Ross reached nearly 500,000.[17]

Inasmuch as the great majority of sociology students do not go on for advanced degrees, it is understandable that materials prepared for classroom use often show little relevance to the requirements of graduate students in sociology. Furthermore, the lack of some single noninstitutional destiny for graduates with B.A. degrees who do not intend to go on for higher degrees in sociology guarantees the lack of any single coherent focus in the materials prepared for undergraduate consumption.

In his attempt to estimate the value of the undergraduate curriculum of sociology as a preparation for graduate work in the discipline, Sibley concluded that it was virtually useless.

The relevance of undergraduate training in sociology diminishes as one advances from the earlier to the later stages of graduate study. Undergraduate courses which are essentially unscientific expositions of popular ideology and discussions of familiar social problems in an esoteric language may well inspire some students to pursue further study in the same field, but many of these drop out after a year or two in graduate school.[18]

Sibley reports that the chairman of one of the nation's leading sociology departments commented that if he were to live his life over he would concentrate his efforts on mathematics, philosophy, biology, history, and economics, since "very few sociology courses cover what is worth knowing."[19]

The discrepancies between undergraduate instruction in sociology and the requirements of a pre-professional program oriented toward graduate requirements cannot be solved simply by tightening up requirements. In 1958, there were 1,930 institutions of higher learning in the United States with a faculty of 344,525 and an enrollment of 2,899,482. At the same time, there had been only 83 institutions in the United States that appeared ever to have granted at least one Ph.D. in sociology. Between 1960 and 1961, only 78 institutions had active programs leading to the degree.[20] By 1974, the number of higher education institutions had increased to 2,720, of which at least 209 were offering at least one advanced degree in sociology and a majority were offering two.

It is idle to ask the 2,511 institutions which do not offer advanced degrees in sociology to streamline their sociology offerings along pre-professional lines, when there exists no profession for sociologists apart from the graduate departments of a few colleges, universities, and professional schools. At the same time, since the holder of a B.A. in sociology has no special nonacademic destiny, there is no objective situation against which undergraduate instruction can be measured. Under such circumstances, one can only expect instruction amorphously to flow along the currents of popular ideologies, with a few appeasing gestures in the direction of preprofessional training.

There is no prospect of an immediate solution to this problem, for it is intrinsic to the situation of the discipline that grants B.A. degrees to students who, nevertheless, have no objective professional destiny against which to test the validity of their training.

Although lacking coherent orientations and prescribed job opportunities, sociology's fortunes rose dramatically during the growth period of higher education, the 1960s. In an attempt to estimate the reasons for the unusual demand for sociologists at the time, *Time* magazine reported in its October 29, 1965, issue that various leaders of the field attributed the demand to the search of masses of students in undergraduate sociology courses for guidance with respect to the complexities of contemporary society.

Why such new success for sociologists. "This is a complicated society with a lot of problems around, and there's a demand for people who are trying to understand them," explains Harvard Sociologist Talcott Parsons. Another reason, says [David] Riesman, is that "the bloom of psychoanalysis is off"; people's problems often have to be related to conditions that lie beyond their family situations. The new drives against poverty, urban blight and crime have also increased the demand for sociologists who, as George Washington University Vice-President Jack Brown says, "want to get out in the field and get their hands dirty rather than just talk about social problems."

For these reasons, student enrollment in sociology courses is rising rapidly at both undergraduate and graduate levels. "Students today want to get involved, to know the society they live in to change it," explains Sociologist Paul Sheldon of Occidental College. They are asking for such courses as "The Modern City," "Social Pathology" and "Intercultural Relations." Harvard's survey course in sociology attracted 250 students last year; this year there are 325. Graduate student enrollment in sociology at U.S.C. has nearly doubled in the past two years. A few sociology departments even keep the names of their best students quiet and offer them graduate fellowships—at up to $4,000 a year—to entice them to stay. Among the most eminent departments are those of Berkeley, Harvard, Columbia, and Chicago.

In an age of specialization, sociology was a generalizing discipline uniquely addressed to the needs of contemporary society. Undergraduate sociology, composed of masses which pay the bills and create the demand for all else, was focused on the ideological preoccupations of contemporary men. Graduate sociology which arose on this foundation, however, aspired to specialization and professionalism which found ideological preoccupations unacceptable.

SOCIOLOGY AND ITS GRADUATE STUDENTS

The most comprehensive of all audiences for sociological literature is provided by undergraduate college and university students. A smaller, different audience is provided by the graduate students in sociology. The production of Ph.D.'s in sociology has been highly concentrated, with three institutions awarding around one-quarter and the top ten awarding more than one-half of all such degrees (see Table 4).

In view of the fact that students taking undergraduate degrees in sociology are usually not prepared for any specific activity outside or inside college life, it could be expected that recruitment to graduate work in sociology was not primarily through undergraduate sociology.[21] Moreover, the recruitment of sociology students for graduate work has been from the group ranking on intelligence tests near the bottom of a list of nineteen fields. Only students in education, home economics, and physical education have ranked below sociology students.[22] In the competition for the Woodrow

Table 4.   DOCTORAL DEGREES IN SOCIOLOGY, 1950-60, AND GRADUATE STUDENT ENROLLMENT AND FACULTY, 1960, IN LEADING DEPARTMENTS OF SOCIOLOGY IN THE UNITED STATES

INSTITUTION	PH.D. DEGREES CONFERRED 1950-60	GRADUATE STUDENTS IN RESIDENCE 1960	FACULTY MEMBERS 1960
University of Chicago	198	73	17
Columbia University	128	109	18
Harvard University	103	47	12
Cornell University	84	43	19
University of No. Carolina	73	55	15
University of Wisconsin	72	65	20
Ohio State University	71	32	22
University of Minnesota	59	53	14
New York University	56	196	10
Yale University	54	28	12

SOURCES: *Degrees Conferred, 1950-1956*, National Research Council; *Doctorate Production in U.S. Universities, 1936-1956* (Publication 582, Washington, D.C., 1958); *Degrees Conferred, 1957-1959* (Washington, D.C., U.S. Office of Education); *Earned Degrees Conferred* (Annual) 1960, Schedule I, Students and Faculty, Schedule I; Sibley, *The Education of Sociologists in the United States*, pp. 65-6.

Wilson National Fellowships, candidates for graduate study in sociology have won only about one-third of their pro rata share of awards.[23]

Typical graduate students in sociology are individuals who, during their undergraduate training, developed an urge to understand and reform society.[24] The tendency to choose sociology is usually a late decision. One-fifth of the recent Ph.D.'s in sociology have held Master's degrees in other disciplines, about one-half of these in fields other than the social sciences.[25] This kind of recruitment for graduate study has perpetuated the wide discrepancies existing between undergraduate and graduate work in sociology. Few if any undergraduate departments can be expected to be concerned with the preparation of future Ph.D.'s, while the diverse origins of Ph.D. candidates limit the capacity of any particular department to specify the requirements for the preparation of degree candidates.[26] A large portion of those who continue to study for advanced degrees in sociology do not have enough knowledge of one or two foreign languages to pass this requirement for the doctoral degree, and "a great majority have not had even one course in calculus, without which one cannot be considered ready for more than superficial study of a hard science involving quantitative methods or formal models."[27]

Sibley's study presented a rather sorry picture of the policies of admission, elimination, and progress of graduate students in sociology.[28] The admission policies of most departments were found to be lax, turning away only a minority of applications and permitting students to proceed at their own pace. Most sociology departments admitted almost any student who measured up to the minimum standards set by the graduate schools as a whole,[29] and they were unwilling to raise standards at the cost of smaller enrollments. For their part, the students frequently applied for admission to several institutions and entered the one offering the most financial assistance.[30] Formal procedures for sifting out unqualified students not only differed from place to place, but often changed from year to year in the same department.[31] Sociology departments seldom told a student frankly that he was unqualified to continue beyond the M.A. level,[32] and when members of the senior staff did so, others usually intervened to reverse the decision. Hence, students often continued in sociology departments long after their presence had become unprofitable to themselves and their schools.[33]

The prolonged stay of graduate students in the sociology departments where they are taking their work has a number of unintended consequences. To incoming students, the old students acquire the character of battle-wise veterans, being virtual treasure houses of gossip about the staff, who and what courses to avoid, and the like. Such lore often has little relation to the facts. As W. I. Thomas used to say, "If persons define a situation as real, it is real in its consequences," and as Merton has insisted, may become "self-fulfilling prophecies."

What the staff and other graduate students often overlook is that such veterans have a psychological stake in delaying the progress and performance of those around them. This is inevitable, for students who pass them by automatically represent a threat. It becomes essential in subtle ways to prevent others from achieving a rate of progress toward their degrees which would call their own performances into question. It is critical to steer the incoming students away from professors inclined to speed them on their way. The veterans may deem it essential to steer the achievers onto the rocks or to drop subtle hints in the right places to create negative opinions about them on the part of the staff.

Meanwhile the laxness of most sociology departments has perpetuated the system. Screening devices such as examinations can usually be deferred. A student very often is given more than one chance at passing the examinations. Ph.D.'s in sociology obtain their degrees at a median interval of 9.9 years after the B.A.[34] Sibley found the median age at the time of the degree to be thirty-three years.

Along with the imprinting of a body of knowledge and development of an array of specialized skills, graduate education is ordinarily expected to develop a sense of professional identification. However, the lack of any clearly defined nonacademic role for the sociologist and the public's consequent vagueness on as to what a sociologist is or does, the lack of pre-professional orientation by undergraduate sociology, and the late commitment by students to sociology make professional identification ambiguous. Many of the courses taken by the sociology graduate student are also open to upper-class undergraduates, depressing the level of instruction on the one hand

and often causing bright undergraduates to believe that grading is more lenient for graduate students on the other.[35]

The lack of any clear conception of the roles for which they are destined is enhanced by disparities between what is taught in most colleges and what is required by a professional sociologist. Hence, graduate students in sociology often gain more of a sense of identification with the profession by participating in the projects of faculty members than from their studies.[36] At the same time, graduate student teaching assistants may find that their duties consist of the routine grading of papers with negligible professional value. Their work as research assistants may be little better, consisting of labor on routine phases of research which are clerical or mechanical in nature. According to a study by the National Opinion Research Center, 23 percent of the first-year graduate students in the social sciences held teaching assistantships, and 3 percent held research assistantships. Sibley observed that "students of sociology appear to be relatively deprived of opportunities to become integrated into their professional community by serving as assistants at a very early stage."[37]

The content of the training of graduate students in theory and methods in most cases is low. The required theory courses for graduates and upper-class undergraduates are frequently described "as consisting essentially of a catalogue of authors' names, dates, and brief excerpts from their works."[38] Even the systematic theoretical work of men who dominated American sociology in its formative period (such as Small, Ward, and Giddings) "have virtually been buried with their authors."[39]

The core requirements in methods are almost as unsatisfactory as the theory requirements. Statistical techniques are often taught in separate courses, but minimally included in methods courses. Students in many departments can often postpone their statistics courses until the late phases of their graduate work, just prior to the Ph.D. preliminary examinations. Courses in methods for the beginning student are found to be "often frustrating to both students and teachers."[40] While some of the M.A.'s and a somewhat larger percentage of sociology's Ph.D.'s at some time have had practical experience in applying methodological precepts and acquiring research skills, "a great many have only a cook-book kind of knowlege of methods, supplemented by the experience of preparing a master's or a doctor's thesis."[41]

The opinion of both graduate students and their professors in sociology tends to polarize between those who deny the need for and utility of formal methodological rigor in sociology and those "who reject as scientific anything that is not stated in the language of mathematics and formal logic."[42] Hence, Sibley observed, despite the sociologist's "proclivity for talking about scientific methods, a student who is not interested in formal methods can get a doctoral degree in sociology from almost any institution without much more than the usual high school graduate's acquaintance with mathematics."[43]

The same graduate students who came late to sociology, delayed taking their examinations until they were sure they could get through, and resisted attempts to tighten up course examination procedures, often complained bitterly about the low level of the graduate training in sociology once they had obtained their degrees. Among graduates there was "a relatively high prevalence of avowed dissatisfaction."[44] As many as three out of ten sociologists indicated that they were not completely sure of the wisdom of their choice of discipline.[45] Moreover, Ph.D.'s in nonacademic careers were "about twice as likely as their academic colleagues to feel that some other discipline would have been preferable to the doctorate in sociology,"[46] dramatizing once again the lack of objective subject matter.

If sociology were to make the bid for full professionalism, no time appeared more propitious than the 1960s. While the number of persons receiving the B.A. or its equivalent in sociology had remained virtually constant between 1950 and 1960 (and in fact had dropped slightly), the number of B.A.'s granted in 1970 (30,848) was more than four times greater than the number granted in 1960 (7,182) (see Table 5).

An indication of the popularity of the field during the decade can be gauged by the devotion by *Time* magazine of a special issue to the subject in 1965. Of the demand for sociologists *Time* observed:

Moonlighting becomes them too. Publishers are peppering sociologists with offers. "I've heard it said that any sociology professor who can't

Table 5.   DEGREES GRANTED IN SOCIOLOGY, 1950-74

ACADEMIC YEAR	DEGREE		
	B.A.	M.A.	Ph.D.
1949-50	7,886	552	98
1959-60	7,182	440	161
1969-70	30,848	1,716	534
1973-74	35,898	2,196	632

SOURCE: The American Council of Education, *Fact Book of Higher Education* (1975, 75.270).

double his salary with extra-curricular jobs shouldn't be here," says Brandeis Sociology Chairman John R. Seeley. A sociologist can command $100 a day as a consultant to industry, up to $90 a day as advisor to such federal agencies as the National Institutes of Health, C.I.A., Census Bureau, State Department, Office of Economic Opportunity and Office of Education. Sociologist David Riesman (*The Lonely Crowd*) left Chicago for Harvard in 1958, not for money ("Any time I'm hard up I can give a lecture somewhere."), but because he was offered a special chair that would permit him to teach undergraduates without restriction. Demographers are in big demand, and so are social psychologists and sociologists with training in medicine. The American Sociology [*sic*] Association, whose total membership runs to 8500, has a medical-sociology section with nearly 600 members.[47]

And while the popularity of sociologists was at an all-time high, Sibley's book, *The Education of Sociologists in the United States*, was a virtual manual ready at hand for the task of achieving full professionalism in sociology.

A monograph would be required to deal adequately with all the efforts to achieve the full professionalization of sociology in the 1960s. However, few of Sibley's suggestions went unheeded: (1) in most departments with graduate programs, undergraduate instruction was sharply downgraded; (2) efforts were made to develop pre-professional major programs in sociology, programs with heavy stress on statistics and methods which, presumably, would transform the discipline into a self-recruited operation; (3) graduate programs were formally organized and partially bureaucratized with the appointment of special (with time off from teaching obligations) administrators and graduate coordinators, often assisted by special departmental committees; (4) major attempts were made to tighten up recruitment policies for the admission of students with new, higher grade point averages, Graduate Record Examination scores, and the like; (5) incoming sociology graduate students were increasingly accepted on a strict quota basis and visualized as a cohort whose members were to be carefully tracked through their graduate careers; (6) promotion and tenure policies for staff members were self-consciously based on professional performance, defined as comprising such things as activity in the regional and national societies, adeptness at obtaining extramural funding, and publication in a limited number of refereed professional journals.

While few of Sibley's suggestions went unheeded in the drive by sociology departments with graduate programs toward full professionalism, only variable success was achieved. Opposition was soon encountered, resulting in a profound cleavage in the ranks of sociologists at all levels.

(1) The downgrading of undergraduate instruction was correlated with a sharp decline in its quality. If promotion, for example, was based on attendance at professional meetings, service on professional committees, the administration of research grants, and the writing of papers for a limited number of refereed journals while no recognition was received for teaching excellence, ambitious individuals took the hint and reduced their teaching obligations to the minimum. Sensitive students were not long in perceiving that the life was vanishing from their sociology courses. They began to give angry voice to their frustrations and denounced the preoccupation by their instructors with professionalism and grant-getting as a rip off. (2) Professionally oriented sociologists interpreted their transformations of the undergraduate program as upgrading it to genuine pre-professional status, loading their programs for majors with methods and statistics requirements. When this backfired and enrollments began to fall, there was often lame concession to the need to retain service courses which preserved the humanistic appeal of traditional sociology for the American undergraduate. As a result of being separated from the pre-professional courses, the service courses tended to become even more ideological in flavor than before, even as the courses for majors became more scientistic

as their substance was removed. The resulting cleavage was exaggerated by the senior staff's inclination to shunt teaching obligations in large undergraduate sections to junior staff members and to graduate assistants. When these tendencies took the form of a two-track sociology major, an almost complete polarization of sociology resulted: ideologically committed humanism versus an arid, value-neutral scientism.

The new policies toward graduate students—(3) the bureaucratization of graduate programs, (4) the tightening up of recruitment policies, and (5) the organization of incoming groups of graduate students into carefully policed cohorts—did, indeed, by and large, accomplish a rise in the level of formal qualification for graduate study in sociology. Unfortunately, in the opinion of many sensitive observers, it also led to the selection of conventional, strictly academic grade getters. The days of the recruitment into sociology of students with rich backgrounds in varied academic disciplines were apparently over. With it too came the disappearance of the individual with an overpowering passion to understand society, who often traversed many diverse academic boundaries (geography, political science, economics, philosophy, history, anthropology, and law) before settling in sociology and who brought rich sophistication in the social sciences with him. Moreover, the tendency to shift teaching responsibilities to the junior staff and graduate students meant that, in the days of the counter-cultural revolt against establishment-dominated research, grantsmanship, poor teaching, and the disappearance of relevant courses, graduate students were tempted to assume the leadership of undergraduate student protest. This activity provided graduate students with an independent power base from which to bargain for concessions on their ancient grievances: the language requirements, the preliminary examinations, the course requirements, and the like. Standards often yielded and broke before the force of student power.

Finally, (6) the narrow professionalisms that inclined ambitious staff members to withdraw from unproductive pursuits, such as undergraduate teaching, placed them in opposition to staff members who bore the primary burden of teaching. With the cleavage that was appearing between an ideologically committed humanism and an arid, value-neutral scientism, some individuals who were disenchanted with the drive toward professionalism sponsored the relatively inarticulate undergraduate student demands for relevance. This provided them with an anti-establishment power base. Moreover, commercial publishing houses were receptive to writers who addressed popular themes and the mass market. From a base in leadership of studied revolts and possibilities for commercial publication, the more radicalized members of the profession were able to launch a counterattack on establishment sociology, a counterattack that even reached into the regional and national associations. Those aligned behind professionalism responded by downgrading, for promotion and tenure purposes, every form of writing other than the monograph or the article for the refereed professional journal.

In the course of all these developments, graduate students found themselves in the classical position of middlemen torn by contradictory influences.

With all the ambiguities of their position, pulled both ways (toward the vague ideological orientations of undergraduate sociology on the one hand and ill-defined professionalism on the other), the graduate students provided a second major audience for the productions of their elders. With considerable skill, many of their elders seized upon the demand for work materials represented by the mixed aggregations of upper-class undergraduates and graduates to assemble an ever-increasing number of compilations, symposia, anthologies, and books of readings comprised of articles and research reports by themselves and their professional colleagues for use in upper-division classes, graduate courses, and seminars. While such symposia permit their elders to publish commercially their articles and research reports, they are frustrating to undergraduates and graduates alike. Such symposia and compilations contribute to the fragmentation of the field, for they normally have little theoretical or methodological unity.

SOCIOLOGY AND ITS TEACHERS

The third major audience to which the writings of sociologists are addressed is composed of other sociologists, primarily in their roles as college professors. Sociology professors perform roles often fractured by internal contradictions.

At the time of the Sibley study, nearly 250,000 persons were engaged in college and university teaching, a number which the U.S. Office of Education estimated would double in the next decade. The professor in America, Robert Knapp observed, is expected to perform three distinct functions: research, transmission of information, and character building.[48] Most of the paradoxes and contradictions in the professor's role arise from mixing these functions.

It is my thesis that the evolving role of the college professor in America has been characterized by a progressive decline of his character-developing function along with a strong tendency for the research and informational functions to part company and form two separate callings.[49]

From seventeenth to the midnineteenth centuries, the professor's role was dominated by the character-building function. The professor was expected to place emphasis on classical education (Greek, Latin, history, and theology). He was "an intellectual generalist who might at once profess natural history, ethics and theology while remaining a Latin or Greek scholar."[50] Among the circumstances in America which shifted emphasis away from character building was the Morrill Act of 1862 and the establishment of the land-grant college. Subjects concerned with status deportment began to give way to technological and practical subjects. The rise of natural science was a component in the rise of the research ideal of the professor, originating in Germany and copied by Johns Hopkins. A development initiated by Harvard and rapidly copied elsewhere was abandonment of the fixed classical curriculum and the substitution of the elective system. Emphasis on science and research, together with the elective system, was correlated with the rise of departmentalism and accelerating specialization.[51]

Character building and the classical curriculum had been closely associated with the training of the clergy. Now theory in a variety of disciplines was correlated with the rise of technical, compartmentalized education. The rise of professional societies and of professional identification enhanced the movement in the colleges and universities toward departmentalization. Professionalism posed a conflict of loyalties, for "on the one hand, [the professors] see themselves as members of their particular academic discipline with its professional journals, annual meetings, employment centers, and committees. On the other hand, they are members of the faculty of an institution which pays their salaries and in other ways commands their loyalty and services."[52] The complex of their loyalties also reacts upon the kind of intellectual fare professors prefer.

Other major trends with effects on intellectual output included the rise of the doctrine of academic freedom, the increased emphasis on research and publication as evidence of professional success and as bases for promotion and advancement, and the evolution of the Ph.D. degree into the union card of the college professor. The decline of the college professor's influence in the management of affairs of the institution and the alienation of the college teaching profession from the managerial class in America have also had repercussions on outlook and creativity. There has been a progressive decline in enthusiasm for teaching, a decline most advanced in the wealthy, prestigious institutions that set the style for others. The main avenue of employment and promotion has shifted to scholarly publications and research.[53]

As the American college or university professor plots a course through the crosswinds of these diverse functions, a number of typical career stages can be isolated. The average sociologist is twenty-nine years old at the time of the awarding of the Ph.D. The sociologist will ordinarily (except for special cases and accidents) be forced to take a first job at a second- or third-rate institution, saddled with a large teaching load. If professionally oriented, he will regularly attend regional and national meetings and make some effort to seek a place on the programs. He will make efforts to publish. If he succeeds by his mid- to late thirties, the opportunity may arise to move from college to university or from an institution offering graduate work in sociology of low prestige to one of higher status. Among the benefits to be enjoyed are higher salary, more research facilities, and a lighter teaching load. If this transition is not made, readjustment in expectations may occur, reconciling the individual to remaining an undergraduate teacher in sociology or to leaving the teaching profession. Inasmuch as fewer than 140 institutions in North America offer the Ph.D. degree, with fewer than 100 additional ones offering the M.A. only, the large majority of sociology teachers are in the category of those forced to consider themselves primarily as teachers.

The second major stage in the career of the aspiring professor, who has managed to pass through the first, usually falls between the ages of thirty-five and forty. By the time he enters this phase, the professor has used up the intellectual capital received from his own teachers, for in the first few years of teaching, the newly christened Ph.D. typically gives lectures drawn in varying degrees from the best of his own teachers.[54]

All in all, it is probably for the overall good of the teaching profession that so many new Ph.D.'s deliver the lectures of the best of their own teachers. It is one of the important ways in which the oral traditions of the teaching world accumulate, for at times the young do indeed "stand on the shoulders of giants." This, in part, accounts for the fact that the young Ph.D.'s are often the electrifying source of new ideas, breathing a new spirit into the institutions they join.[55] However, by the end of the first four to six years of teaching, the new Ph.D. has either used up the intellectual capital from his home department, in which case his lectures may have begun to jell into permanent stereotypes, or he has begun to work out his own point of view.

To the individual who successfully enters the second stage, an assault on the field is possible with any ideas he has independently generated. During this second period, depending upon success, the professor may occupy successively higher positions on the committees of the regional and national societies. A major component in the rate of salary increase and promotion will be his rate of publication. And if he becomes successful, invitations from more prestigious institutions may be forthcoming.

Among the big opportunities for the individual able to pass through the first stage of the academic career in the social sciences to the second is an increased possibility of obtaining research funds. Nothing succeeds like success. Research funds, in turn, permit direct competition for the services of graduate student assistants. The nucleus is present for the formation of a small power circle. Drawn to the professor for support during their academic studies and for possible data for their dissertations, graduate students supply energies and intelligence which may be exploited by the professor for the promotion of his personal research concerns. To be sure, the student benefits as well. A complex symbiotic relationship may develop between the project director and the student assistants.

Bernard Berelson explored the feelings of new Ph.D.'s that they had been exploited by their major professors. In his sample he discovered that

. . . recent recipients in the sciences complain in substantial numbers (46 percent agree to 34 percent disagree) that major professors often exploit doctoral candidates by keeping them as research assistants too long, by subordinating their interests to departmental or the professor's interests in research programs, etc."[56]

However, in a secondary analysis of Berelson's data, Hagstrom discovered that only 29 percent of the doctoral candidates in sociology agree with the statement that graduate professors exploit their students.[57] At least in sociology, it would appear, the graduate students' sense of exploitation was not as intense or as widespread as in other sciences.

Hagstrom also believes that the dependence of students on professors has an influence on the kind of research performed in universities. Students, he suggests, are less likely to engage in long-term research than professors. They have precarious status and receive minor material rewards.

Since research is done in organized groups, the status of the group leader is dependent on success in attaining group goals. Failure may mean a loss of status for the leader, or at least the leader may expect this to happen. He will therefore be tempted to avoid problems in which failure is likely.[58]

The leader, according to Hagstrom, acts in a manner intended to increase his personal prestige and to diminish risk taking. Moreover, professors who must compete for student assistance may avoid topics or techniques that students perceive to be unfashionable or avoid tasks they cannot perform.[59]

To hold students or to induce them to join their projects, professors may extend opportunities for the joint publication of papers. "Today in the United States, professors are probably more apt to give students credit not really due them than to appropriate the work of students for themselves."[60]

Phase two of the professional career (the gathering of graduate students around the individual, the competition for foundation grants, speeded up production of research papers and reports, pressures to obtain positions in the regional and national societies) is a time of feverish activity for the ambitious sociologist. Depending on a combination of chance factors and his research and writing skills, the individual may be ready either to make the last flight to the top ranks of the profession or to turn his sights upon lesser but more accessible objectives.

Usually by his late thirties or early forties, the professor knows whether attainment of the top ranks of the profession with various attendant honors is possible: invitations from the most prestigious institutions, offers of chairs or distinguished professorships, high office in the professional societies. At this time and with special frequency, able individuals who realize they will never achieve top rank redirect their expectations to the local college or university, aspiring for chairmanships or deanships. The palace revolutionaries in academic life are usually individuals in their forties. In ten years or so, if not earlier, they will in turn face the possibilities of palace revolutions from new groups on their way up.

Anywhere from his mid-forties to the time of retirement, the professor who has passed through the other stages and has achieved primary position either in the professional society or in the local milieu finds himself fighting a holding action, seeking to retain whatever fragments of prestige remain. At best, the individual in the fourth stage will be treated as an elder; at worst, he will be viewed as an intolerable old fool who is undoubtedly senile. Where the individual still retains the trappings of office desired by younger aspirants, a ruthless assault may be made on his person. In some instances, individuals with major reputations have even been driven from their home schools shortly before they could qualify for retirement.

In retirement, the individual is suddenly removed from the competition. If his wits and energies hold out, however, he may suddenly find numerous opportunities for short- or long-term lectureships. The academic person occasionally ends his days with a long and happy Indian summer.

The academic sociologist's period of greatest productivity usually falls in the second and third career phases. It is also at this time that he is most apt to be research oriented and to view the imparting of information as an unnecessary obstruction to career goals. The ambitious academic social scientist turns toward securing foundation or other grants to support research, while winning freedom from undergraduate teaching obligations, if not graduate teaching. Among other things, research funds permit the individual to hire numerous research assistants. At the same time, in his academic role the professional research academician often bends every effort to raising the methodological and statistical requirements for the graduate degree, thus doubly validating his claims to scientific and professional standing.

However, sociology's general lack of objective subject matter, apart from the material worked up specifically for various academic needs, also reacts on the research sociologist. He often searches for the latest mathematical devices and techniques from a wide variety of surrounding disciplines. These techniques are, at times, precipitously introduced into his own research and into the training of the graduate advisees long before the patient work has been done to adapt them to sociological subject matter. The selection of problems is often determined by the methods available rather than by theoretical considerations or antecedently existing problems. If no problem can be found to fit the techniques, artificially created or simplified situations must be designed to give plausibility to procedure. Especially designed "experimental" situations are not per se scientifically useless. If they arise in service of theoretical considerations, they may represent a step toward exactness; but if designed to employ methodological techniques, they have at best only a training function.

RECAPITULATION

The sociologist has no clearly defined role apart from his position as a teacher of sociology. The primary audiences for sociological works of all sorts are academically anchored as undergraduate students, graduate students, or other professors. Sociology presents the rare spectacle of a discipline with no other task than to work out its own salvation, enjoying freedom from external obligations in the search for its self-definition. Sociology became popular as a promise to square the circle of the sciences, to bridge the humanities

and the sciences. It became a general point of view uniquely qualified to adapt man to the contemporary world. However, in an age
in which everything is a specialty, sociology has turned itself into a
specialty in search of an identity. Offhand, it would seem to be
brilliantly placed to achieve a maximum of unity, inasmuch as the
one point at which its adherents can make common cause is in their
positions as teachers or students. This, however, has proved to be
an illusion.

By the mid-1960s the demand for sociologists primarily by the
colleges and universities was, according to *Time* magazine, at an
all-time high.

"We've come into a new day," says Dr. Dan Dobson, chairman of N.Y.U.'s
department of sociology and anthropology, while complaining that he
sought seven new sociologists for his staff this year, but could snare only
three because of the nationwide competition. "I fully expected to retire at
$10,000 and live a fairly spartan life," beams a young Emory University
sociologist who got 14 job offers—one at $18,000 a year—even though he
was not seeking a change. "I hardly know what to make of what's happened."

The Berkeley campus of the University of California—where some people
would say a need has been demonstrated—has offered more than $25,000
a year to a few renowned sociologists, $20,000 to others less well known.
The University of Southern California will pay $20,000 for a top professor,
as will New York University. A big name can try for $25,000 at Harvard
and probably get it. A sociologist at Tulane who only five years ago was
drawing $10,000 now gets $21,000. And average pay is also rising. Median
salary at the universities is $10,000, only slightly below economists.[61]

However, by the mid-1970s, the split between the scientific and
humanistic branches of sociology, the collapse of the War on Poverty,
the partial drying up of foundation funds and government grants
for research, and the shift of undergraduate students into the professional schools and more vocationally promising programs had
largely isolated professional sociology from the old foundations of
the discipline's mass appeal. Sociology's splendid freedom to work
out its own destiny without external commitment (that is, in an age
of specialization, it is an intrinsically unspecializable point of view)
has turned out to be a booby trap. It has permitted the conflicting

currents of contemporary higher education to pull it in contradictory directions. A discipline with subject matter definable apart from the position and activities of its teachers and students has an objective reference point and the possibility of a mission that permits it to resist trends in the educational process. Lacking such an objective reference point, sociology is destined to experience internally all tensions playing upon higher education itself.

Hence the fascinating spectacle: in its undergraduate teaching, sociology has unconsciously taken over the role vacated by the decline of the classical ideal of scholarship; it has undertaken a character-building or status orientation function and, on many campuses, has grown into the single largest department of the liberal arts college. In its graduate teaching, on the other hand, such ideological and evaluative orientations are abandoned as unscientific for an insistence on various sorts of methodological, mathematical, and statistical gadgetry which, when employed at all, is applied to such trivial problems as to lead C. Wright Mills to characterize it as "abstracted empiricism." Finally, in its professonal research activities, sociology has been propelled toward the ideal of becoming a research specialty, often by borrowing techniques and skills from other disciplines and choosing problems for study on the basis of how well they fit the method or research technique.

The consequence of this remarkable adventure is the appearance of a voluminous, largely ideological, literature for undergraduates in isolation from any exacting methodological requirements. It has led to a considerable literature for training in methods in isolation from clearly defined content. It has led to a considerable production of research reports and studies chosen not for the solution of theoretical problems, but because a technique or research method was available.

Nowhere are the ironies that haunt contemporary sociology more apparent than in the statement by one of the outstanding sociologists of contemporary America, Robert Nisbet, Albert Schweitzer Professor of the Humanities at Columbia, member of the American Academy of Arts and Sciences. He has argued that sociology is not even a science but an art form and that the view that sociology advances ideas (theory) and employs empirical methods to prove or disprove them is an illusion.

For of all the Idols of the Mind or Profession regnant today the worst is that which Bacon might have placed among his Idols of the Theatre: the belief, first, that there really is something properly called theory in sociology, and, second, that the aim of all sociological research should be that of adding to or advancing theory. At its worst this idolatry takes the form of veneration for the grand system.[62]

Having denied to sociology both ideas and method, Nisbet makes an argument for visualizing the essence of sociology as consisting of aesthetic insights. This noble vision of sociology is worthy of translation into the form of a Shakespearean sonnet.

> Give up the myth that scientists never weary
> In trying to account and to explain,
> Like patient hunters with a net of theory
> Who all too often set their snares in vain.
> Abandon it, that fanciful old story
> Of the empiric edifice of thought,
> Erected stone by stone, as from the quarry
> Each new won piece is mined and shaped and wrought.
> The splendid insights that illuminate
> Leap, rather, full-fledged from the mind and heart
> Of that Fine Being not destined by his fate
> To work and sweat and grunt and strain and fart.
>   In Social Science the Greatest of the Great,
>   On broad behinds do sit and scintillate.

NOTES

1. Elbridge Sibley, *The Education of Sociologists in the United States* (New York: Russell Sage Foundation, 1963), pp. 22, 46.

2. Ibid., p. 47.

3. Lester F. Ward, "The Place of Sociology Among the Sciences," *American Journal of Sociology* 1 (July 1895): 16.

4. Talcott Parsons, "Some Problems Confronting Sociology as a Profession," *American Sociological Review* 44 (August 1959): 559.

5. C. Wright Mills, *The Sociological Imagination* (New York: Oxford University Press, 1959), p. 13.

6. Harry Alpert dates it from the first appearance of the newly coined word "sociology" in the forty-seventh chapter of Auguste Comte's, *The Positive Philosophy*. Harry Alpert, "Sociology: Its Present Interests," in

Bernard Berelson, ed., *The Behavioral Sciences Today* (New York: Basic Books, 1963), p. 52.

7. Frank L. Tolman, "The Study of Sociology in Institutions of Learning in the United States," *American Journal of Sociology* 8 (July 1902): 86. Quoted in Sibley, *The Education of Sociologists in the United States*, p. 18.

8. Albion Small, "Fifty Years of Sociology in the United States (1865-1915)," *American Journal of Sociology* 21 (May 1916): 828-9.

9. Ibid., p. 829.

10. Ibid., p. 834.

11. Ibid., p. 825.

12. Leonard S. Cottrell, Jr., Unpublished Memorandum quoted by Sibley, *The Education of Sociologists in the United States*, p. 18.

13. Howard W. Odum, *American Sociology* (London: Longmans, Green, 1951), pp. 10-11.

14. Sibley, *The Education of Sociologists in the United States*, p. 48.

15. Ibid., p. 49.

16. Odum, *American Sociology*, p. 12.

17. Ibid., p. 13.

18. Sibley, *The Education of Sociologists in the United States*, p. 48.

19. Ibid., p. 87.

20. Ibid., p. 64.

21. Ibid., p. 76.

22. Ibid., p. 179.

23. Ibid., p. 82.

24. Ibid., p. 83.

25. Ibid., p. 84.

26. Ibid., p. 85.

27. Ibid., p. 88.

28. Ibid., pp. 89ff.

29. Ibid., p. 93.

30. Ibid., p. 94.

31. Ibid., p. 96.

32. Ibid., p. 87.

33. Ibid., p. 98.

34. Ibid., p. 99.

35. Ibid., p. 105.

36. Ibid., p. 106.

37. Ibid., p. 109.

38. Ibid., p. 117.

39. Ibid.

40. Ibid., p. 119.

41. Ibid., p. 121.

42. Ibid., p. 134.

43. Ibid., p. 34.

44. Ibid., p. 158.

45. Ibid., p. 159.

46. Ibid., p. 170.

47. *Time* (October 29, 1965).

48. Robert H. Knapp, "Changing Functions of the College Professor," in Nevitt Sanford, ed., *The American College* (New York: John Wiley & Sons, 1962), p. 291.

49. Ibid., p. 292.

50. Ibid., p. 293.

51. Ibid., p. 294.

52. Ibid., p. 295.

53. Ibid., p. 298.

54. It was a considerable surprise to me the first time young men who had completed their Ph.D. preliminary examinations sat in on my lectures for the express purpose of getting a set of lecture notes to use in their own forthcoming teaching jobs. Over the years I have also known professors who attend summer sessions for this purpose. When Louis Wirth visited the Minnesota campus in the early 1950s, students of one of Wirth's own former students who was on the faculty at the time discovered that they had already heard Wirth's lectures, second hand, down to and including his very own jokes.

55. The ideas are new, of course, from the standpoint of the students at the institution the young professor joins. For example, when C. Wright Mills first joined the faculty at Columbia and filled his lectures with ideas he had obtained from the lectures of Hans Gerth, Mills was the electrifying source of new ideas to Columbia students, who marveled at hearing so many things in Mills's classes that they had not heard in the classes of other Columbia professors.

56. Bernard Berelson, *Graduate Education in the United States* (New York: McGraw-Hill, 1960), p. 153.

57. Warren O. Hagstrom, *The Scientific Community* (New York: Basic Books, 1965), p. 134.

58. Ibid., p. 137.

59. Ibid., p. 138.

60. Ibid. If Hagstrom is right, sociology graduate students have a control over the research projects of their professors that their counterparts in the broad sciences could not possibly have.

61. *Time* (October 29, 1965).

62. Robert Nisbet, *Sociology as an Art Form* (New York: Oxford, 1976), p. 20.

4 SIL DONG KIM

The Student Pawn in Professorial Power Politics

The story of Ri Sing Moon illustrates how graduate students become pawns in professorial power politics. Moon was born on January 17, 1942, in Pusan, Korea, to a family of poor farmers and was raised on a combination of Christian doctrine and traditional Korean custom, norms, and values. Thus, he was taught family principles, such as patience, not to talk when unsure, not to betray others, to help the poor, to compete fairly, to have faith that justice always wins, to study hard and be diligent, to accept responsibility for one's own actions, to respect all human beings, especially teachers, elders, and particularly, to love one's family.

Because of his family's great respect for education, Moon's brothers and older sister were among the lucky few who managed to continue their education during the Korean War.

The South Korean educational system is highly competitive. The schools from the junior high through college level are ranked according to prestige. If a child completes his education at one of the top junior and senior high schools and graduates from a top college, his future in Korea is secure. Moreover, if a graduate from the top schools in Korea obtains advanced education in the United States and other developed countries, his future is virtually assured in the positions of higher social status and prestige. Money cannot buy entrance to a top school in South Korea; access is possible only through competition among the thousands who apply each year.

The alumni of these top schools form an elite with strong brotherhood attachments throughout life. Moon studied diligently for the entrance exams at each level, even to the extent of cloistering himself in a Buddhist temple for three months before one of them. His upwardly mobile family pinned their highest hopes on him and his brother.

Moon placed seventh for entrance to the top junior high school and was later admitted to the most prestigious high school in Korea. At the high school, he became the captain of the ping-pong team and of the gymnastics team. An incident during these years illustrates Moon's competitive drive and will to succeed. During gymnastic exercises, when he was pressing himself to unusual lengths, he broke an arm. Determined to prevent future accidents, he took up karate, earning the black belt. He was to become the karate representative from his high school, and he won a national gymnastic championship in an inter-high school tournament.

Despite Moon's heavy involvement in sports, he did not neglect his academic pursuits. He gained entrance to the top Korean college and to its law school, the most difficult to enter in the whole nation.

During his college years, Moon began to make plans for study abroad. At that time, his brother was already attending the University of San Carlos in Guatemala, the first Korean student to study in any Spanish-speaking country in Central America. When Moon was a senior in college, through his brother's efforts, he received a summer internship assisting a professor of law at the University of San Carlos. In March 1964, Moon graduated from college, placing ninth out of approximately 300 graduates. Two months later, he was on his way to Guatemala. The stipend from the internship paid his travel and his living expenses for the summer. In September 1964, after his brother had earned the degree of Licenciado en Letras and Moon had finished his internship, the brothers arrived in Miami, Florida, with plans to continue their studies in the United States.

Moon's brother was admitted to the Department of Political Science at the University of Florida with a teaching assistantship. Moon, on the other hand, was admitted to the Department of Political Science of Midwest University as an unsupported graduate student. Both chose political science as a major because of their strong interest in political careers cultivated primarily by their leadership in the April 19, 1960, Korean student movement and their personal experiences with high-ranking government officials.

INTO THE CROSS FIRE OF AN ACADEMIC BATTLEFIELD

There was nothing in Ri Sing Moon's experience to warn him that he was about to find himself in the cross fire of an academic battlefield. He had no way of knowing that American education was about to undergo a convulsive ground movement that would polarize the academic generations before the inevitable conflicts had run their course.

On September 20, 1964, a week after his arrival in Watertown, Moon presented himself at the office of Professor Edward McDougal, the chairperson of the Department of Political Science. McDougal had joined the Midwest faculty in 1945 or 1946. At this time (the early 1960s), the most prominent member of the department was an internationally known pacifist, Oswald Ripley. Ripley was revered by Midwest's students who, whether or not they agreed with his theories, were impressed by the lucidity and insight of his teaching. By the 1960s, McDougal and Ripley had the longest tenure in the department. Meanwhile, a new group of younger professors was beginning to make its presence felt on the Midwest campus. These hard-nosed scientific professors were about to challenge McDougal, Ripley, and others of the older generation for power over university and departmental affairs. At the same time, the civil rights movement and the Vietnam War were causing unrest, and the Chicano, American Indian, gay, and women's liberation movements were beginning to polarize both the faculty and the student body.

When Moon introduced himself to McDougal, the chairperson immediately invited him to sit down, had the secretary get all the materials in the department files on him, and proceeded, through interrogation and inspection of the files, to work out a plan for Moon's graduate studies at Midwest. McDougal suggested that he (1) take the mandatory English examination for foreign students and proceed immediately to improve his English; (2) choose Oswald Ripley as an adviser because of Moon's interest in political philosophy; (3) spend at least a year taking undergraduate courses inasmuch as his degree in law in Korea was insufficient preparation for political science; and (4) apply for financial assistance for graduate study if he proved a good student. Moon unhestitatingly accepted all of McDougal's suggestions. There is a Korean saying that "Words from a respected professor are more valuable than 1,000 gold bars." Because of his traditional Asian value system, it would have been disrespectful for him even to think about alternatives to those suggested.

Thus, Moon's academic life at Midwest began with courses for which he would receive no credit toward an M.A. program. He took the English proficiency exam offered by the Foreign Student Office and was advised to take grammar, conversation, and writing classes simultaneously for at least one year. He combined these classes with undergraduate political science classes, taking fifteen credits a quarter in the first year and nine a quarter in the second— a heavy load for any recent immigrant. Moon also had to struggle to support himself completely and to meet the high cost of nonresident tuition. After two years of this existence, his weight had dropped from 145 to 108 pounds. All the while he tried to earn respectable grades, for, as one of his Korean friends informed him, "If you don't get at least B's in your course work, you will get kicked out of the university. If you get kicked out of the university, you will be deported from the United States by the Immigration and Naturalization Services. If that happens you will be too humiliated to face your friends back home and your family will be disgraced."

The special pressures foreign students felt had been tragically illustrated during that year, when one of Moon's former classmates from Korea committed suicide in his room at Centennial Hall. Another, who had been studying mathematics at Midwest, had broken under the stress, flunked out, and was deported.

Few American students or professors have an adequate understanding of the difficulties faced by a foreign (particularly Asian) student for whom English is a second language. Moreover, the financial difficulties are especially severe when, as in the case of Korea, the law forbids that more than $100 be sent out of the country annually. Thus, even if the famiy at home is wealthy, the Asian student must live in poverty. Moreover, the immigration laws of the United States prohibit the foreign student from working during his first year of study.

Only four days after arriving in Watertown, Moon was working in a Mexican restaurant as a ceiling washer for $1.00 an hour. Although it was illegal for a student to work during the first year of study, the Korean student community did seek jobs, since they had no other option for survival. This was the beginning of a long series of such jobs. He worked as a pot washer, bus boy, waiter, car washer, and laborer at a paper factory. Added to this economic pressure was the psychological pressure of being nameless and faceless in a new land and of working as a menial while in his own country Moon was considered a success.

These pressures may have contributed to Moon's car accident in his third year, which almost brought his studies to a halt. As a result of the accident, he was forced to register for only three credits during the winter quarter of 1966.

Before the car accident, Moon had managed to earn Bs in his courses and was not in debt. He believed he had successfully fulfilled McDougal's suggestions, which were also approved by Ripley. His English was improving rapidly, and he had finished three courses offered by Professor Brian Grossman and five by Ripley. In order to do so, he was sleeping only about three hours a night. He did not complain, however, for he was proud to keep his promise to Mc-Douglas. His employment picture had also improved: he was now teaching karate at Midwest University, at St. Thomas College, and at a karate center.

In early 1966, while Moon was preparing to take graduate courses in the Department of Political Science, Joseph Schneider replaced McDougal as chairperson. At this time Moon did not fully appreciate what had happened. A coup had taken place, with the old guard, epitomized by McDougal and Ripley, falling from power and the young Turks, epitomized by the new chairperson, Joseph Schneider, and the new graduate coordinator, Richard McCafferty, taking over the leadership of the department. Suddenly, there was a great emphasis on quantitative methodology, and it was stressed that political science students should also take additional quantitative methodology outside the Department of Political Science. The new chairperson informed Moon that if he hoped to major in political theory, he had to take courses from professors other than his adviser, Oswald Ripley. Many other students were also being advised to drop Ripley's courses. Rumors were continually being floated to the effect that Ripley was leaving Midwest University. Alarmed, Moon asked Ripley about the rumors. Ripley denied any knowledge of the matter and said he could not imagine who was instigating such talk. On one occasion, however, he did express the fear that some people wanted his removal. Moon became even more apprehensive when McDougal, the man whose advice he had been following so conscientiously, began talking rather defensively about retiring to Hawaii.

It was some time before Moon realized that the new chairperson of the Department of Political Science did not have the slightest intention of honoring arrangements the graduate students had made with the former chairperson. By this time, he had developed an intense admiration for Ripley and clung to him desperately as the troubles in the department deepened.

SHAPE UP OR SHIP OUT

Moon had spent the academic years 1964-65 and 1965-66 on the program McDougal had worked out for him. By the fall of the academic year 1966-67, he was ready to undertake formal graduate work in Midwest's political science program. At this time, however, he was involved in the serious automobile accident mentioned earlier and, as a consequence, his progress during the academic year was slowed considerably. Meanwhile, it became emphatically clear to him that the young group that had succeeded to power in 1966 severely disapproved of Ripley. Both the new chairperson and the new graduate coordinator first advised him to study political theory with other members of the department, and when he rejected that advice, they counseled him to transfer either to philosophy or to history. Moon resisted this suggestion as well, but he did make one compromise. He signed up for Schneider's methodology course, which he hoped would both meet the methodology requirements of the new scientism and give him an opportunity to demonstrate his competence to the new chairperson. He also hoped the compromise would both save the faces of the young Turks and give him an opportunity to continue to pursue his interest with Ripley.

During the fall quarter of 1966, every paper Moon wrote for Schneider's class was given a grade lower than a B. Since he never received a grade higher than a C in the course, he asked permission to drop it and retake it when he had further time to study. Only after he had taken the final examination on which he again received a C was he permitted to drop it.

At the beginning of the winter quarter in 1967, Moon received Schneider's permission to retake the course which was a prerequisite to the Ph.D. program. Schneider signed the entry form with no suggestions or comments. Again Moon received no grade higher than a C on any paper or exam. By now, he knew the course by heart, but nevertheless labored endlessly to improve on every assignment. Once again he asked permission to change the course to audit to avoid getting a C. Again Schneider granted him permission without comment.

At the beginning of the spring quarter of 1968, Moon again asked Schneider's permission to take the course. By this time, he knew the course so well that he was informally tutoring a new student in the department in it.

Moon told Ripley what was happening in the course. While Ripley was sympathetic and angered by the attempt to intimidate him through Moon, he emphasized that he had no power to interfere with the grading of another professor. When Moon asked him about the continuing rumors that Ripley would imminently leave Midwest University for another position, he was assured that they were not true.

In the fall of 1967, Moon asked Schneider directly what he could do to gain good standing in the political science program. Schneider replied that Moon had to take, and complete with a good grade, two seminars offered that quarter. He did take both seminars and he earned Bs in both. The paper he wrote for one course was graded A and was praised as excellent. Parts of it were mimeographed and handed out as a model to other members of the seminar as illustrating ideal compliance with the seminar requirements. Nevertheless, Moon was given only a B in the seminar. When he protested, the professor was embarrassed but refused to change the grade. By the end of 1968, Moon had completed the courses needed for an M.A. and the courses Schneider had indicated would take him off the probation set by Schneider's arbitrary standards in early 1968. However, when Schneider was approached about continuation toward the Ph.D. program he remained cold and noncommital.

Meanwhile, the new department clique was insisting that all students shape up, according to their special criteria, or ship out. Ripley's graduate students had all but disappeared from the scene. In one of Ripley's seminars, Moon observed, nine out of ten students were from departments other than political science. By the end of 1968, Ripley did not have new Ph.D. students who would major in political philosophy supervised by him.

FALSE HOPE SPRINGS ETERNAL

As previously described, on the one hand, Moon's hard struggle for survival in academic life and the United States went on endlessly with an optimism that someday he would adjust well to the new systems and once more be successful in his pursuits. However, on the other hand, by the fall of 1967, right after he failed to obtain a passing grade of B from Schneider's course, despite attempts in three consecutive quarters, Moon had begun to realize that the chairperson and graduate coordinator of the Department of Political Science probably intended to eliminate him from the graduate program no matter what he did. His friend, Jee Rak Kim, newly from Korea, urged him to consult with his own adviser, Ron Hollywell, and to transfer to the Department of Social Science, as by this time Ripley was the only professor Moon trusted. All the same, he did take Hollywell's theory course, which was considered one of the toughest courses on the Midwest campus. It was in this course that he earned his first A at Midwest. As a result, Moon concluded that, unlike the Department of Political Science, the Department of Social Science was not using grades as weapons to destroy the graduate students' careers for political reasons. Reassured by this experience, Moon consulted with Hollywell on the possibility of transferring from political to social science.

Hollywell listened closely to Moon's account of his academic experiences to that date, and reviewed his records, advised him to wind up the M.A. in political science as expediently as possible. He was quite pessimistic, however, about Moon's prospects for transferring to social science. As Hollywell explained (1) Moon's grade point record was low and had to be raised; (2) a student's formal and informal reputation followed him around, and it was unlikely he would be admitted to another department at Midwest after being eliminated from one; (3) the same division between old guard professing a humanistic social science and young Turks professing a form of hard-nosed scientism had emerged in social science as well as in political science at Midwest; and finally, (4) the graduate coordinator and Admissions Committee in social science imposed unusually tough admissions requirements on entering students. Only if Moon considerably raised his grade point average and completed the M.A. could he even hope for consideration—and, even then, it would be well to consider applying elsewhere just in case.

Moon was not discouraged by these rather severe judgments. At the very least, it was clear that Hollywell was attempting to be completely honest with him. Moon went to work with renewed enthusiasm, devoting the same long hours and intensity of effort to his studies that he had at one time invested in his studies in Korea and earlier at Midwest. Hence, by the end of the spring quarter of 1969, he had completed not only his M.A. in political science but had also thirty credits of sociology courses in the Social Science Department. He had earned nine A's and one B. By this time, he had completed eighty-four credits of graduate work and had raised his grade point average to over 3.25. Only eighteen of these credits were not applicable to a Ph.D. program. He was now in a strategic position to pursue the Ph.D. degree in either political or social science.

Despite the fact that Jonathan Kresge of the Graduate School, who was also an instructor in political science, had put a fourth man on his M.A. committee in February 1969, Moon was ready to make his bid for admission to a Ph.D. program. Since he was now becoming more interested in social science, he once again met with Hollywell. Hollywell, however, remained pessimistic about his prospects.

Now that he completed the M.A., Hollywell said, political science should be ready to reconsider his prospects. Hollywell repeated his warning that the Department of Social Science was very tough on admissions. Nevertheless, Moon persisted in his desire to transfer to social science. Hollywell then advised him to first check out the possibility of his being acceptable to the Department of Social Science. As Hollywell explained, if Moon left political science to apply for social science, he would be dropped by political science, and if social science did not then accept him, he could be out in the cold. As a way out of such a predicament, Hollywell suggested that he see Brian Grossman, the chairperson of the Admissions Committee for social science. Although Grossman was not in political science, he originally earned the Ph.D. in political science under Oswald Ripley. Grossman would therefore probably be sympathetic to Moon's case. Hollywell advised Moon that he should not make formal application until he could be certain it would be acted on favorably. He should therefore ask Grossman whether he would be willing to review his file with his committee in advance and give him assurance that he would be accepted before formally applying. In that way, Hollywell said, Moon could attempt to transfer without risk.

Hollywell accompanied Moon to Grossman's office, and together they explained that Moon wished advance clearance, informally, as to his acceptability to the department. Grossman very cordially agreed to this, and Moon's file was turned over to him for the committee's perusal.

In the winter quarter of 1969, after Moon had completed his M.A. requirements in political science for graduation in June 1969 and had taken four graduate level courses in social science, earning A's in all of them, he returned (again accompanied by Hollywell) to Grossman's office and asked him what decision had been made on his case. Grossman stated that Moon was acceptable and that he should not hesitate to apply for admission to the department. In the spring quarter of 1969, to Moon's great surprise, he received a notice from the Department of Social Science informing him that they were rejecting his application on the grounds that they had too many students. He had, after all, carefully explained to Grossman that he did not want to submit his application if he was to be rejected.

When Ripley heard about the actions of his former Ph.D. advisee, he, too, was dismayed. He advised Moon to reapply for admission to the political science Ph.D. program, and he asked for a recommendation from Hollywell. Hollywell wrote a strong letter to the chairperson of the Department of Political Science, asking that Moon be readmitted to its program and expressing his outrage at the events that had occurred. The Department of Political Science rejected Moon's application for readmission and transmitted Hollywell's letter to the chairperson of the Department of Social Science,

Mario Petrocelli. Petrocelli thereupon requested Hollywell to report for a meeting, the agenda of which he did not specify.

Petrocelli also invited two full professors to the meeting: the subchairperson for agricultural social science, and the assistant chairperson and head of the Social Science Center for the Study of Death. Hollywell, sensing that a disciplinary action was going to be staged and determined that it would not obscure the fundamental issues of the case, brought Ri Sing Moon to the meeting, being prepared to send him away if the meeting turned out to be on a different matter.

Though seemingly taken aback by Moon's presence, Petrocelli opened the meeting abruptly and aggressively. He announced that he had called the meeting because Hollywell had written a "nasty" letter about his colleagues in the department. Petrocelli also informed Hollywell that he had written a letter about the matter to the administration.

Hollywell interrupted Petrocelli, saying that before going into that, they should review the facts to which the letter was addressed. He then introduced Moon and, thereupon, proceeded to question Moon about every meeting and every conversation that had taken place. At each step Hollywell asked Petrocelli and the other two professors present to question Moon further. At the end of the questioning, Petrocelli proposed that a committee be formed to review the case. For his part, Hollywell voiced regret that he had expressed value judgments about his colleagues. He promised to write letters of apology to the parties involved, and to ask that his letter to the chairperson of the Department of Political Science be withdrawn. Now that Petrocelli had agreed to form a committee, he was satisfied.

Hollywell kept his part of the bargain. Two days after the fateful meeting, however, Petrocelli reported that he could not form a committee to review the case, for no one in the department was willing to serve on it. No such committee was ever to be appointed.

A few days later, Hollywell learned of an opening for a social scientist in the Sioux branch of Dairy State University just across the state line. Hollywell thought that the experience would be valuable for Moon, for he would be in a position to establish a reputation as a social science teacher and would have an ideal basis from which to apply for admission to the Ph.D. program in social science of some graduate school, either Midwest University (which, after all, had agreed that he was acceptable and had excluded him only on the grounds that its quota was full) or some other university. Hollywell strongly emphasized that when Moon applied for admission to a graduate program he should by no means apply at Midwest University alone. Moon immediately telephoned for an appointment and was granted an interview at the Sioux branch. He was hired on the spot.

Moon had yet another shock awaiting him that fateful June of 1969. He invited his wife and inlaws to the June graduation M.A. ceremonies, rented a cap and gown, and attended only to find his name missing from the program. Humiliated, he wrote to the president of the university who assigned an associate dean of the Graduate School to investigate the incident. In due time Moon received an apology from the dean and was sent his diploma in the following quarter (Summer) of 1969.

In the fall of 1969, Moon began his teaching assignment at the Sioux branch. His courses quickly became popular, becoming known as some of the best offered on the campus. When it was learned that he also held the black belt in karate, the students urged him to open karate classes. These too were enthusiastically patronized. By the spring of 1970, Moon had established so solid a reputation that he was offered a permanent position at the university.

By the winter quarter of 1970, Moon had already made application to the graduate social science programs not only of Midwest University but also of three other universities. Midwest was the first to reply: Ri Sing Moon was rejected.

Moon sent a vigorous letter of protest to the president of Midwest. When Hollywell learned about Moon's action, he wearily observed that Moon should not expect any results. Moon, he explained, had put the Department of Social Science on the spot and he should expect that its members would now move heaven and earth to prove that they were right and he was wrong. If he received any offers from his other applications, Hollywell suggested, it would be highly desirable for him to accept one.

Before the end of March 1970, all universities to which Moon had applied contacted him. All three of the schools other than

Midwest not only accepted him into their graduate programs but also offered him some form of financial assistance. Following Hollywell's advice, he accepted the best of the offers; he made plans to transfer his family to the new location and to begin his Ph.D. work.

Meanwhile, he had received no response from the president's office. Some time later, Moon received a letter dated August 24, 1970, from Associate Dean Roger Form of the Graduate School. When later, Moon speculated as to why such a communication was even written, he could see no reason other than Midwest's desire to "paper" its official files with a self-indicating document. Quite possibly the deans or the president feared the entire case might be released to the press. In his letter, the dean reported that as a result of extensive review and investigation, the Graduate School could find no fault with the Department of Social Science—neither with their methods of evaluating the record of prospective students nor with their actions as regarding his original or subsequent applications. As the dean explained, the department had to be very selective in view of the small number of places available and the large number of highly qualified applicants for these places. While Moon's overall record in social science was very good, it was not considered to be as persuasive as that of other applicants. In addition to the general quality factor, Moon's background in sociology was judged to be less well developed than that of other applicants. Moon's difficulties, the dean stated, arose out of the fact that one or two members of the department believed his record was sufficiently strong to justify reconsideration. As the dean maintained, unfortunately, they could not have complete knowledge of the qualities of the other competing applicants, nor could they speak for the Admissions Committee or the graduate faculty in social science as a whole. The dean concluded that he believed the department and the Graduate School made a conscientious and unbiased review of the original decision, and of Moon's request for reconsideration.

At the very time the dean was writing this letter in which he stressed the small number of places available in the department and the large number of highly qualified applicants for these places, the Department of Social Science was unable to fill its teaching assistantships and was advertising for applicants.

SUMMARY

Ri Sing Moon had been caught up in two conflicts: one involving the changing character of educational policy and the other involving his experiences with two, somewhat antithetical cultures.

Conflict in many of the social sciences centers around two orientations: the qualitative and the quantitative. The qualitative stresses undertanding and meaning, whereas the quantitative strives for precise numerical formulations. When problems involving concerns over power emerge, battle lines are frequently drawn around the qualitative-quantitative axes. This was true for the Department of Political Science at Midwest University.

Though Moon was unaware of the storm gathering at Midwest when he arrived, it was soon clear that he had been swept up in the final stages of a confrontation that had been unfolding since the mid-1960s. By that time, the prestige of the department in terms of national rankings had dropped by a big margin. Furthermore, Ph.D.'s in qualitative disciplines who obtained their degrees at Midwest were having difficulty finding jobs at other prestigious institutions. This situation alarmed various persons at Midwest for it seemed to confirm the general impression that the shift from qualitative to quantitative concerns was more than a local phenomenon.

In an effort to effect program changes, the Department of Political Science appointed a new chairperson, whose first task was to discourage, if not "wipe out," faculty with qualitative orientations. In this process, he maintained that retraining qualitatively oriented students to the quantitative approach was inefficient to the department and, hence, to the university. He argued that it would take longer for these students to get the Ph.D. than it would for new students who would begin immediate training in quantitative orientations. Discouraging the older, qualitatively oriented student by giving low grades was (and still is) the most effective means for accomplishing this end. Finally, he maintained that professors committed to the qualitative approach were, as he stated, "cancerous tumors" to the university and to students.

As this protracted conflict reached its final stages, and as Moon was to witness, older faculty such as the previous department chairperson and his chosen advisor, Oswald Ripley, were singled out.

Even though both had tenure and were widely known to most political scientists in the United States, they were subjected to covert forms of intimidation which neither had confronted before. As a result, they were unable to focus their resistance on many of the programs and policies the new chairperson was establishing.

For Moon, these circumstances were disastrous. As Ripley's student he needed Ripley's protection from the new chairperson's efforts against the older, qualitatively oriented students such as Moon. Ripley himself, however, became a target of the chairperson, who worked gradually, often covertly, and carefully abided by university rules and regulations in advancing the general outlines of program change. His efforts gained legitimacy in the eyes of supporters at the expense of Ripley and the qualitatively oriented students.

Schneider and his supporters, as well as some hapless persons, campaigned against Ripley on two fronts. First, persistent rumors began to be circulated that Ripley was leaving Midwest. Second, active efforts were made to dissuade students from taking Ripley as an advisor, if not a teacher, because his qualitative orientation, it was held, did not have much promise for the field; students so trained could not be employed. Thus, by the end of 1968, Ri Sing Moon was the sole new student advisee of Oswald Ripley.

Moon, of course, maintained that he had the right to choose his advisor according to his academic interest; this right was legitimate and was officially recognized in Midwest's procedures. He admired Ripley deeply and was impressed by the profundity of his intellect. Moon was unaware of the developments within the department prior to his arrival, and, later, never sought any active role in intradepartmental strife.

As Moon became apprised of the circumstances engulfing both himself and his major advisor, he remained loyal to his traditional value orientation. From that perspective it was dictated that he continue allegiance and respect to Ripley to whom he owed much for his intellectual development. Thus, he became an unwitting part of the intrigues which were unfolding and which were directed at Ripley. The result was that he would suffer under the arbitrary actions that would sustain the new quantitative orientation in the department.

The conflict he had encountered in the Department of Political

Science was not, as Moon would discover, unique. When he turned to the Department of Social Science, he witnessed a similar scenario: a new, aggressive chairperson stressing quantitative orientations was aligned with supporters against Ron Hollywell, a qualitatively oriented social scientist with whom Moon desired to study. Again, Moon was victimized.

Moon was caught not only in the intrigues of academic power politics but also in a conflict that has been of great concern to numerous social observers: the conflict between individual rights and organizational imperatives. In the effort to maintain the corporate integrity of various academic endeavors, sometimes sweeping transformations are undertaken without regard for the immediate costs to those caught in the middle. In Moon's case at Midwest University, expediency in advancing bureaucratic professionalism responsive to perceived needs and the imperatives of control came to dominate. Moon's rights to choose his own course of study, which was seemingly sanctioned by university policy, and to receive fair treatment were swept away. Moon's experiences were exacerbated by his commitment to traditional culture; loyalty and respect were deeply ingrained in his formative Korean years. His sense of traditionalism increased his liability in confronting the events at Midwest. Even native Americans such as his first advisor, Oswald Ripley, seem disoriented. For Moon the outsider, the lessons he was learning were sobering.

5 ARTHUR S. WILKE AND LEE KRUEGER

Due Process: In the Shadow of North Mountain State

After graduating from college in the 1960s Dennis Russell enlisted in the navy. While in the navy, he was trained in Russian and subsequently spent a long tour of duty in Spain where his wife François joined him, and they enjoyed the delights of Spain's countryside. Spain, as he would later discover, was far from the social unrest the United States was experiencing.

Uncertain of what he wanted to do after his service in the navy, Russell decided to take advantage of the GI Bill. In the fall of 1972, he enrolled at North Mountain State, a small university of less than 10,000 students. Prior to going into the service he had graduated with a B.S. in psychology. After some initial uncertainty, he decided to complete a second undergraduate degree, this time a B.A. in foreign languages and social science. With his previous degree and military training in foreign languages, it would take Russell only a year to complete the degree.

During the year in which he would complete his second Bachelor's degree, Russell first experienced the effects of the cultural and political turmoil that had erupted in the 1960s. It was a culture shock for him to confront the questions and concerns his generation had been asking. Without the tempering influence of day-to-day affairs, lost to him while stationed in Spain, Russell was amazed at the variety of expressions and of the experiments in life-styles being entertained within universities.

In many settings, what Russell was encountering was simply a historical artifact, but North Mountain State was an anomaly. Since North Mountain was out of the mainstream, structural developments and student consciousness had lagged there, and the campus violence of the 1960s had not touched it. North Mountain did not have its first student strike until after United States forces invaded Cambodia from South Vietnam in the spring of 1970.

With his second Bachelor's degree in hand, Russell entered graduate school in the fall of 1973 to study social science. However, the deeper he got into graduate study, the more he found that his sentiments did not lie in what was rapidly becoming a "professionalized" field, dominated by what seemed to be an overly detached perspective on human affairs. His, by contrast, was an activist orientation. He was dissatisfied with a passive chronicling and analysis of human events. The recaptured images of the 1960s so recently embraced continually returned. He thrust himself into community action projects and the more he did so, the more he seemed to be at odds with some of the dominant members of the social science faculty.

Not content with his prospects in social science as they unfolded during the 1973-74 academic year, Russell turned to law. Russell still under the GI Bill, was employed in a part-time job he found most satisfactory, and he and his wife had found a comfortable network of associates in North Mountain. When North Mountain's law school accepted him for studies in the fall of 1974; Russell had, it seemed, found his niche.

THE NORTH MOUNTAIN STATE LAW SCHOOL

North Mountain State's School of Law was founded in the late nineteenth century. It had an undistinguished history, preparing students for practice in the local area. In the 1970s, there were some changes, however. Through the political maneuvering of the law faculty and with the assistance of the American Bar Association, the school won a professionally competitive salary schedule. This, it was widely rumored, had been won at the expense of faculty in other schools of the university. In addition, a major building program was undertaken to respond to the growing demand for admission to the school and increases in enrollments. When Russell entered in the fall of 1974, the student body numbered around 250. The faculty consisted of 11 instructors in the professional ranks and several lecturers.

The first-year courses in the School of Law involved principally the case study method. Although the school's bulletin indicated that this approach was designed to challenge the imagination and ability of the student, Russell found classroom sessions organized around this method to be more of a trial. Nonetheless, he endured. By the end of the first semester, however, he had failed to make the necessary 2.00 grade point average and was placed on probation. He was givern one semester to raise his cumulative grade point average to 2.00 or better. The dean of the School of Law offered to meet with him regarding his academic status, if he so chose.

In assessing his situation, Russell was convinced that neither his classroom performance nor his comprehension was deficient. Rather, he surmised, it was his inability to write adequate final reports and examinations that kept his grades so low. When he met with the dean, he inquired if the university offered a remedial legal writing program. He was informed that there was none. The dean then proceeded to urge Russell to contact his instructors of the past semester. Russell complied, making appointments to see two of them, Professors Frank Lofton and Louis Bonard.

Russell's meeting with Lofton was cordial. Lofton's advice was to study examples of A papers which were on file in the law school library. Russell then met with Bonard. Bonard also advised studying A papers, but then the apparent harmony, as he would recall, was shattered. Bonard charged Russell with being a class cutter. Russell denied his charge, stating that except for an occasional, minor illness, he had dutifully attended class regularly. Angered, Bonard took the inquisitional stance he was well known for both within class and in other dealings with students who proposed to resist authority. Was Russell calling Bonard a liar? Without waiting for a reply, Bonard reminded Russell that he had the power to "make or break" him in law school. The experience was unnerving. Russell confronted not only the threat of his probationary status, but the spectre of a professor who singlehandedly could seal his fate. The central role Bonard occupied in the law school along with the legion of claims made about his personal demeanor made the vulnerable Russell even more wary.

Russell's performance in law school deteriorated further in the second semester, and he was notified in a letter of May 19, 1975, from the dean of his elimination from law studies. Pursuant to the provisions of the retention policy, the dean wrote, Russell could petition for readmission. To do so, he had to submit evidence of extenuating circumstances or support of his contention that there was a high likelihood that he would raise his cumulative grade point average to 2.00 by the end of the first semester of the next academic year.

The dean's letter, which accurately summarized the school's retention policy, informed Russell that there wasn't much time for a petition since some of the faculty were leaving for the summer. Quickly, Russell attempted to contact Dean Pladsen, but found that he was out. So too were the members of the Retention Committee, Professors Harold Gottfied and Bonard. Eventually, Russell was able to arrange a meeting with the dean on May 24. The dean urged Russell to file his petition immediately because both Bonard and Gottfied were about to leave town. When Russell asked about procedures regarding the petition and whether oral presentation and character witnesses could be used, the dean indicated that he did not know. These concerns, it seemed, were in the domain of the Retention Committee.

Later that day, Russell contacted Professor Gottfied. Gottfied was unable to clarify procedures any more than the dean had, deferring, it seemed, to Bonard. He did, however, reiterate the issues identified in the policy—"high likelihood of success" or "extenuating circumstances"—as critical factors. In conclusion, he advised Russell to put together the "best legal argument" he could in his own defense.

After his meeting with Gottfied, Russell contacted Bonard over the telephone. While Bonard left questions of procedure unclarified, he opined that Russell should concentrate on developing "extenuating circumstances" because he felt that the "high likelihood of success" in raising the grade point average was not a realistic argument. Questioned as to examples of "extenuating circumstances," Bonard gave examples such as a death in the family or serious illness within the immediate family. His final advice was that Russell should "give it his best shot." With that, the conversation ended.

Russell remained unclear as to procedures. He seemed to be getting two types of advice. One type encouraged a fight, while the other was less encouraging, being more proscribed and formally legalistic. Confused, Russell faced the prospect of mounting compelling arguments in his petition in less than two days. The Retention Committee would address his petition on May 27.

Russell sought counsel with Professor Richard Hebert who, because of his own battles regarding procedures within the university, might be of some assistance. Hebert said he could not advise him regarding the course of action Russell should pursue, but once Russell reached a decision he could suggest some tactics. After some discussion in which his options were discussed and assessed, Russell concluded that he did not have a compelling case involving extenuating circumstances—not at least as Bonard portrayed it. Hence, his only option was to make a fight of it, to give as it were his "best shot." To do so, he would be required to challenge the very procedures or lack of procedures that were in operation. The lack of clear procedural directives and the constraint of time seemed to be most significant. If Russell could combine this challenge with some competency having bearing on legal studies, he might be able to present a prima facie case that he would be a credit to the legal profession. It was a long shot. No other approach appeared possible at that time. With that, Hebert suggested some general areas Russell might wish to explore in the university library.

For the next forty hours, Russell worked on preparing his case. He outlined his strategy and researched some of the ideas suggested to him. By the morning of May 29, he gave his text to a typist. By noon the same day, Russell delivered a ten-page paper to the dean's secretary.

Russell's petition consisted of three parts. The first was a general introduction. The second was an appeal, challenging the lack of clairty in the procedure he was being subjected to and pointing to the general lack of due process. The third was a wide-ranging argument which attempted to broaden the narrow bases for the extenuating circumstances argument. Russell's argument was that while his previous training did not seem to relate very well to the current training he was receiving in law school, he could link his previous intellectual orientation to a school of jurisprudence, namely sociological jurisprudence. With that, he pointed out that the critique he was mounting had standing among some comentators on the current educational scene. This was an intellectual challenge to the law school's predominant mode of study, the case study approach. It was a long shot, but if the reviewing committee could see him operate under fire, perhaps there was a chance. After all, legal procedures existed for reconsideration, so why couldn't administrative procedures in a law school?

THREAT, INTIMIDATION, AND DENIAL OF DUE PROCESS

The response to Russell's petition was rapid. Shortly after noon, Professor Bonard called Russell's home. Russell's wife, alone at home, answered the phone. Bonard informed her that if Russell did not come to the law school immediately and retract his protest regarding the lack of due process, his petition would never be read.

Russell was now even more confused. He spoke briefly with Hebert but was uncertain as to his course of action. Russell returned to the law school and met with Bonard who confirmed that the petition would not be read unless he submitted a retraction. Russell complied and withdrew those portions of the petition challenging the lack of due process, conceding in writing that the North Mountain State School of Law could review, per the regulations, his petition at any time between the close of law school in the spring and the beginning of the fall term.

This was a strange turn of events. Russell, who had sought out information on the procedures had been advised to submit his petition quickly because the members of the Retention Committee were leaving. At one point, he was told that they were not contracted to work in the summer and that his petition was being accommodated at some personal sacrifice. The law school's procedures were unclear in this area. However, Bonard's demand of Russell's retraction would pose another dilemma: that is, the full process to which Russell's petition could be eventually subjected could not be resolved before the beginning of the next term's classes. Thus, a procedure was being forged in which the lack of detail constituted a punitive action. It appeared that Russell had stumbled onto a lacuna and that the perceptive Bonard had responded to head off the challenge. Unfortunately, Russell's first year of law training had not prepared him for this other face of the law, where extralegal maneuvering predominates. Furthermore, he faced the problematic situation in which advice, interpretation, and review all issued from one person, in this case, Professor Bonard. The very conditions of the adversary system to which Russell was being groomed in law school were denied him unless he wished to press on into a terrain that was quite uncharted. Not all, indeed very few, are able to persist in the face of such odds. Russell was among the many who chose to capitulate.

With the keystone of Russell's argument knocked out and Bonard's cryptic assurances that "due process is alive and doing well in the School of Law," Russell's situation was bleak. It was made bleaker the following day when, in a letter from Dean Pladson, it seemed that Bonard was going all out to vindicate his actions. The dean noted, in accordance with Bonard's acknowledged instructions, that Russell had misinterpreted the rule regarding petitioning and had, in fact, submitted an appeal. He made this claim even though the appeal portion of the document had already been deleted. In effect, the Retention Committee was not going to act on Russell's document of May 29. Neither accepted nor rejected, the document was in effect declared null and void by the gesture to give Russell a second chance to petition. Pointing out that Russell misunderstood the procedure (the same one he had attempted to get clarification on and had challenged), a ruling was now made that Russell could, if he so chose, submit another petition, no later than August 16, 1975, providing it dealt specifically with either (1) high likelihood of success or (2) extenuating circumstances. It was becoming increasingly clear that the evolving procedure and rules of evidence were becoming more explicitly defined. Personal problems of a transitory nature or factors amenable to short-term corrective action were being reemphasized. Among the examples mentioned in conversations with Russell by members of the Retention Committee were a death in the family or a short-term illness. Still, how transitory or how short-term the problems had to be was unclear, and there was no procedure for establishing clarification on these matters. The very foundations of a legal-rational social order, particularly one in a bureaucratic setting, are predicated on making such distinctions clear and unambiguous. How much grief associated with a death in the family or how long a short-term illness is become critical issues in forging procedures aimed at general application as well as some modicum of fairness. Yet, these concerns were not to be open to review by the interpretation that the petition process was not merely laying a case before a deliberating body, as it is in the case of the law, but that it was to be treated as a request for grace before a sovereign power. Hence, Bonard's advice to make the best legal case was a fool's errand.

Confronted with the narrower interpretation of the petitioning process and the kinds of examples being cited by the Retention Committee as constituting extenuating circumstances, Russell sought to establish some extenuating circumstances that would carry compelling weight in the petitioning procedure. He consulted Dr. Marvin Tenoule, a counselor specializing in problems in academic performance resulting from stress. After the initial consultation, Russell became Tenoule's client and was diagnosed as exhibiting "acute anxiety reaction to situational stress." This, Tenoule stated, could be an extenuating circumstance. In Tenoule's estimation, there was a high likelihood that Russell could be helped by counseling, and as a result his performance in law school might improve. Although this argument was far from compelling, Tenoule's support of Russell was strong, in part because Tenoule was looking for some way to present to the faculty of the law school a more sensitive, "humanized" view of their students. It was widely felt in some circles that the university's professional schools, the School of Medicine and the School of Law, were rampant with cases of personal psychopathology, a psychopathology that was being shrouded and yet nurtured under the generally repressive ethos of "professionalism."

Russell detailed his extenuating circumstance in a petition he submitted to the School of Law's Retention Committee on August 13, 1975. The committee, now consisting of three members—Professors Bonard, Lofton, and Hector Galton—met on August 18 and rejected Russell's petition. No extenuating circumstances were recognized, and as a result the committee concluded that there was not "a high likelihood" that Russell could succeed in school by the end of a third semester. With the Retention Committee's rejection,

Russell could now appeal that decision to the School of Law's faculty at large.

THE ACTIONS OF THE LAW SCHOOL FACULTY

Several days after the fall session began, the faculty of the School of Law met to consider Russell's appeal of the Retention Committee's action on his petition. Russell appeared before the faculty in person together with two supporting witnesses, Professors Hebert and Tenoule.

Russell presented his appeal, along with documents relating to his case, to the faculty. He was particularly concerned with laying before the faculty a documented history of events, judiciously including the conflicts of the past spring. He also indicated that in his estimation he could show that there were extenuating circumstances in his case and that those circumstances were of a temporary nature. Once these circumstances were resolved, he expressed confidence that he would have a high likelihood of success.

Hebert followed Russell. Based on his familiarity with Russell's biography as well as his past work, both as an undergraduate and graduate, Hebert highlighted Russell's capabilities. He pointed out Russell's facility with foreign languages, the speed with which he had completed a second Bachelor's degree, his adequate graduate school record, and the growing social consciousness Russell exhibited prior to his enrolling in law school. He also revealed how Russell, after facing the disastrous news of his fate in law school, had resumed work on his Master's degree and had undertaken a community action project in the local public schools. Hebert was questioned as to whether training in the social sciences and law were incompatible, and he responded by indicating that in general he did not know. However, he was aware that in "leading" law programs the social sciences were integral to the training of law students. Thus, he suggested that these modes of study might not be incompatible.

Following Hebert came Tenoule who addressed the specifics of Russell's case. He discussed his work, emphasizing the success he had achieved in treating students such as Russell. He indicated that "acute anxiety reaction to stress" was a very widespread phenomenon. In particular, he noted that Russell had a very good prognosis and that the symptoms Russell exhibited constituted, in his estimation, extenuating circumstances that were capable of remission in less than a semester of therapy. Indeed, therapy had already commenced.

The faculty response to Tenoule's presentation was polite, though guarded. Asked about the nature and legitimacy of his field, counseling, Tenoule deftly handled the question. Sensing that the question was designed to provoke, Tenoule quietly summarized counseling as the accumulated wisdom of the ages brought to bear on problems of living. At this point, tensions appeared to ease somewhat. Tenoule was asked to reiterate points he had already covered. The most damaging question dealt with Tenoule's assessment of Russell's abilities once there was a remission of stress symptoms. Here Tenoule could not comment; he did not know if Russell would perform significantly better in the absence of stress, although he opined that his scholastic record would likely improve if stress was the precipitating condition.

In retrospect, the question of Russell's abilities may very well have been the most critical in the appeal proceeding, although this area of inquiry seemed to be beyond the scope of a procedure dealing with extenuating circumstances. A sense of the ambiguity that was apparent in the meeting emerged with a general discussion about the character of the lawyer and the law student. In a particularly graphic instance, one professor admitted that he suffered from acute stress, vomiting before court appearances, but the important thing was that he still functioned. There seemed to be a general assent to this testimony. Acute situational stress was being ruled out as an extenuating circumstance by personal testimony, and in the process not only were procedures being forged, but also the portrait of what constituted an ideal character type for the lawyer and the law student emerged.

Several days later, the verdict came in. The Retention Committee's rejection of Russell's petition was upheld. In denying his appeal, Russell's suspension from law school became permanent.

There was no denying that Russell's performance was unsatisfactory. It was ironic, however, that when he had challenged procedures the previous spring, in a fashion not unlike the faculty testimony regarding their responses to stress, he has been chastised. Despite the portrait of cool professionals at work, in his efforts to exercise as many rights as possible, he had encountered intimidation at the hands of Bonard as well as a lack of critical attention to procedural detail when it came to handling his first appeal petition. The law, as Russell was belatedly discovering, was not simply the pursuit of justice but involved human beings who could employ legal resources to dominate, if not repress.

Russell's actions did not appear to have been wholly in vain, for they encouraged several other students who had been dismissed from the law school to pursue appeals through to the faculty. It seemed that the tenaciousness of students in pursuing their cases had increased and that the favorable rulings by the faculty in several instances was out of the ordinary. Meanwhile, Russell's challenge of the procedures, even though not central to the final decision regarding his retention, was vindicated. In the late fall of 1975, the School of Law revised its readmission policy and then detailed procedural rules for readmission. Though the same criteria—high likelihood of success and extenuating circumstances—remained intact, a more detailed agenda of notification, petitioning, and a time schedule were instituted. Tenoule's proposal to expand the interpretation of extenuating circumstances was not, however, incorporated.

A few months later, Russell had an occasion to read the 1975-76 bulletin of North Mountain State's School of Law. There he read how the school emphasizes that understanding is more important than the mere accumulation of information. A student, he read, must know not only the formal operations in creating and interpreting the law, but also the legal process in which decision-making takes place. Such understanding might be important, but if his case was indicative, in this school of law such concerns remained academic.

6 ARTHUR S. WILKE AND HARVEY R. CAIN

Vendetta

It was a cold afternoon in mid-December 1972. First semester classes at Fremont State University had come to a close. Faculty and students awaited the final examination period that would be completed by the end of the following week. The brief holiday vacation was looked upon with great anticipation.

Bounding up the creaking stairs of Wilcox Hall came the bundled figure of Frank Herndon, a first-year graduate student in the Department of Sociology. In his arms were two large frozen turkeys, giving him the general appearance of a Santa Claus. The turkeys, which Herndon, the department's representative, had been charged with obtaining, were to be gifts from the department's faculty and graduate students to the department secretary and the building custodian. They were to be presented at the annual Christmas party later in the afternoon.

Arriving on the second floor where the department offices were housed, Herndon met Adam Ibsen, the department chairperson. After a customary perfunctory greeting, Ibsen summoned Herndon to his office. Placing his bundles in an inconspicuous place, Herndon ambled down to Ibsen's office.

AN ADMINISTRATIVE "ACCIDENT" AND A LACK OF DUE RESPECT

Herndon was still in a happy Christmas mood as he walked down to Ibsen's office. He little dreamed that the next few weeks would turn into a nightmare because of an administrative "accident" and of conflicting suggestions and requirements.

Once inside the office, Herndon was asked to close the door. That done, Ibsen began. He had been informed by one of Herndon's professors, Vincent Nelson, that there was a very good possibility that Herndon would receive a C in Nelson's methods seminar. This came as no surprise to Herndon. Given the deterioration of their relationship (at one point in the semester, an angered Nelson had hurled a list of books he claimed he had been required to read when he was in graduate school on the floor and complained bitterly that Herndon's work load of class assignments was light in comparison), Herndon had long ago resigned himself to getting a C. Ibsen urged Herndon to placate Nelson and to do his best. Herndon indicated to Ibsen that he doubted much could be done and that he was not expecting much. Ibsen pointed out that this was no position for a student such as Herndon to take; after all, Herndon was on probationary status. Thus, not only did he have to attain a B average, which was likely, but also he could not have any grade lower than a B. A C in Nelson's seminar would mean the loss of his teaching assistantship as well as permanent suspension of graduate study.

The news of his provisional status was shattering to Herndon. There must be a mistake, he thought. It was impossible; that's all there was to it and he so informed Ibsen. A conflict was unfolding. In such circumstances, Ibsen was always uncomfortable. He did not like these nasty chores, but he did them. Once done, however, he expected that, as far as possible, everything should quickly return to normal. Herndon was behaving in an unreasonable manner. Ibsen was personally sympathetic, but he had his administrative duties to perform, and Herndon's insistence that other conditions obtained appeared, at least to Herndon, to frustrate Ibsen. That Herndon was not, as he asserted, on probation and that a serious error was being compounded did not appear to register with Ibsen. Yet, Ibsen was not without feeling. He offered to meet with Herndon the next day to talk things over. The current conversation could not continue because the department Christmas party was about to get under way, and Ibsen did not want to miss it.

The next day Herndon met again with Ibsen. Angry and frustrated, Herndon demanded action, insisting that he could not be on probationary status. Herndon's reaction, as he later recalled, was disconcerting to Ibsen who simply wished to talk things over. Certainly, Herndon argued, the Graduate School could be contacted to confirm his status. Ibsen recoiled at the suggestion; he did not wish to disturb the dean. Herndon remained insistent, however. Ibsen simply shrugged his shoulders, indicating that he didn't really know what to do about the "Frank Herndon case." If Ibsen didn't know, Herndon did: he would march over to the Graduate School himself. Reluctantly, a weary Ibsen relented and called a staff member at the Graduate School. He was assured that an answer would be forthcoming very shortly. Ibsen hung up, and he and Herndon waited.

Not long after the initial call, Ibsen got a return call. The Graduate School representative reported that when Herndon's application for graduate school had been processed the previous year (based on work through his junior year), his record clearly indicated that he had less than the required 2.75 grade point average (on a 4.00 system) for admission to graduate study in full standing. Ibsen relayed this information to Herndon. Herndon protested, arguing that this computation could not have taken into consideration his performance at Fremont during his senior year in which he had demonstrated continued academic improvement. Ibsen relayed Herndon's argument, and the caller indicated it would take a few minutes to recompute Herndon's undergraduate grade point average.

Herndon was bewildered by the turn of events. After all, the faculty in the Department of Sociology had approved his admission to graduate study while he was a senior and had seen fit to offer him a part-time teaching assistantship, something that is not done for those on probation. Something was awry.

A second call to Ibsen from the Graduate School came within fifteen minutes after the first. Herndon's position was vindicated: based on his full college record, he was not on probationary status. Even if he received a C from Professor Nelson, he could not be dismissed from graduate school. His status was confirmed in a memorandum Herndon received the following day. He had specifically requested this memorandum as he had already learned that documented evidence was required for proper defense.

Ibsen expressed general regret over the situation, intimating that the difficulty had arisen because of actions at the Graduate School. To Herndon he seemed oblivious of the favorable actions the Department of Sociology had taken toward him and to the fact that if the Graduate School's original interpretation of Herndon's probationary status was upheld, a serious error had been made internally in awarding Herndon an assistantship.

Regardless of who was responsible, Herndon had been traumatized. Because he was so upset, he attempted to have his final examinations postponed. All his professors, including Nelson, acceded to his request. Nelson, in fact, agreed to permit Herndon to take the final examination in the seminar three days later. Herndon was relieved, but his relief was short-lived. Later the same day, Herndon ran into Nelson and found that Nelson had changed his mind: Herndon, Nelson said, should present himself for the examination the following day. Herndon protested that he had to proctor the final examination for the introductory course as part of his teaching assistantship duties and had scheduled another one of his final examinations. To that, Nelson replied that Herndon would have to make other arrangements, which Herndon did.

The next morning Herndon presented himself for the final examination in Nelson's seminar. The examination, an open book type, consisted of nine essay questions. Nelson informed him that he could take as much time as he needed. With that, Herndon retired to his office, one he shared with two other teaching assistants who were also in Nelson's seminar. There was no other available place in the building to take the examination. The conditions proved less than ideal.

During the course of the morning, Herndon was interrupted several times. He administered several final examinations to students in the introductory class who had schedule conflicts. In addition, he assisted, as he had done throughout the semester, several fellow graduate students on some computer-related statistics and methods problems due in another course. He was also interrupted by his office mates. Seeing that he was working on Nelson's examination, they joked about how formidable it had been. They had taken it the day before. It was so "terrible," they reported, that the last examination was completed at approximately 6:30 P.M. This was later confirmed by others, including another faculty member.

At approximately 2:00 P.M., Nelson entered Herndon's office and demanded his examination. Herndon protested, relating that he had heard that students had worked until 6:30 P.M. the previous evening on their examinations. Nelson denied this allegation, maintaining that all examinations had been handed in by 3:00 P.M. Nevertheless, he would give Herndon another hour to complete his work. With that he left. Herndon's office mates, fellow graduate students, were astonished and fearful, too, thinking ahead to a sequel seminar they had to take under Nelson the following semester. On that dismal note, a dejected Herndon completed the examination. He was not surprised to receive his final grade—a C.

Except for some minor skirmishes with two other graduate students over how he conducted the discussion sections of the introductory course, none of Herndon's other experiences in his first semester as a graduate student had dampened his enthusiasm for graduate study. True, he faced yet another semester with Nelson, but this could be managed. He derived enormous pleasure and value from the discussion sections he directed, conversations with other graduate students, and encouragement from other professors.

AND THEN THE ROOF FELL IN

Herndon's next surprise came in the spring of 1973. At this time, the faculty conducted an annual review of graduate teaching assistants, traditionally a pro forma exercise. Unless there were extraordinary factors, a student who received an assistantship the first year would automatically receive one the second, the maximum period of time any student was to be supported. The review usually provided the faculty with an opportunity to assess where some students were in the program and to make decisions regarding applicants for vacated assistantships. The meeting had just opened when Vincent Nelson moved to strip Frank Herndon of his assistantship. His motion was seconded by Nicholas Gustafson, an associate of Nelson's since their days as undergraduates.

Several faculty were surprised by these developments. Most startled was Jonathan Stebbins, the professor in charge of the introductory course. Stebbins asked for the reasons for this move. Gustafson's short response was "Frank's problem in communicating." No further clarification was forthcoming. As Stebbins and others were to learn, Nelson, Gustafson, and Ibsen frequently used the phrase "a communications problem" to cover a wide range of affairs from inchoate personal dissatisfactions to expressing disagreement over policy matters. This disconcerting phrase was a means to turn an interlocutor's questions around without answering or providing critical information.

With regard to Herndon's alleged communications problem, Stebbins had heard nothing directly. In fact, the only negative comments on Herndon's performance had come from a graduate student, Naomi Smith. Throughout the first semester, she made a special point of commenting on the need for people in the profession to be tough and people such as Frank Herndon, she asserted, simply couldn't "cut it." People such as Frank, she maintained, had to be cut loose. To Stebbins this statement sounded strangely like something Vincent Nelson would have said. Smith and Nelson were in frequent conference, and Nelson was known to share his frustrations on a wide range of issues with sympathetic graduate students. Smith was clearly sympathetic.

Stebbins spoke up for Herndon, suggesting that at present there was no critical information on any of the graduate teaching assistants. With no other information than Gustafson's comment about Herndon's communication problem, a vote was taken. Herndon's teaching assistantship would not be renewed for the 1973-74 academic year.

AFTERMATH

Frank Herndon has come to view the termination of his graduate assistantship by Fremont as the most significant learning experience of his graduate career. No other experience has provided equivalent insight into the discrepancy between appearance and reality, between the alleged reasons (difficulty in communication) and the real reasons for his persecution by a faculty elite. His real difficulties originated in the ill will and vindictiveness of a professor and in the embarrassment and discomfort to the chairperson brought about by the Graduate School's administrative error in putting him undeservedly on probation. The termination of his assistantship was so evidently an expression of disapproval and no confidence that he considered dropping out of graduate school altogether. Upon reflection, he resolved to complete the M.A.—an accomplishment he managed within a year and a half.

Herndon gained further bitter insights into the workings of the academic personality during his final work at Fremont. Outcasts, he found, were forced together for self-protection and were radicalized by their experience (Stebbin's who became one of his few sponsors was himself fired from the faculty); other students readily joined the faculty in the scapegoating of one of their number; and faculty members were endlessly ingenious in giving allegedly principled reasons for actions based on questionable motives and emotions. For Herndon, the true drama of social science became the tracking and elaboration of these types of human encounters.

PART I.

The Rocky Road to Tenure: Profiles in the Hidden Professoriate

Colleges and universities are bureaucratic organizations. According to classical formulations, such as the one by the eminent German sociologist Max Weber (1864-1920), bureaucracies operate according to the following:

1. There is the principle of fixed and official jurisdictional areas, which are generally ordered by rules, that is, by laws or administrative regulations.
2. The authority to give the commands required for the discharge of these duties is distributed in a stable way and is strictly delimited by rules concerning the coercive means, physical, sacerdotal, or otherwise, which may be placed at the disposal of officials.
3. Methodological provision is made for the regular and continuous fulfillment of these duties and for the execution of the corresponding rights; only persons who have the generally regulated qualifications to serve are employed.[1]

Weber's view is decidedly rationalistic. It presupposes that stable goals and purposes for organizational life exist.

The very nature of education, involved in creating and transmitting new knowledge, does qualify, if not outright challenge, notions of stable goals and purposes. New knowledge and new teaching missions may affect the corporate character of higher education in dramatic ways. Furthermore, under conditions of rapid change, the goals and purposes of education may be further obscured. The fixed areas of jurisdiction may give way to emergent ones, authority systems may be challenged, and the procedures for continuous fulfillment of duties may be altered in an effort to respond to changing conditions.

The fact that many large-scale organizations are seen as operating in a world of flux has led to some different conceptions of organizational life. Instead of stressing the rationalistic dimensions of organization in which procedures are seen as inextricably tied to well-known purposes and goals, perspectives emphasizing more flexible agendas are now in evidence. A spokesperson for this new orientation is Charles Perrow. Perrow distinguishes two major categories of goals, official versus operative. "Official goals," he states, "are the general purposes of the organization as put forth in the charter, annual reports, public statements by key executives and other authoritative pronouncements."[2] They are usually characterized by a high degree of generality, if not obscurity. The history of education reveals that these goals have often changed.[3] Nevertheless, they serve as sources of authority for the actions taken in colleges and universities. In recent years, for example, with increasing rapidity, it has been observed that general goals for education have regularly alternated in many large institutions between teaching and research. Despite the alternation, the achievement of these respective goals is often difficult to ascertain.

In contrast, operative goals are the "ends sought through the actual operating policies of the organization; they tell us what the organization actually is trying to do, regardless of what the official goals say.[4] Perrow states that "the discernment of operative goals is . . . difficult and subject to error."[5] He suggests that the researcher may have to focus on relatively minor decisions to develop an understanding of the character of complex organizations. Case studies, as suggested at the outset of this volume, particularly those employing deviant case analysis,[6] provide a valuable probe into this important area of organizational life where the discrepancies between official goals and actual practices are often most pronounced.

As the case studies in this section show, the changing nature of operative goals not only mirrors forces leading to the expansion of the hidden professoriate, but also suggest that higher education, like many segments of American social life, is embroiled in what Jurgen Habermas has termed the "legitimacy crisis."[7] That is, there seems to be no steadying mechanism or appeal to steer conduct and thought consistently. Instead, as Weber warned generations ago, if rationality persists it takes on formal characteristics, not substantive ones. There is a tendency, when adherence to rules is in evidence, to look upon rules and laws in strategic terms, determining what is warranted and what is not. The isolated faculty member against whom such rules are invoked experiences them as repressive conditions, not constitutive. Various dimensions of this form of repression are observed in the case studies reported in Chapters 8, 9, and 10.

Employing a series of vignettes describing the problems facing academic women, Fran French (Chapter 7, "The Rules Keep Changing Every Day") shows how operative rules can result in discrimination. Often such rules are contradictory as well as at variance with official goals and guidelines. Nonetheless, their effect has been particularly damaging to women. Indeed, long before the current problems in higher education, women along with other "undesirables" (e.g., ethnic and ideological minorities) constituted core categories in the hidden professoriate. Even today, because of the unique twist encountered in operative rules, women often find themselves to be premium candidates for the ranks of the hidden professoriate.

The following three chapters are devoted to case studies of nontenured faculty. Each subject of these chapters developed a sensitivity to the changing climate of the 1960s in that each responded variously to the issues of that period: active involvement in community affairs and teaching, as well as a tolerance for a variety of expressions that were emerging in this decade. Because of these concens, each resisted or was singled out at some time.

The three principals of these chapters — Clyde Matuse, Richard

Stewart, and Gerald Franklyn—faced a common situation: termination, and each responded in a way that became increasingly common in the 1970s: resistance. As each drama unfolds, competence becomes the focal concern for those in superordinate positions only after resistance is encountered. While the locus of such judgments varies, the ambiguous position of the nontenured is revealed, along with the machinations inherent in the operative goals. Although operative goals have long been known in "the academic marketplace,"[8] these case studies reveal that their construction and use are expanding. Out of this vague milieu of operational goals, often rapidly changing, the kind of concerns as well as the type of procedures that are evolving as a result of cases such as these are laying the foundations for the future of higher education. The significance of these circumstances is still to be appreciated. Finally, the three cases illustrate the strategies that can be employed in resisting not only the immediate threat of termination, but also the means by which such actions are taken. In the case of Clyde Matuse (Chapter 8), resistance was limited to his department. In the case of Richard Stewart (Chapter 9), a protracted conflict occurred, marked by the emergence and withdrawal of allies and issues. Finally, in the case of Gerald Franklyn (Chapter 10), a court battle was the strategy used.

Clyde Matuse's experience (Chapter 8, "The Trials in a Little Gemeinschaft") demonstrates the all too common tendency for academic procedures to slide into informal ones, which give rise to operative goals. Although a faculty member's contract is a formal document, the day-to-day affairs of the academician are very often undertaken and evaluated in an informal context. This is stressed by appeals to a small "community," a Gemeinschaft. In Matuse's case, the informal approached the irregular. In all of his encounters with his chairperson, Derrick Egon—from the first meeting in which he was given a job offer to his subsequent ones—an Alice in Wonderland aura predominated. When operative goals are in such constant flux, the individual's personal character ultimately comes up for evaluation, and it can endlessly be discussed and evaluated. In many bureaucratic settings, including education, conflicts involving character are portrayed euphemistically as "personality conflicts." This signals that the official goals or public procedures used in dealing with personnel have little, if any, standing in the social realities upon which a concern is focused. Thus, the struggle comes down to whose version of character is to be believed: that circulated by those wishing to pass judgments, which are often negative in nature, or that offered by the person for whom the question of character is an intimate concern, the person affected. Time after time, Matuse fends off erroneous judgments of his conduct, and even though no substantial critical public support can be garnered for such evaluations, when uttered by a powerful figure, such as his chairperson, these judgments have devastating effects. Meanwhile, the chairperson is not held accountable for his judgments. A condition which Marcuse describes as "repressive tolerance" thus prevails.[9] That is, numerous statements are considered to have standing, if not conclusive standing, simply because the right to speak is inherent in a position. Matuse too can speak, defending himself, but in the end the most important determinant is not truth or falsity, not adequacy or inadequacy, not fairness or unfairness—but power.

As Mirandé notes, Egon is not a shrewd Machiavellian, but an individual beset with contradiction. How, then do some of his actions assume such enormous significance? In the first place, it is simply a matter of formal power. Chairpersons have a control over organizational affairs which is not available to the faculty, particularly the nontenured. Second, position carries with it the important element of mystification, which is highly prized in many academic circles. That is, despite the apparent irrationality that confronts the puzzled individual such as Clyde Matuse, damaging information is often said to really exist, but "confidentiality" makes it impossible to divulge the nature of the information. As a result, in Matuse's case, other faculty members, some of whom had earlier supported him but were personally insecure, eventually capitulated.

For Matuse the unwholesome atmosphere in which he was ensnared was, at least temporarily, escapable. He did not join the ranks of the hidden professoriate, although if his case had occurred only a few years later, he could very well have been a prime candidate. Belatedly, "justice" conquered in Matuse's case, although he did not personally benefit. It appears that his resistance did serve as a focal point for subsequent developments in the department he left.

Matuse had few allies: a close friend and several sympathetic, but not openly political, colleagues. In contrast, Richard Stewart (Chapter 9, "Stewart's Folly") had aggressive, tough colleague and student support. While Matuse would never know if any truly damaging confidential items against him did exist (although there were probably none), Stewart finally discovered, through an examination of administration files, that the cloak of confidentiality was nothing more than a smokescreen. This discovery did not radically change his fate, which was very similar to Matuse's.

Stewart, like Gerald Franklyn in Chapter 10, was hired without having completed the Ph.D. His study reveals the fragility of colleague and student alliances. Where public procedures are not clearly detailed, formal records can become a collection of meaningless statements, with the result that personal demeanor becomes the critical feature of a case. Stewart, facing dismissal, had only two possible alternatives: resistance or capitulation. He chose resistance, even though it was the more troublesome of the two—particularly in the form of resistance he decided to take. Stewart, along with a supporting faculty member and a cadre of students, made intense investigations of various rumors and innuendos that were being circulated about Stewart. This investigation was very much in keeping with academic procedures, but it was met with great resistance—which suggests that truth-seeking efforts can themselves be proactive.

Like Clyde Matuse and Gerald Franklyn, Stewart undertakes a search for meaning, the search for "dependable responses to ... objects."[10] The portrait that was being painted of him did not coincide with his own perception of his character and abilities. Stewart was nevertheless able to entertain scholarly doubt because his allies, many of whom were students, were committed not simply to vindication, but to determining if there was any basis for the widely discrepant portraits of Stewart. The result is the exploration of a labyrinth of little encounters and hearsay.

Stewart's case possesses an electric, if not chaotic, quality, in part because of the extremely political environment at Baldwin University. Facts and rumors were continually intertwined. As challenges were mounted or critical questions advanced, new actors and issues emerged, seemingly from nowhere. Stewart and his dogged band of allies investigated each new twist and turn. While there was always the possibility that fabricated statements were being issued, there was a concern that they might contain a scintilla of truth, or at least that there was a plausible reason for their existence. Moreover, if Stewart's claims of unfairness were to be supported, all forms which the claims against him took had to be noted in order to point out how selective perceptions as well as the filtering of information took place regarding other faculty. If, as some administrators were claiming, the labyrinth of rumor and innuendo was the "procedure" in evaluating faculty, the nature of that procedure had to be fully exposed.

Stewart was not content merely to dismiss his adversaries as maleovolent. While this assessment would have simplified his position, it would have contradicted his own academic standards. Furthermore, it would have discredited him in his efforts to be retained and obtain tenure. If he considered his colleagues less than noble, why would he want to be part of their community?

Many of Stewart's clashes over procedures and interpretations have the character of guerrilla warfare. His most pointed conflict was with Dean More, with Stewart advocating open, fairly administered procedures and the dean more covert ones. The dean did not take kindly to the challenges mounted by Stewart and his allies. In the heat of the controversy, the dean resorted to tactics ably detailed by Harold Garfinkel: he undertook degradation ceremonies at Stewart's expense.[11] A degradation ceremony, as Garfinkel uses the phrase, involves addressing a person's character as a public commodity in such a fashion as to discredit the person. In so doing, the merits of contesting claims are simply brushed aside. The dean was not alone in using these tactics, for rumors regarding Stewart's unprofessionalism, his incommunicability, and his being "too good" for the environment originated from several sources. Stewart resisted by attempting to make his detractors accountable for their statements, not simply in an operative sense but in an official sense as well. His effort had the dimension of folly.

Organizational controversies that focus on personal character can take on a variety of guises, as happened in Stewart's case. Yet, Stewart was able to find the source of each new claim and to determine if there was a plausible reason for its existence. As a result, he got caught up in the small, embryonic intrigues and conflicts of interest involving graduate students, faculty, and administrators. With each new discovery the conflict intensified. Instead of establishing that the case against Stewart was suspect, his discoveries produced renewed resistance.

Stewart never suggested that he was without fault; his position, rather, was that the process of fault-finding had to be undertaken openly and with fairness. This desire earned him and his supporters the label "troublemakers," and troublemakers they in effect became.

The persistence of Stewart and his allies paid off when the president of Baldwin University mandated special hearings. Though the need for such procedures would on the face of it have seemed to vindicate Stewart's original claims about faulty procedures, the issue was not that clear cut. Now new actors came on the scene. Although Stewart would be vindicated, the actions of the special reviewing committee did not have complete support within the university. New forms of resistance were in evidence, and meanwhile Stewart suffered the inevitable fate of an individual whose major support comes from students — attrition.

Stewart was returned to full contract status, but while awaiting a final tenure decision, he found himself embroiled in the same kind of controversies as in the past. Claims that had no standing or which had been conclusively disproved continued to haunt him. The same processes of corrupted communications remained. With each passing day, it became more urgent to decide how much of his life and thought was to be devoted to an enterprise which both he and those close to him were more and more viewing as a folly. As is true of any solitary individual, his financial and emotional resources were simply inadequate.

Like Clyde Matuse, but unlike Richard Stewart, Gerald Franklyn (Chapter 10, "Due Process in Higher Education") had a clear picture of his opposition. From the outset he was clearly involved in a conflict with the administration, first in his support of more democratic procedures within his department, and second, in the area of community service where his actions brought him into direct conflict with representatives of the university's administration.

Among the formal goals used in conjunction with evaluating faculty members are teaching, research, and community service. These goals are often vague and subject to a wide variety of interpretations. Good teaching may be defined as an intense devotion to one's field, with a genuine interest in sharing the problems and adventure of the discipline. Or it may be defined as the ability to attract large numbers of students. Those in administrative circles can choose either definition to suit their own purposes. Community service, too, is open to administrative interpretation. Service may be deemed acceptable if someone is willing and able to respond to community concerns, or it may come to mean involvement in only noncontroversial political activity.

Franklyn's case has numerous merits, and it appears that he will be able to get sufficient standing to pursue his case through the courts. Here again, however, roadblocks confronting the isolated individual emerge: time and resources. Franklyn must grapple with the various demands placed upon him. Despite the dismal results of his case, he remains committed to a set of ideals which are highly supportive of education, especially higher education.

NOTES

1. Max Weber, *From Max Weber*, translated, edited and with an introduction by H. H. Gerth and C. Wright Mills (New York: Oxford University Press, 1946), p. 196.

2. Charles Perrow, "The Analyses of Goals in Complex Organization," *American Sociological Review* (1961) and reprinted in John G. Mauer, ed., *Readings in Organization Theory* (New York: Random House, 1971), p. 460.

3. Ernest L. Boyer and Martin Kaplan, *Educating for Survival* (New Rochelle, N.Y.: Change Magazine Press, 1977).

4. Perrow, op. cit.

5. Ibid., p. 461.

6. Discussed in the Introduction to this volume.

7. Jurgen Habermas, *Legitimation Crisis*, translated by Thomas McCarthy (Boston: Beacon Press, 1975[1973]).

8. Theodore Caplow and Reece J. McGee, *The Academic Marketplace* (New York: Basic Books, 1958).

9. Herbert Marcuse, "Repressive Tolerance," in Robert Paul Wolff, Barrington Moore, Jr. and Herbert Marcuse, *A Critique of Pure Tolerance* (Boston: Beacon Press, 1965), pp. 81-117.

10. Ernest Becker, *Angel in Armor* (New York: George Braziller, 1969), p. 9.

11. Harold Garfinkel, "Conditions of Successful Degradation Ceremonies," *American Journal of Sociology* 61 (1956), pp. 420-24.

7 FRAN FRENCH

The Rules Keep Changing Every Day

Every year Alice in academe learns the lesson the queen taught in Wonderland: There are rules that are not on the books, and we can invent new ones as fast as you can break them. In American colleges and universities, administrators and faculty alike have established and adhered to unwritten rules reserved exclusively for women. Women professors are subject to the same threats as men and in addition must face the jeopardy of violating rules applicable only to women. Frequently, the woman in academe does not become aware of these rules until she herself becomes the victim of their application. This may help explain why awareness never comes to most men.

Jessie Bernard's influential book, *Academic Women*,[1] suggests that only the "elite" or the "most talented women," and not the "rank and file," are discriminated against. Ever since the book's appearance in 1964, a few researchers, women's organizations, and committees of professional, scholarly, and scientific organizations have been attempting to demonstrate that such discrimination affects both the elite and the rank and file in academe. These investigations have concentrated on comparing women and men of similar credentials in terms of salary and length of service required to obtain promotion and tenure.

Governmental agencies have made some effort to investigate claims of sex discrimination. One of the principal agencies charged with such investigations is the U.S. Department of Health, Education and Welfare (HEW). HEW's efforts, however, are not universally or uniformly applied since an HEW investigation, consisting of a search for the presence or absence of discrimination "patterns," depends on the willingness of women to file complaints. Many women do not complain to HEW because they must grant HEW permission to use their names in the investigative process.

The right of the accused to face the accuser is a well-established canon of Anglo-American law, but the principle as applied in discrimination cases in higher education produces questionable results because of the immense structured inequality existing between the single faculty member and the school administration. The faculty member, concerned with earning a living, must do battle with a system whose legal and political resources are enormous and often repressive. For the isolated female faculty member, the dangers of HEW's procedure are therefore magnified.

As do her male colleagues, a woman faculty member recognizes that the "right" to accuse with immunity resides with administrators and their surrogates. In some cases, unfounded if not inappropriate claims are used in decisions regarding tenure, promotion, and pay. In addition, the prospects of revealing one's name, of becoming overtly identified as a "troublemaker," regardless of the merits of the complaint, has a chilling effect. Consequently, nontenured, often temporary, women faculty members may be dissatisfied but not willing to risk everything. Instead, they choose to move to another college, to go into nonacademic work, or to remain in a low ranking position. As a result, the extent of sex discrimination cases goes underreported.

In addition, the rules employed against women are unwritten, and those administering and interpreting rules regarding their employment—administrators and male colleagues—often do not make decisions in a consistent fashion.

If all the unwritten rules were ever published in the local faculty handbook and if the administrator and male colleague's undisputed rights to make up new rules were stated in contracts, then all discrimination investigations would be easy. Lacking such signed confessions, however, the case history approach may be used, especially if no names are published. The following highlights of cases have been selected to indicate the scope of the woman professor's problem. They come from universities in four states.

—In a school of business, a woman professor who had taught there seven years and who had twice won a school-wide Most Outstanding Teacher Award was denied tenure, but was told she could stay on indefinitely as a temporary instructor. She was informed that such an arrangement was necessitated by the fact that her husband had tenure in another school of the university.

—A woman political scientist was denied tenure because she had not qualified for the graduate faculty. Earlier, when she expressed a desire to teach at the graduate level, she had been told that students had more confidence in male professors. Further, she was informed that the chairperson felt that women did their best teaching to freshmen and sophomores who needed a little "mothering" to help them establish good study habits.

—Once a month all the male professors in a department held a poker party at which they exchanged departmental and university gossip, established friendships, and sometimes made informal departmental decisions. The two women in the department were excluded from this fraternity. One, who had been an assistant professor for twelve years, met her classes, published a little, and kept her own counsel. The other, unmarried and new to the department, was eager for departmental involvement and often contributed her views at departmental meetings. She sometimes introduced issues in faculty meetings before the men, and on occasion she took the "wrong" position on issues. After all, she was not privy to the information shared at the monthly poker session. When she discovered why she was "out of step," she mentioned that she, too, played poker and she offered to hold the poker party at her house. When she issued invitations, only two of her male colleagues appeared. Although she was willing to try again, she did not after one professor explained that the "wives objected." Her contract was not renewed.

—An instructor in mathematics was fired after twelve years with the explanation that she did not have a Ph.D. and the department could now get a Ph.D. for the same salary she was being paid. When she appealed through the local administration and then through the AAUP, the head of the department said, at a meeting of AAUP officers and administrators, that no one had thought she took her job that seriously.

—An instructor in sociology, told that no one without a Ph.D. would be considered for tenure, requested a leave of absence without pay to return to graduate school for one semester to complete her residence requirement for the doctorate. Several men, she noted, had been granted such leaves. The vice-president denied her request, asking her why she should want a Ph.D. since her husband already had one.

—An assistant professor of English submitted a request for summer teaching and was informed that the university always gave summer jobs to men because they had families to support. He suggested that inasmuch as she was up for tenure the following year she should guard against acquiring the reputation of being overly competitive with her colleagues. She didn't teach that summer. Nor did she get tenure the following year.

—A paleobotanist who was professionally active (publishing, reading papers at national meetings) was told by the chairperson that she would no longer be granted money to attend meetings because her husband would probably not like her to go to meetings with a bunch of men. When she came up for tenure two years later, she was told she could not be recommended by either the chairperson or her male colleagues since, for the past two years, she had not been professionally active.

—A woman and her husband, each with a Ph.D. in speech from the same university, had very similar qualifications, except that the woman had published more. When interviewed by a university, the husband was offered an assistant professorship but the woman only an instructorship. When the woman objected, she was asked why she would want to compete with her own husband.

—A nationally known artist was denied tenure because she had not been sufficiently active in departmental and university service, especially on committees. (Service on such committees is by appointment of administrators.) In order to qualify for tenure, she actively sought committee appointments, ran for the faculty senate, and was very vocal at departmental meetings. At the end of the year she was terminated on the grounds that she had been too "aggressive."

—Finally, a department hired its first woman professor and assigned her the last private office available. The rule of the department was that junior faculty had to share offices if no private offices were available. A year later, another young assistant professor, a man, was added to the department. The woman professor was told that the department would not be able to keep her after the current academic year, since as junior faculty she couldn't have a private office and as a woman she couldn't share an office with a man. For the remainder of her stay, the new male assistant professor shared an office with a senior faculty male.

Most of these instances of discrimination involve women who are not elite but rank and file, trying merely to hold onto their jobs. The situations presented portray ordinary academic events—tenure decisions, assignment of office space, teaching assignments, applications for travel funds and leave. In no case was there either a personality clash or charges of professional incompetence—just different rules for women. If each of these vignettes were rewritten substituting a male for every female character, the results in every case would be quite different. (In those instances involving a married couple, a set of brothers or a father-son duo could be substituted.)

As reflected in these cases, the following unwritten rules are seen to have served as guidelines for administrative decisions:

1. A woman professor must not be married to a tenured professor, and competence in one's job is not sufficient grounds for the granting of tenure.

2. Women professors are employed to teach lower level courses, not graduate courses.

3. Women professors should not socialize with male professors, especially if the women professors are not married, and women should not offer their opinions or ideas in faculty meetings.

4. It is not unethical to fire a woman professor without cause since women don't take their jobs seriously anyway.

5. Men get leaves of absence for professional improvement; women don't. And one Ph.D. in a family is enough.

6. Women should not ask for summer employment unless

there are no married men in the department; women do not have families to support and if a woman professor is competitive at all, she is "too competitive."

7. Women faculty have family obligations; men do not. Professional women must not travel to professional meetings with professional men; fringe benefits, such as travel money for professional activities, are not available to married women faculty. (If the first part of rule 7 seems to contradict the second part of rule 6, you are a woman, a woman-lover, or "soft on women.")

8. Women faculty should not marry men in the same academic discipline.

9. Women should wait quietly to be appointed to committees or to be asked to serve the department in some capacity. A woman who seeks such appointments is too aggressive and therefore not fit for tenure.

10. Something terrible will happen to a male professor if he shares an office with a female professor.

NOTE

1. Jessie Bernard, *Academic Women* (Philadelphia: Pennsylvania State University Press, 1964).

8

ALFREDO MIRANDÉ

The Trials in a
Little *Gemeinschaft*

Toward the end of his interview at Southern State University, Clyde Matuse received a written offer of appointment by the chairperson of the Department of Sociology, Derick Egon: an associate professorship and a substantial increase over his current salary as assistant professor. Matuse considered the appointment and accepted it two days later. On January 23, 1970, Egon sent him this short note:

There is rejoicing on the fourth floor of Abbott Hall this morning what with the news that you accepted our offer. Our invalid, Tom Drake, in a hospital recovering from serious surgery, bubbled at the news when I called him. Naturally we are all convinced that you made an excellent choice!

Though Matuse wasn't really sure of his opinion of Egon, he was generally pleased with his appointment. The associate professorship in what promised to be a growing department was a recognition that the twenty-nine-year-old Matuse, only three years after the completion of his Ph.D. and with four years of teaching experience, was on his way up. He had already demonstrated much promise as a researcher and scholar, having already published a number of articles, and was working on a book. Southern seemed ideally suited to his career objectives. Furthermore, his friend from graduate school days, Jake Kennedy, also an associate professor, was on the staff. Kennedy had encouraged Matuse to take the position at Southern.

and his presence on the staff was reassuring. Matuse was slated to join the staff in the summer of 1970.

THE SMOKE OF CAMBODIA LINGERS

When Matuse arrived to teach summer school at Southern, the campus was alive with the issues surrounding its demonstrations of the past spring. At Southern, as at many other campuses across the country, the U.S. invasion of Cambodia and the killing of students at Kent State by the National Guard had sparked violent passions. At Southern, bomb threats had been made, a campus building had been occupied, and ROTC military drills had been interrupted. Eventually the National Guard was called. Students in the occupied building were removed, herded into large moving vans, and taken into police custody.

For Matuse, the Department of Sociology seemed a refuge from these unsettling events. His knowledge of Egon's approach to the chairpersonship had reinforced this impression. While Egon was deeply dedicated to building his department into a reputable one, he also appeared to care about faculty sensitivities and rights. On occasion Egon voluntarily voiced his support of the faculty, portraying himself as a liberal beleaguered by conservatives on all sides.

Ideological sympathies, as well as Egon's concerns for the development of the department, drew Matuse to Egon. Soon after he arrived, Matuse found that Egon frequently sought out his opinions and counsel. Matuse readily gave his advice and regularly informed Egon of his concerns and activities. The only distracting element in this relationship, as far as Matuse was concerned, was Egon's preoccupation with appearances. A carefully attired individual himself, Egon insisted that the office be as businesslike as possible. He even went so far as to suggest proper housing for staff members. Matuse easily tolerated this idiosyncrasy for it did not seem to be overly critical.

Meanwhile, Jake Kennedy was always present to help Matuse interpret his new environment. It was Kennedy, for example, who reassured Matuse that the disturbances on campus during the previous spring were not as they appeared. Other factors may have influenced some of the current controversies.

For Matuse, the drama of the spring riots was not easily dismissed. He was particularly disturbed by reports that two young faculty members had been terminated because of their involvement in the demonstrations. The two were Art Burns, a statistician, and Ron Ravowitz, a historian, both of whom had addressed student gatherings. Both, however, had denied making inflammatory statements or inciting the students, even though they had been served temporary injunctions by the County Sheriff's Office to desist in "engaging in riotous and disorderly conduct and acting with others threatening to continue these acts." Since they were fired in the aftermath of these events, the university's denial that their political activities had influenced its decision to terminate their contract was met with suspicion.

The more Matuse familiarized himself with the situation at Southern, the more a consistent, but troublesome, picture emerged. The school was definitely being run in an authoritarian manner by its president, George Hunnell. A politically ambitious individual who had long devoted himself to the well-known military education program of Southern, Hunnell, it seemed, wished to keep his credits with legislators as well as with the public. With the support he had on campus, it meant that activist faculty, if the Burns-Ravowitz encounter was indicative, were in difficulty.

CRACKS IN THE "GEMEINSCHAFT"

Egon was fond of describing his department as a "little *Gemeinschaft*," a small, tight-knit community. It was an image that he continually cultivated. His administrative style involved a "drop in" method whereby he would selectively solicit advice and counsel from some persons in the department, and not from others. Because of Matuse's rank, he was frequently consulted in those early days.

Egon had taken a fatherly interest in Matuse, periodically drawing parallels between Matuse and his oldest son, a graduate student at another university. Eventually, Matuse learned that the relations between Egon and his son were strained, which made Egon's remarks about how his son's tie to the youth culture made it easier for him to relate to Matuse somewhat puzzling. Nevertheless, Matuse continued to seek Egon's advice on a variety of matters.

Egon and another staff member, Jim Bandeagle, were the oldest members of the department. Bandeagle had become director of Operation Bootstrap, a program designed to help underprivileged youth attend college and was increasingly detached from affairs in the department. After some preliminary debate over office space and the eventual relocation of Bandeagle's Bootstrap office to another building, Bandeagle became more withdrawn. At midyear, he moved into a new office with the Office of the Dean of Arts and Sciences as an assistant dean. The *Gemeinschaft* was cracking.

Bandeagle and Henry Gibson, an assistant professor, had been on the staff prior to Egon's appointment. Both had obtained tenure by default because Egon was unaware of the university's tenure regulations; they had been automatically renewed without review and had taught sufficient time at Southern to warrant automatic tenure.

Gibson was only an assistant professor because he had only recently completed the doctorate. Although though he did not have a prolific publishing record, Matuse was favorably disposed to him. Gibson, it was rumored, had "Egon's ear." On several occasions, Egon publicly voiced his approval of Gibson's work with the graduate program.

Gibson had a close friendship with John Campesino, a young, popular instructor, who was in his second year at Southern. Like Matuse he taught classes that dealt with contemporary and controversial issues. But Campesino had reached an impasse in his career. Having failed his Ph.D. comprehensive examination, his chances for completing the doctorate were virtually nil. Egon, realizing that it would be difficult for Campesino to get either tenure or promotion without the Ph.D., made an agreement with him. If the book Campesino was working on dealing with the drug subculture were published, he would recommend him for assistant professor. It was Jake Kennedy's view that Campesino was in good standing with Egon because he was a good teacher and had played a conciliatory role in the demonstrations of the past spring. Egon had, on occasion, mentioned Campesino's role.

The department's "mystery man" was Joseph Sane, a young man of about twenty-six who had just received his Ph.D. Joe's long hair appeared to link him to the youth culture, but with his quiet, introverted manner little was known about him. Rick Wong, another assistant professor, likewise did not play a central role in departmental affairs.

Another assistant professor, in his second year in the department, was Bill Hoffman. It was rumored that he had difficulties with Egon and in addition was having trouble adjusting to teaching. Egon had confided in Matuse that Hoffman, having done graduate work at a large, prestigious university, felt demeaned having to teach at the less prestigious Southern. Hoffman, a methodologist, had apparently expected too much from his students; he was rumored to be "above their heads." To the contrary, Matuse found that Hoffman was relatively well liked by students and easily accepted by his colleagues.

Probably the best liked and most respected member of the department was Tom Drake. Previously a minister, Drake had later come into sociology. A private person, Drake worked to keep his public and private life separate. Accordingly, he lived with his wife and daughter in an old farmhouse situated on a beautiful tract of land about fifteen miles out of town. He accepted many committee assignments from Egon. Privately, he did not care for Egon's interest in the private lives of the staff.

Egon's concerns as reflected in his cryptic phrase "little *Gemeinschaft*" were ever-present reminders of his interest in the private lives of his department members. Nurtured in a fundamentalist religion, Egon looked askance at any moral trespass. Earlier, at another university where he was the chairperson, he dismissed a faculty member for carrying on an open liaison with a graduate student. His views on morality and appropriate behavior made the position of the Gibsons, Henry and Betty Lou, precarious. They had been married in their teens, and Betty Lou was a constant reminder of Henry's working-class background. Aggressive, loud, and crude at parties, she was often observed openly flirting with other men. Their marital discord seemed to be well known. Rumor had it that Gibson had been involved in several affairs with students; rather than discourage the rumors, Gibson seemed to thrive on them. Yet, strangely, Egon was unaware of this situation or chose to ignore it.

In spite of the variety of personal backgrounds and interests of the department members, Matuse observed that most of them acted out Egon's "little *Gemeinschaft*" scenario. The small staff seemed cohesive, especially in informal settings; they would drop by one another's homes unannounced after classes. Jake Kennedy's home was often the site of unplanned get-togethers for the young faculty. There were also planned activities, attended by all except Egon and Bandeagle. One of the first was a potluck dinner at the home of the Campesinos, where Campesino, Gibson, and Sane were observed to have smoked pot. Matuse could only speculate what Egon's reaction would have been.

The last party of the year was a departmental Christmas gathering. The highlight of the event was the search for Henry Gibson who had mysteriously disappeared. Jake Kennedy and John Campesino proceeded to check out several student apartments where Henry was known to hang out, including that of two graduate students in the department, Joanie Olson and Carrie MacDonald's. Henry's disappearance remained a lively topic as Carrie MacDonald contacted Rick Wong to express dismay not only at the search by Campesino and Kennedy, but the fact that Betty Lou Gibson had on several occasions previously come over to the apartment in search of Henry.

EGON'S PUBLIC EYE

Despite the seemingly repressive climate, the general affability of his colleagues and the challenge of his classes more than compensated Matuse. Many of the students were conservative, but there was also a core of radicals. The students were generally competent and academically well prepared. Matuse's classes were lively and somewhat controversial, though he tried very hard to maintain a low profile and to refrain from becoming involved in campus politics. Since he taught the course Crowds and Social Movements and other courses dealing with timely social issues, however, it was impossible to avoid controversial issues or to remain completely anonymous. Students were attracted to him, especially those who identified with the New Left or the counter-culture. Many felt free to drop into his office to chat.

In the process, Matuse developed close ties with two groups—those interested in utopian societies and communal living and an enclave of gay students. These ties emerged from his research interests. He had started a study of a rural intentional community located in the state and was also doing research on homosexuality.

At the close of the fall quarter, Randy Thomas, the student body president and other students who lived on a farm, approached Matuse about offering an independent study course on experimental communities during the second quarter. Their interest was of a practical nature. They wanted to read about and discuss historical communities so that they could design a successful community at their farm. Matuse was excited by the idea. He asked them to write a course proposal for the chairperson and the dean.

Egon was not enthusiastic about the proposal because on principle he opposed independent study courses. His fear was that such courses might lead to increases in departmental teaching loads, especially if it looked like the faculty had spare time on their hands. Moreover, in Egon's estimation, Thomas, a sociology major, was an irreverent radical. Although Matuse agreed that independent study courses should not be abused, noting that he had rejected frivolous requests for independent study, he assured Egon that these were serious and highly motivated students with a worthwhile project. Egon reluctantly signed the necessary forms and sent the proposal to the dean for his approval.

Among graduate students, Matuse developed a close relationship with Ivan Boroff. An ex-athlete who had joined the counter-culture, Boroff had the appearance of a gentle giant. A sensitive and inquisitive young man, Boroff struggled to overcome the image of his past identity. This was no easy task as he was frequently dismissed as merely a "jock."

Boroff came into the graduate program with a mediocre undergraduate record. Nevertheless, he worked hard during the fall quarter, and the faculty generally agreed that his performance was more than adequate. He learned very rapidly. Even Henry Gibson, who taught graduate theory and was considered a formidable teacher, judged that he was making good progress. Only Egon was openly critical, referring to Boroff as that "big Russian kid" or the "revolutionary." Boroff was neither Russian, nor a revolutionary. What particularly piqued Egon was Ivan's long hair and casual dress of bib overalls and red plaid shirt. This was not the style Egon had earnestly advocated for himself and his "little *Gemeinschaft*." For the status-conscious Egon, Ivan Boroff was suspect. Nothing else was necessary to threaten the public relations image Egon continually cultivated.

MARIJUANA, ASSASSIN OF YOUTH AND OTHERS

It was January 1971. The winter quarter had just started. Betty Dukes, a graduate student in the department, had recently moved into a new apartment. She and one of her roommates, an undergraduate in one of Matuse's classes, invited Matuse, his wife, and their daughter to a housewarming dinner. The Matuses accepted.

Matuse was the only faculty member present at the dinner. After dinner people sat around talking and drinking inexpensive wine. The Matuses were among the first to leave.

Two days after the party, on a Saturday morning, Matuse received a phone call from Egon. Egon told Matuse that he had a problem and wondered if he would come down to the office and talk it over with him. What, he wondered, could be the problem? Was it, possibly, the discovery of Gibson's escapades? Or was there another problem with Bandeagle? The previous fall, Egon, puzzled over how to handle office assignments and not wishing to offend Bandeagle, had consulted with Matuse and Jake Kennedy. Even then, Bandeagle's relationship to the department had cooled. What could be the problem?

When he arrived at Egon's office, Matuse sensed immediately that the situation was serious. Egon's appearance conveyed the weightiness of some problem. He closed the door and asked Matuse to sit down in one of the easy chairs in the room. Egon, in uncustomary informal attire, sat down in front of him.

After lighting his pipe, Egan began to speak,

You know that I like you and think of you like a son. What I am going to ask you is as your friend, not as head of the department. It has been said that the other night Clyde Matuse, his wife, and little daughter attended a party and that during the course of the evening Clyde smoked marijuana. More importantly, that a young female student was present who refused to smoke and that Clyde demeaned her and tried to coerce her into smoking marijuana.

Clyde was taken aback. Furious, his first impulse was to walk out, but he quickly reconsidered. Derick did not deserve that.

"Derick," Clyde began, "my initial reaction is that the charge is so ludicrous that it doesn't deserve a response, but since you ask me as a friend, I can assure you that I have never belittled anyone for not smoking marijuana, nor have I ever tried to coerce anyone into smoking." For Clyde, that was all that was critical in terms of his relationship with the university. His own personal conduct was not the university's business.

Egon sat quietly for a moment reflecting on Matuse's answer. Then in an effort to respond to Clyde's last statement, he said, "Well, the dean thinks it *is* our business." It was the dean who had passed on the information Egon had relayed. If Matuse denied the charges, the dean would consider the case closed.

Matuse was anxious to know who was making the charges, but Egon did not know the source. If he wished, Matuse could consult with the dean. On the following Monday, he did so.

Dean Princeton greeted Matuse cordially. After some pleasantries, Matuse stated that he considered the charges slanderous and that he wanted to know the identity of his accuser. The dean attempted to mollify Clyde and related how a student had called him the previous Friday afternoon. It seems the student's ex-girl friend had attended a party where marijuana was smoked. He reported that she had claimed Professor Matuse had tried to force her to smoke. It was, of course, hearsay, but the student was upset by the situation and threatened action with the FBI.

The dean's responsibility, as he explained it, was to investigate the situation, but the student's name was a matter of confidentiality. If Matuse denied the charge, the case would be dropped. Matuse said he would forget it if he could be assured the accusation would not be on record as a part of his personnel file. The dean assured him.

Before Matuse left the dean's office, the dean attempted to counsel him: avoid situations where other people might be using drugs or engaging in illegal or illicit activities. Matuse acknowledged the soundness of the advice. However, for a sociologist carrying out research on drugs or other illicit activities, it was not always easy to avoid such situations.

EXERCISES IN THOUGHT REFORM

Matuse recounted his meeting with the dean to Egon, who indicated that the matter was "dropped." Sometime after the marijuana
"incident," Egon called Clyde into his office and began a rambling
discussion. He talked about his friendship for Matuse. It was possibly the only friendship, besides that with Jake Kennedy, that
Matuse had in the department. Although Egon understood young
rebels like Matuse and Campesino, it was important, he stressed, to
know the academic environment. Matuse, it seemed, didn't. Furthermore, he was too defensive, carrying a chip on his shoulder. Egon
maintained that Matuse had completely alienated his colleagues.
When pressed for details, Egon indicated that this was a matter of
confidentiality, but colleagues had indeed complained.

Leaving Egon's office, Matuse sought counsel with his old friend
and colleague, Jake Kennedy. There was a general bewilderment.
In their search for a plausible explanation for Egon's sudden attack,
Ann Kennedy somewhat reluctantly volunteered that Betty Lou
Gibson had made derogatory ethnic remarks about Matuse, but
little was made of it.

Several weeks after his encounter with Egon, a representative of
Southern's Department of Public Relations asked Matuse for an
interview. She was interested in publicizing his course, Crowds and
Social Movements. At first he suggested she interview Campesino
instead since he taught the same course. But the reporter was persistent, and Matuse finally agreed to the interview.

Matuse described the course as dealing with protest, crowds, and
civil disorders. Was the course, she asked, designed to encourage
student protests and disorders? It was not, he replied. Nevertheless,
it had to be remembered, he noted, that the right to peaceful protest
was a constitutional guarantee. As far as the study of collective
behavior was concerned, it could be used to avert violence. An
article based on the interview appeared later in the student newspaper.

Several days after the article was published, Egon called Matuse
to his office. He was upset by the article. The dean, he reported,
had expressed concern over the image of the department such
publicity created and over the number of lower division courses
such as Crowds and Social Movements and Racism in America.

Such courses, the dean supposedly maintained, were of questionable academic quality and attracted revolutionary students. Matuse was perplexed. The article had contained some factual errors, but overall it could not be said that it cast a bad light on the department.

Somewhat later, Matuse happened to see the reporter. He related his meeting with Egon. On her own initiative, she went to visit Dean Princeton, apologizing for any errors that might have occurred in the article. After her meeting, she returned to Matuse's office. The dean, she reported, had not been upset by the article. He had, she noted, wondered about the advisability of offering so many lower division courses that were oriented toward social problems. This was ironic. It was Egon, after all, who had introduced these popular level courses in lieu of the traditional social problems course in an effort to attract students. By contrast, Matuse early on had proposed that these courses be dropped and a more traditional problems course be reinstituted.

Soon thereafter, Matuse was confronted with yet another challenge. At the end of the winter quarter, a group of students from the Gay Alliance approached him about becoming their faculty sponsor. He explained that given the political climate, it would be risky for any faculty member to sponsor the organization. The students agreed. Would it be better, they wondered, if an entire department sponsored the organization? Matuse said he could sound out the possibility with Egon, or, they might wish to approach him directly. The students decided on the latter course of action.

Roger Maynard, president of Gay Alliance, sent a letter of inquiry to Egon on March 8, 1971. It accurately summarized the concerns discussed with Matuse and indicated Matuse's willingness to discuss the matter. That afternoon, Matuse received a handwritten note attached to the letter. It read:

Would you agree that you are a little too "hot" right now to champion this organization just now—also in view of the image the dean has of "sociology and its 200 courses?" Reply.

Egon had viewed the letter as an attempt to embarrass the department, and not as a legitimate and confidential request for aid. Matuse immediately asked for a meeting.

Egon was visibly upset. Matuse stated that the Gay Alliance did not wish any individuals to stick their necks out. As far as he was concerned, it was a matter to be discussed in the department. Egon was in no mood to be appeased, however. Matuse was not, he observed, in any position to champion "a bunch of homosexuals." Matuse replied that he was not "championing" the group, but he knew and respected the students and felt they had a legitimate cause.

Unmoved, Egon reminded Matuse of his vulnerability, given the marijuana incident and the dean's opinion of the department's lower division courses. When Matuse became angry, Egon backtracked, returning to his original position: Matuse was in no position to sponsor "a bunch of homosexuals." Egon concluded that the department would not sponsor a group of homosexuals and that he would not meet with them.

After the meeting, Clyde sought counsel with Jake Kennedy. It was agreed that Clyde should keep a low profile and preferably stay out of Egon's sight until the situation cooled down. This Clyde did, and things returned to normal.

Several weeks after the incident involving the Gay Alliance letter, Matuse was summoned to Egon's office. Egon appeared uneasy, and looking out the window, he began: "You know that I'm trying to help you. I think I'm the only one who understands you. You have such a lovely wife and daughter, such a nice family. Aren't you concerned about them?"

CLYDE: "Yes, I care a great deal about my family, but I don't see what you are getting at."

EGON: "What am I going to do with you?"

CLYDE: "What are you talking about?"

EGON: "You have completely alienated your colleagues."

CLYDE: "I don't understand. Which colleagues? I'm very happy with my colleagues."

EGON: "All right, let's take your colleague down the hall, Henry Gibson. Gibson's done a great job as head of the Graduate Committee, and you come in here and try to take over the chairmanship of his committee. We had a little *Gemeinschaft* here, a small community of scholars, before you came but you seem to thrive on conflict."

CLYDE: "Wait a minute. I don't want to take over that committee.

When I first came here you asked me what committee I wanted to be on and I said the Graduate Committee, but I'm very satisfied serving on the Undergraduate Committee. I don't have anything against Henry."

EGON: "Allright then, what about the marijuana incident?"

CLYDE: "What marijuana incident? I thought that was dropped. If I have done something wrong, I'd like to know what it is."

EGON: "What am I going to do with you?"

CLYDE: "I don't know what you're talking about. What have I done?"

EGON: "You don't know what you've done" You don't know? Do I have to tell you?"

CLYDE: "No, I don't know. You have to tell me."

(*pause*)

EGON: "You just had a class, didn't you?

Clyde nodded in the affirmative.

EGON: "For Christ sake, Clyde, wear a tie."

Matuse sat dumbfounded. Not believing what he had just heard, he spoke slowly, indicating that this was distressing news. Egon maintained that Matuse did not look or act like an associate professor. "I'm trying to build a department and when the dean or some other administrator comes over here they think that my young professors are a bunch of radical students."

In the ensuing weeks Matuse avoided Egon. The departmental routines were tolerable except for those strange encounters with Egon. Neither Matuse nor, it seemed, his close associates suspected the objectives of Egon's actions. Attention was focused on the technique, a form of thought reform, made famous by the Chinese during the Korean War as well as the police in the United States through their "Mutt and Jeff" routines of interrogation. Matuse, the prisoner, was confronted with Egon, the friend. Egon, the helpful individual, was continually thwarted by Matuse. If only Matuse would confess to a series of unknown or unnamed crimes, Egon was there to help. After the accusations were made repeatedly, Matuse, the prisoner, was made to feel guilty without knowing the nature of his crimes or having the opportunity to face his accusers.

Whether it was his lack of success in reforming Matuse or a general disdain for certain appearances, Egon settled on another target, Ivan Boroff. Boroff worked as Matuse's graduate assistant. As the relations between Egon and Matuse cooled, the attacks on Boroff became more direct. On several occasions, Egon urged Matuse to tell Boroff that he was too much of a revolutionary for the department and university. When Matuse sought clarification, Egon noted that both the posters adorning his office and Boroff's dress gave the department a bad image. Matuse was instructed to tell Boroff that he had to start towing the line or be dropped from the program.

Matuse was in a difficult position. He spoke with Boroff about the situation and urged him to consult with other faculty. These conferences were generally reassuring. When he questioned Matuse about retaining the posters, he had no advice. Boroff, he pointed out, did have a constitutional right to display those posters, but the decision was Boroff's.

At this time, graduate student morale was at a very low point. Many of their problems stemmed from their dissatisfaction with Henry Gibson's graduate courses. By spring, the dissatisfaction bordered on rebellion. There was some criticism of course content, but the most serious complaints centered on the issue of Gibson's favoritism in grading. Some students, no matter what the quality of their work, received A's. One specific accusation was that Gibson gave preferential treatment to Joanie Olson and Carrie MacDonald. It was rumored that Gibson was having an affair with Olson.

Tensions increased even further when it was learned that Mac-Donald had received an A in Gibson's course, even though she had not handed in the final paper. Those who had handed in papers and received low grades were naturally upset.

In April 1971, most of the staff, except for Rick Wong and Clyde Matuse, were away at a professional convention. The graduate students decided this was a good time to hold a meeting to air their grievances. Frightened at the prospects of discovery, they attempted to keep the meeting secret. The meeting was attended by most of the students in the program, even Joanie Olson and Carrie Mac-Donald. From reports, the discussion was wide-ranging, though a portion of it centered on Gibson's treatment of students. No proposals for action came from the meeting.

Joe Pine, a graduate student working with Bill Hoffman, confided in Joyce Hoffman about the meeting. When Hoffman called home from the convention, Joyce relayed the information she had. Word spread quickly among the faculty that "the students are out to get Henry."

When Jake Kennedy returned from the convention, he told Matuse that his name would probably be linked to the student meeting. Gibson and Egon were implying that some faculty (i.e., Matuse) were responsible for organizing and encouraging the "student" revolt. Matuse assured Jake that this was not the case; in fact, he had learned of the meeting only the day it took place.

Egon spent the weekend ferreting out the troublemakers. He spoke with Rick Wong, Carrie MacDonald, and Joanie Olson among others. He isolated three culprits: Joe Pine, Betty Dukes, and Ivan Boroff. On the following Monday, he summoned them along with several other students to his office. Dukes was reminded of her tenuous status, and Pine was ridiculed. Boroff was treated the most harshly. If he did not immediately remove the posters from his office, Egon said, he would recommend to the dean of the Graduate School, B. Toro, that he be dropped from the program for unethical conduct. Boroff did not take down the posters and within a week he received a letter from Egon advising that his moral and ethical conduct left much to be desired and that if not improved, Egon would be forced to recommend to the dean that Boroff be dropped from graduate study at Southern State University.

Shocked, Boroff turned to Matuse and Kennedy for help. Kennedy suggested that he contact the other members of the Graduate Committee and inform them of the situation. In addition to Kennedy and Egon, the other members were Wong, Gibson, and Bandeagle. Wong and Gibson were encouraging; only Bandeagle was incommunicative.

Matuse was in a difficult position once again. Egon had not discussed the student meeting with him nor had he discussed the letter he had sent Boroff. It seemed clear to Matuse that Boroff was being persecuted for his association with him. Meanwhile, Kennedy and Bill Hoffman assured Boroff that Egon would not carry out his threat. If he tried, they counseled, the department would not let him get away with it. As a result, there was no direct faculty response to Egon's letter to Boroff or to his threats to other students.

Matuse continued to keep a low profile. In the last five or six weeks of the school year, he seldom saw Egon except at faculty meetings. These were usually perfunctory affairs, but at one meeting Matuse again was on center stage.

Earlier in the year, Egon had appointed Matuse to chair an ad hoc committee made up of Matuse, Tom Drake, and Joy Pinkerton, a part-time instructor. The committee was charged with making recommendations regarding establishing a permanent executive committee to advise the chairperson on important personnel questions such as tenure, promotion, hiring, and dismissal. At the time, the department had no established procedures for these questions.

In the last weeks of the school year, Egon requested a report from the committee. It was in agreement on the importance of establishing an executive committee that had authority. Matuse prepared a detailed report highlighting the major issues and questions raised during the committee's deliberations and forwarded the specific recommendations, including random selection and fixed membership on the proposed executive committee.

At the meeting where the committee report was presented, intense discussion followed. Egon and Gibson led the opposition. They viewed it as a device to undermine the authority of the chairperson. The meeting broke up in the midst of a heated discussion. The recommendations were never voted on either at that meeting or subsequent ones.

Until two weeks before the end of the spring quarter, Egon had never confronted Matuse publicly. It was always an informal, private conversation. Now this changed. At the last faculty meeting, Egon began to attack Matuse, indicating that his preliminary comments were off the record and were not to be included in the official transcript of the meeting which was to be distributed to the faculty and the dean. He first implored the faculty to get their wives to "hold their tongues." He then paused and said, "And what am I going to do with this fellow to my left, Clyde Matuse? He's morose, withdrawn, and has completely alienated his colleagues."

Egon spoke so casually that Matuse was caught by surprise. He was about to continue when Matuse calmly interrupted: "What are you talking about? I get along very well with my colleagues. If there are specific charges you would like to make, I wish you would bring them up right now."

Egon again returned to his long-established ritual. He claimed friendship for Matuse. If that were so, Matuse countered, "Who's on the other side?" Egon mumbled something about confidentiality while Matuse eyed his colleagues. Campesino entered as arbitrator, suggesting that the issue might be discussed at a later date when cooler heads prevailed. The meeting then began with its normal agenda.

After the meeting, Tom Drake, Joe Sane, and Bill Hoffman stopped by Matuse's office and expressed their sadness over the incident and Egon's blatant attempt to discredit him.

Matuse hoped that the year would end without further incident, but on June 2, Egon asked that they have a meeting on June 4 at 10:00 A.M. On the morning of June 4, however, Matuse asked that the meeting be rescheduled for the following week at Egon's convenience. June 4 was the last day of the quarter and graduation was scheduled for the next day. That very afternoon a special delivery letter arrived from Southern State University. Inside the envelope were two letters. The cover letter was dated June 4, 1971. It read:

This morning I received the message from your wife that . . . you would be unable to confer with me at 10:00 A.M. I had hoped that we could chat about our mutual difficulties this year with a view to resolving them.

Under AAUP rules, it seems, I have no alternative but to submit the enclosed letter to you on this date. Naturally I will welcome a conference with you at later date and at your convenience.

Sincerely,
(Derick Egon)
Professor and Chairman

The second letter, dated two days earlier, June 2, was a notification that Matuse's contract for the 1971-72 academic year would be terminal. If Matuse chose to resign formally, effective June 20, 1972, the notice would be honored and supersede the terminal notice. It was the second paragraph that Matuse studied:

This decision has been reached after consultation with your colleagues. While your activities in research and publishing have been satisfactory during your brief tenure at Southern State University, your human relations skills have failed to reinforce the spirit of cooperation we have tried to engender in the department. A weakness in the supportive role in department development has been observed.

WITH A LITTLE HELP FROM FRIENDS

For the remainder of the afternoon and evening, Matuse sought out members of the staff. One by one—Bill Hoffman, Joe Sane, Tom Drake, Rick Wong, Henry Gibson, and John Campesino— they indicated that they had no knowledge of Egon's decision. From their shock and dismay—it was obvious that Egon had seriously misjudged the mood and sentiment of the department and had probably expected his decision to be more broadly supported than it was. It was Matuse, not Egon, who garnered the initial support of the faculty—an intense, friendly support.

The next afternoon the young members of the department gathered at the Kennedy home. Kennedy, usually the mild and cautious figure, urged those assembled that they should go to the dean and "try to get Egon's ass fired." Others were more conciliatory. The decision was made to send Campesino and Drake to see Egon that evening.

When Drake and Campesino returned later that evening from their meeting, they reported that Egon seemed shaken by the faculty reaction. Egon claimed that he had tried to meet with Matuse to iron out their differences. When confronted with the fact that the letter of dismissal was written two days earlier, Egon indicated that he had only hoped to show it to Matuse, not send it! He claimed he had not yet sent a copy of the letter to the dean. Campesino and Drake persuaded the reluctant Egon to consider forming a departmental committee to investigate the dismissal and make a recommendation to the department faculty. While Matuse had hoped for more direct action, he looked on Egon's willingness to compromise as a good omen.

On Monday morning, following the actions of the past weekend, Egon called a staff meeting which he said, would be off the record since the academic year had ended. He was not, he maintained, authorized to call a meeting during the summer. He then outlined the purpose of the meeting—to discuss the desirability of setting up a committee to investigate Matuse's dismissal.

The meeting was turned over to Tom Drake. There was general agreement that an investigative committee should be established. Debate centered on when it should be formed—immediately or, as

Bandeagle was urging, in the fall. The vote was for the immediate establishment of the committee.

Although his colleagues were reassuring, time passed with no word. After a month, Matuse called Drake to inquire about the committee's progress. There was hope that the committee would meet and report shortly, but as the summer wore on it became clear that they would not make a recommendation on the case. All they did was pass a motion that a permanent standing advisory committee be established—an issue that had already been brought before the faculty under Matuse's guidance. Egon, it was reported, refused to cooperate. He told the committee that the documents in his possession were confidential and therefore could not be divulged. Furthermore, the committee did not have legitimacy because it was not established at a "regular" faculty meeting. The committee was running down a blind alley. More critically, Matuse still did not know the reasons for his dismissal.

Matuse next went outside the department for help. As Southern State's procedures regarding appeal of dismissal were very unclear or nonexistent, he consulted the Reconciliation Committee of the local chapter of the AAUP and, in July, met with its president to inquire about the possibilities of appeal. He was informed that the AAUP did not have an appeals procedure, but merely offered a means of reconciliation, with no power or authority to implement recommendations. Like so many nontenured faculty on trial, he learned that moral persuasion was of little practical use. In fact, the burden of proof lay with Matuse, and, as he could not determine why his contract had not been renewed, he was stymied.

While Matuse was pondering his situation at Southern, another university offered him a teaching position. At first, he considered declining and instead try to be reinstated at Southern, but once he assessed his relations with Egon and his poor future prospects, he saw that he had only one clear choice: take the new job.

AFTERWORD

Before he left Southern, Matuse wrote Egon a final letter. In his letter, he stated that he did not know why he had been terminated as he had established himself favorably with both students and colleagues. He accused Egon of engaging in "vicious personal attacks." He, therefore, asked that his record at Southern State read that he was dismissed because, to quote Egon's earlier letter, his "human relations skills have failed to reinforce the spirit of cooperation we have tried to engender in the department." Matuse refused to resign.

On the same day Matuse sent a letter to his colleagues detailing Egon's lack of good faith and noting that the ad hoc departmental investigation committee's questionable authority was countermanded by an interpretation by Dean Princeton. In short, Egon was lying. Finally, he pointed out that some myths had been shattered. "It would be difficult for anyone," he wrote, "even Egon, to say that we are a *Gemeinschaft*." He closed his letter with an expression of thanks to his former colleagues.

The next day, he sent a letter to all of the graduate students, briefly sketching the circumstances surrounding the nonrenewal of his contract and the nature of Egon's claims. He noted that in the atmosphere that had been created, students had been "pitted against one another and against faculty." In addition, student rights had been ignored, especially Ivan Boroff's. Nevertheless, he noted, the department had great potential. He urged students to assist in preserving the constitutional and academic rights of students "by encouraging the kind of intellectual exchange that will help the department develop into a small community of scholars."

In January 1972, Matuse received a long-distance call from Jake Kennedy. "I have some news I thought you might be interested in," Jake said; "Egon was pressured into resigning the chairpersonship."

9 ARTHUR S. WILKE

Stewart's Folly

For the Richard Stewart family—Dick, Jean, and their two young sons—the Christmas holidays of 1973 were a time of unusual happiness. Stewart, an assistant professor of sociology at Baldwin University, had finally completed all the requirements for his Ph.D. earlier in the month. Adding to the family's delight was the knowledge that Stewart had met the deadline on the conditional rider of his 1973-74 contract. Had he not completed the requirements for the Ph.D. by January 1, 1974, his current appointment would have ended that spring.

Several days before Christmas, the holiday atmosphere was interrupted by a letter Stewart received from the Office of the Dean of the School of Arts and Sciences. The letter was from the dean, Lewis T. More, addressed to Stewart's former graduate adviser, Paul Bellamy, at Grant University, where Stewart had completed the Ph.D. More thanked Bellamy for his letter informing Baldwin University that Stewart had completed all requirements for the Ph.D. In his letter, Dean More conjectured that Bellamy and his colleagues may have had to make extra efforts with regard to the timing of Stewart's completion of the Ph.D. requirements, with a view to helping both him and Baldwin University. Both for himself and the department, he expressed deep appreciation of any special consideration Bellamy and his colleagues may have shown in this matter.

As he read the letter, Stewart experienced momentary uneasiness. From his previous encounters with the dean, he knew him to be a man who chose his words carefully and deliberately. At the least, the letter seemed tactless. The intimation that Bellamy and the remainder of Stewart's Ph.D. examining committee knew of the pressure he was under to complete the degree and therefore extended every consideration was not only untrue but also a serious misreading of how Stewart operated. Stewart's professional code in these matters was very rigid. Anything that compromised the integrity of an intellectual relationship was for him unconscionable. It was one's responsibility to distinguish the professional from the personal; otherwise, the value of his degree and the integrity of Grant University would be blemished. He could not remember ever discussing his situation at Baldwin with any of the faculty at Grant. To be sure, he called Bellamy. If nothing else, Stewart was embarrassed at the mere suggestion that his committee at Grant University had made "extra efforts" regarding the timing of the requirements. This was not what the Ph.D. was all about for Richard Stewart.

The dean had written to Bellamy just before the Christmas holidays. When Stewart called, Bellamy had not yet received the letter. He assured Stewart that More's "conjecture" was off the mark. After Stewart read the letter, Bellamy became alarmed however. He thought that the dean's letter discredited Stewart's completion of his degree and made it appear to be a special act of mercy by his examining committee. He promised to write the dean as soon as he received the letter and to clarify the situation.

In his letter, Bellamy told More that he had been unaware that Stewart was on a terminal contract. He also stated that his original letter to More regarding Stewart's completion of the degree was not written at Stewart's request, but was routinely done for all advisees when they completed their work. He then took the opportunity to offer a full appraisal of Stewart's abilities. He placed Stewart in the upper 20 percent of doctoral candidates who had worked under his direction. He considered his strongest assets as a scholar to be a high level of autonomy, imagination, and discipline. In personality he found Stewart somewhat shy, but also warm, compassionate, and intensely loyal. . . .

Stewart was both embarrassed and delighted by Bellamy's appraisal. The only significant change that he would have made in the letter would have been to state that he had now become more open in seeking opinions about teaching and freely informed his colleagues of his activities. Stewart considered Bellamy's reaction to More's letter unnecessarily alarmist. He had notified President Harold Ledgecross in a memorandum on December 18, 1973, that he had met the terms of his contract as he understood them. He confidently awaited the events of the new year.

On the afternoon of New Year's Eve, Stewart stopped by the Sociology Department to pick up some materials. He had heard nothing from the administration regarding his compliance with his contract and was beginning to be a bit concerned. While he was there he saw his chairperson, Bart Adams, whose irregular routines were well known. In the course of their brief conversation, Stewart casually inquired about his faculty status, especially as it had a bearing on his appointment to the graduate faculty. The second semester was about to begin, and several graduate students were very interested in having him serve on their committees. With uncharacteristic bluntness, Adams replied that nothing had been done about the matter and that the dean said Stewart had a terminal contract. Stewart was disarmed. Stewart stated that this was not his understanding of the contract; there must be, he reasoned, a misunderstanding. Some type of redress was necessary. Adams refused to elaborate, leaving a dazed Stewart to figure out what had happened.

The dean's letter to Bellamy, then, had been very significant. As the dean later confirmed to Stewart, it was a signal. The apparent letter of thanks was actually an announcement that Stewart's achievements were incidental to the behind-the-scenes scenario that had moved, however surreptitiously, to determine Stewart's future at Baldwin University.

TO WITHDRAW OR NOT TO WITHDRAW THE TERMINAL NOTICE

When Stewart arrived at Baldwin in the fall of 1970, he had completed all the requirements for the Ph.D. except for the preliminary examinations, dissertation, and final oral defense of the dissertation. His decision to take a position at Baldwin rather than complete his doctorate first was prompted by his family's dire financial needs.

In taking the assistant professorship at Baldwin, Stewart realized that his progress toward the Ph.D. would be slowed. Virtually no semester went by without new course preparations, and in addition, he made himself available for overload teaching assignments, some of which were directed from Dean More's office. At first, the dean seemed pleased with Stewart's industry. At the same time, Stewart managed to complete his preliminary written examinations at Grant University and immediately began work on the dissertation. Without shirking his teaching duties and doing more than his proportionate share in terms of the department and school curricula, he was making steady progress toward the completion of the degree.

Completion of the Ph.D. was expected for continued employment at Baldwin, although no time limit was ever stated formally. The only pressure on Stewart for completion surfaced during the annual review conducted in December 1972, his third year at Baldwin. For the first time, Stewart was formally apprised of the two-year-rule; the Ph.D. was expected within two years after initial appointment. Though he had heard the rule mentioned, its formal standing was not known. It was not written down nor was it a condition of initial employment, at least not in Stewart's case. The tenuous status of the "two year rule" remained for some time.

In December 1972, the Department of Sociology recommended that beginning in the 1973-74 academic year a terminal contract should be instituted with the proviso that only if the Ph.D. was earned in a specified time, would continued employment be considered. The vice-president for Academic Affairs, Adolf Guerin, questioned this move, pointing out that the department was suggesting that the only factor that was critical to reemployment was attainment of the Ph.D. Might the department reconsider? Much of January and February of 1973 was taken up with an unprecedented review of Stewart's case. After extensive student interviews and meetings, where the most scurrilous rumors regarding Stewart's teaching were entertained and disposed of, Bart Adams wrote a memorandum to Dean More on March 19, 1973, clearly making Stewart's continuation at Baldwin conditional on the completion of the Ph.D.

The associate professors from this department and I have carefully considered and investigated the teaching and scholarly activities of Mr. Stewart as requested. We all agree that he has made a strong and positive contribution to the education of a large number of Baldwin students. We are particularly impressed with his teaching at the 300, 400, and 500 levels (upper division and graduate).

Our conclusions are based on extensive discussions with sociology graduate students (including all his GTA's [graduate teaching assistants]), sociology majors, and other undergraduates. We discreetly surveyed students registered in three of the recitation sections of the introductory course.

It is our recommendation that Mr. Stewart's contract for the coming academic year be terminal but that the possibility of employment beyond May 1974 be considered if all requirements for the Ph.D. are met by January 1, 1974.

Dean More forwarded the memorandum to the Office of the President and the Office of the Dean of the Graduate School with the notation of More's concurrence and the indication that only completion of the Ph.D. stood in the way of Stewart's reappointment to the faculty beyond the 1973-74 school year.

Stewart was aware that letters and memoranda such as he had received customarily went out to faculty members in efforts to upgrade institutions; he was confident that he would meet the standards. In addition, he knew of no instance where an institution had terminated a faculty member who had completed the required degree within a previously agreed-upon time. Hence, he was deeply shaken by Adams' 1973 New Year's Eve announcement that the dean considered his termination final.

Earlier that fall, Stewart had had a somewhat unpleasant encounter with Dean More over the dean's pressures on the Department of Sociology to choose a new chairperson. The department members had been rather unceremoniously notified that Chairperson Adams would be stepping down the next spring. The dean requested that the department members submit their recommendations for a new chairperson within the week. Several faculty members objected to the haste, feeling a broad discussion of departmental needs should precede the appointment of Adams' successor. Stewart brought this faculty concern into the open in a memorandum he circulated within the department. The dean duly chastised Stewart for interfering with his procedure. While the matter seemed to have ended amicably, Stewart recalled it with some anxiety now.

Reappraisal

Stewart's first move was to review the documents leading to his 1973-74 contract. The department recommendation was strong, and again the dean's indication that the lack of the Ph.D. being the "principal" reason for a terminal contract was clearly stated. He then proceeded to contact several faculty who had been principals in the decision to reconsider the initial December 1972 recommendation. In the seven-member department, only three persons held ranks above assistant professor in the winter of 1972-73: Bart Adams, Muhammad Aquabar, and Robert Masters. Stewart knew where Adams stood. Aquabar was on a leave of absence and out of the country. That left Masters. Masters confirmed Stewart's interpretation of his contract status as would Aquabar some time later via a letter. Masters recalled that while he had not known Stewart particularly well at the time Vice-President Guerin had suggested another review of Stewart in early 1973, he had been impressed by the student support of Stewart uncovered in the senior staff's review. The procedures were clearly extraordinary. No other probationary faculty member, indeed not even those being considered for tenure, had been reviewed with such thoroughness as had Stewart. Masters also recalled, as did others, that Bart Adams had termed the extraordinary review procedure necessary and the "only one" they could use if they "wanted to keep Dick." Masters, as well as Aquabar and several others privy to these events, concluded that Adams had been very supportive of Stewart. Indeed, when the departmental recommendation was accepted by the administration, it was Adams, many recalled, who heralded it as a departmental "victory." Yet, less than a year later, the same Bart Adams was saying that it wasn't a departmental matter; it was the dean who was now dictating policy and Stewart was to be terminated.

The fact that his own reading of the file materials and the understanding of a number of the principals in the original actions taken on his appointment coincided (i.e., they were agreed that only the completion of the Ph.D. stood in the way of his continued employment as well as his appointment to the graduate faculty) made Stewart suspicious that More and Adams were conspiring against him. Why, after all, had he been given only until January 1, 1974, to complete the Ph.D.? Why not several months longer? Contracts were not sent out before April 1. Generous-minded faculties urging delinquent faculty members to complete their degrees normally extend the period to the end of the academic school year or even, in some instances, to the end of the following summer. Was it possible that More and Adams had set a date they assumed would be impossible for him to meet? Had they been in fact annoyed when Stewart completed the dissertation and final oral within this awkward deadline?

An Unprecedented "Tenure-like" Review

The early weeks of 1974 found Stewart unable to sort out recent events regarding his status. Nor did Masters or any other member of Stewart's small circle of confidants have a clue. Was Bart Adams being pressured to dismiss him? Adams continually spoke of Baldwin's higher administration in negative terms, and in departmental affairs, his opinions of Dean More and Vice-President Guerin were not flattering. Adams, Stewart thought, had shown himself to be a principled person, but why would he now be so uncommunicative on the interpretation of Stewart's current contract? These and many more questions surfaced, leaving Stewart in a quandary.

Stewart's immediate reaction to Adams' New Year's Eve revelation regarding his contract was one of defensiveness. Clearly, he thought, not everyone could be trusted. For the first time in his association with Baldwin, he took measured interest in idle gossip. His interest was piqued when, in the early weeks of 1974, a graduate student, Don Doolittle, told him that at least some of the faculty in the department "knew" he had a terminal contract, which presumably meant that Stewart would be finished at Baldwin at the end of the 1973-74 academic year. Doolittle also said that during the fall of 1973 he had pointedly told these mysterious others that Stewart was operating under significantly different impressions. Doolittle later repeated the same story to Robert Masters, detailing a consultation with Bart Adams who, he reported, was very distressed over the "Stewart matter." Doolittle's first revelations were discounted; he simply could have misunderstood. Further, if such a monstrous deception had been perpetrated, one in which Stewart, Masters, Aquabar, and numerous students had been misled, there must be some explanation. It would be best, however, to wait and see what official action might be forthcoming.

Two weeks after the disastrous New Year's Eve encounter, Adams summoned Stewart to his office. He detailed a review procedure for Stewart, requesting his concurrence. This procedure, Adams noted, was not fully precedented in that it would involve a review of Stewart by the senior staff in what was later described as a "tenure-like" review. The senior staff involved would be Adams, Masters, and Nicholas Hartman. Hartman had been promoted to associate professor effective in the 1973-74 academic year. He had, unknown to Stewart, participated in the earlier deliberations regarding Stewart's 1973-74 contract. Initially, Stewart was in agreement with the procedure, although he noted the omission of Muhammad Aquabar. Then Adams unveiled some of his own as well as Hartman's concerns. There were the questions of where Stewart "fit in," of his "teaching effectiveness," of his alleged "communications problem." It was apparent that Adams was repeating the same list of concerns he had introduced a year earlier, with one modification, the matter of where Stewart "fit in." In early 1973, when Vice-President Guerin had suggested that the department review their recommendation of Stewart for the 1973-74 contract, Adams had called Stewart in. At that time, as Stewart recalled, Adams said he was baffled as to what to do. He had then recited some of the same concerns, providing no more detail at that time than later. Stewart viewed these complaints as unfounded allegations. He could point to the accomplishment of many students with whom he worked, the outstanding caliber of students he had in class, the favorable student evaluations of his teaching, and a generally high regard he sensed he was held in by many students. Of course, there was always the chance that these were self-delusions, but as far as Stewart could tell, any negative reports on his teaching effectiveness reflected little more than general student disgruntlement regarding any professor. He had heard far worse remarks about many of his colleagues. Therefore, unless there was a clear indication of malfeasance, he believed his professional responsibility was to treat the statements about teaching effectiveness or communication as nothing more than idle gossip.

In 1973, Adams gave Stewart the impression that he should respond to these rumors, and in the process, it became obvious to

Stewart that his conduct as a teacher was being impugned. Reluctantly, he allowed Adams and other senior staff members to conduct interviews with any of his students, past and present, in order to see for themselves that the negative statements regarding his teaching were unfounded. His reluctance in this matter stemmed from his worry that students would be unnecessarily politicized. He communicated this concern to Adams, but Adams nevertheless proceeded with the interviews. Later, Stewart learned from Aquabar and Masters, as well as from several of the students interviewed, that Adams had expressed great pleasure at what he had heard. With good reason, then, Stewart believed the charges against him were found to be without merit. Moreover, he did receive the memorandum regarding his 1973-74 appointment, which likewise seemed to confirm the favorable reading on his teaching. Yet in 1974, Adams was again dredging up the same old issues. When would they cease?

Neither Stewart nor many others, within and outside the department, suspected Adams' conduct. He portrayed himself as a harried department chairperson who worked hard against the stifling influences of higher administrators. If he was faced with unsavory duties, many agreed that he was probably being "pressured" into them.

The startling aspect of the 1974 situation was that the concerns Adams was now raising were being advanced as an agenda for what Adams clearly indicated was an unprecedented "tenure-like" review. Furthermore, none of the official records apparently counted; otherwise, Adams could not have brought up the overworked charges without providing some substantive proof. Stewart was being placed in a position where he was to be treated uniquely, something he would reflect upon after his meeting with Adams.

Stewart's Uninvited Second

Unsettled by Adams' proposal for a "tenure-like" review, Stewart returned home. After some deliberation, he called the president of the local chapter of the AAUP, Luther Arnoldson. Indicating that it was to be an *informal* conversation, Stewart outlined his situation. Arnoldson opined that what was happening to Stewart seemed somewhat suspicious. Stewart thanked him for his time and indicated that he would keep in touch but, in his judgment, it was premature to involve the AAUP.

The next day, unknown to Stewart, Arnoldson delivered AAUP rules on reappointment to Adams and conferred with the dean. In doing so, he had announced that Stewart was ready to fight and that he would not leave willingly. Possibly Arnoldson saw an opportunity to advance AAUP concerns; if this was the case, Stewart was not the immediate beneficiary.

The Shadow of Legal Opinion at Baldwin

On January 15, the same day the AAUP president was visiting the university, Stewart asked Adams to suspend any action on the forthcoming review until he could deliver a reply. Stewart's reply was in the form of a lengthy memorandum addressing the issues and questions Adams had raised in their January 14 meeting. He indicated that the charges against him were without foundation, contradicted the available record, were unfair and punitive, reflected lack of good faith, and were arbitrary and capricious. Instead of the proposed procedure, Stewart suggested that the issues be discussed informally. If this could not be done so that all parties would know the scope of concerns, Stewart suggested a more formal mechanism, one including an AAUP observer.

Stewart personally handed Adams a copy of his memorandum in the presence of student body president Jerome Pleasance who happened to be conferring with Adams in the hallway. Adams immediately retreated to his office and hastily read the memorandum. Pleasance, whose discussion with Adams had been interrupted, waited at the open door of Adams' office, but their conversation was not to be completed. An angry Adams quickly jumped up from his desk, brushed past Pleasance, and left the department. As Adams later admitted, he had gone to consult with Dean More.

Several days after Stewart delivered his memorandum, he encountered Adams in the hallway of the department. Adams said that the dean had instructed him to say nothing and to do nothing in his case until the university's attorney rendered an opinion.

Nearly three weeks passed. According to Adams, the university attorney concurred with Dean More that Stewart's contract was

terminal. More directed the review to proceed as Adams had originally proposed to Stewart.

Later investigation did not uncover any record of the attorney's
opinion, and with the untimely death of the attorney shortly after
his supposed advisement in the Stewart case, it remained a permanent mystery. Meanwhile the dean became more legalistic in his
dealings with students and faculty. A master rhetorician, the dean
seized opportunity upon opportunity to communicate the most
recent term or phrase, particularly if it had legal significance. After
attending a national meeting of university administrators, he began
to describe the proposed review of Stewart, not as one involving
the recommendation of continuing appointment, but as one determining whether there should be, as he phrased it, a "withdrawal
of the terminal notice." He thereby aligned himself with a strict,
legalistic interpretation of Stewart's contract.

While Stewart continually confronted a series of directives, no
senior staff person in the department or higher level university
administrator explicitly informed him of the various legal and
organizational issues in his case. Yet, as a nontenured faculty member, he was dependent upon these very same persons for whatever
procedure was to exist. At this point, even if he had wanted to, he
was not in a position where he could profitably explore legal action.
Meanwhile, if there was to be legal recourse (something that was
increasingly becoming a distinct possibility to Stewart), he needed
a record of what had taken place. Preparing for an adversary
stance, he decided that direct challenge was the best means of obtaining information on procedures whose rationale was far from
clear. All that Bart Adams could tell him was that he had to follow
through with procedures, but where they came from, how they
were formulated, and what risks were involved—none of these
things were explained to Stewart. If no one could understand his
initial quandary, it was now doubtful, at least to Stewart, that he
would be given any quarter in any subsequent dealings.

On February 8, Adams told Stewart that the "tenure-like" review
he had outlined to him on January 14 was to proceed. Apparently,
the objections Stewart had raised to the procedure were dismissed.

Upon hearing that the review originally proposed was to proceed,
Masters became quite concerned. Like Stewart, Masters questioned

the appropriateness of the procedure, especially in light of the re-
sounding support the department had given Stewart a year earlier.
He also was concerned that Stewart was not being treated by the
same set of standards applied to other nontenured faculty. When he
sought to clarify these matters with Adams, all he could get from
Adams was the general reply that the department had to use this
procedure because Stewart was "in trouble." When Masters pressed
for details, Adams exhibited increasing displeasure at being questioned so closely. To compound the matter, Adams placed Masters
in an adversary position, urging him not only to defend Stewart
against unspecified charges but also to convince Nicholas Hartman
who, Adams indicated, had doubts about Stewart. Masters viewed
the scenario as incredible. Without getting any specifics, he was to
defend Stewart who was "in trouble" and who was not favored by
Nicholas Hartman.

Masters, having not obtained tenure at another institution, was
familiar with the tenuousness of academic procedures; he therefore
began to write a series of memoranda detailing his meetings with
Adams to provide supporting evidence for this unbelievable turn
of events. Moreover, he was still quite unconvinced of the rationale
for the procedure. His series of brilliant memoranda not only
revealed the lack of clarity in the procedures, but also showed that,
as a senior staff person, he had been systematically excluded from
critical information in the formation of departmental policy, information that Adams and Hartman operated upon. Masters' efforts
only earned him reproach. Adams, as he would later write in his
assessment of Stewart, now considered *both* Stewart and Masters
obstructionists. Meanwhile, Dean More maintained that Masters'
and Stewart's actions were inappropriate because they were attempting to influence a procedure to which Stewart was being
subjected. Masters and Stewart remained adamant that the procedure was questionable and that it had only tenuous authority.
Masters thus found that his position as associate professor gave
him no access to the university's inner workings.

Student Support

As the attempt to discredit Stewart's teaching continued to unfold
during the early weeks of 1974, student interest mounted. The first

to be concerned was a group of highly capable graduate students, some of whom had been Stewart's teaching assistants in the introductory sociology course in 1972-73, and leading undergraduates. Many had been interviewed in connection with the review to which Stewart had been subjected in 1973. Many had personally heard Adams praise Stewart in the past. Many sensed that if a fair evaluation of teaching effectiveness was used, Stewart would certainly not be at the bottom of the list. Adams' reluctance to use the standardized teaching evaluations, in which Stewart had ranked highly, heightened suspicions that an administrative plot might be in effect, but the exact dimensions could only be speculated upon. As a result, the students first attempted to modify some of the interdepartmental contentions that had been building. When this effort failed, they began in-depth consultations with the principals who would influence Stewart's future: Adams, Hartman, Dean More, and Vice-President for Academic Affairs Adolf Guerin. What they discovered was a series of contradictory rumors and rationalizations. The effect was demoralizing and frustrating for those who had identified not only with Stewart but also with an ethos championing truth-seeking and the exercise of reason anchored in verifiable evidence.

The movement for student participation in university decision-making peaked on the Baldwin campus much later than it had at many of the nation's major universities. By 1974, this movement was riding a crest, directed by Jerome Pleasance, a particularly able student body president. Pleasance's response to the first group of students was immediate. He seized the opportunity to follow up on the precedent set in the Stewart case a year earlier, one in which the departmental decision included active student participation. Though rebuffed, he continued. Through his efforts, he was able to establish a record of the shifting rationales used in the Stewart case and to highlight the workings of the administrative mentality being manifested at Baldwin. In a meeting with many of the principals (Adams, Hartman, More, and Guerin) in the Stewart case, administrators were questioned as to what their responsibility was to a faculty member in informing such a person of factors considered critical for reappointment. The response was direct: none. Thus, all the posturing over effective teaching was revealed to be part of a grand strategy to remove faculty members. For clearly if the concern had been to "improve" teaching and if this was critical in

Stewart's case, either he should have been dismissed much earlier or he should have been informed of the "problem." The dean, in characteristic fashion, seized upon this in a conference with Stewart, suggesting that because Stewart did not know these concerns, it was Stewart who was revealing his own inadequacy. The same position was relayed to numerous students. They were not impressed with the dean's logic, nor was Stewart.

Pleasance's actions in pursuing student rights and student participation in the department made him a bête noire for Adams, Hartman, More, and Guerin. Still, efforts to discredit Stewart continued, even in settings where the student body president had authority. During an early 1974 meeting of a faculty-student committee considering nominations for the Outstanding Teaching Awards, a student complained to Pleasance that Vice-President Guerin, an ex-officio member, openly discredited Stewart's nomination. No other nominee had been singled out. Pleasance appealed to the local AAUP, suggesting that the vice-president's actions were detrimental to Stewart. A standing committee found these concerns to be without merit, although their investigation only consisted, as they admitted, of several phone calls among committee members.

Each successive wave of negative responses to student concerns further politicized the students. The last group of students to be politicized consisted both of persons who embraced alternative life-styles and "average" students who were being "represented" by Adams, Hartman, More, and Guerin as the source of the undocumented "numerous student complaints." Their sentiments began to crystallize in late January 1974 after the discrediting of Stewart took a somewhat new turn. Now Stewart was portrayed as "too good" for Baldwin students. According to one faculty member, he did not cater to "our kind" of students. This view was advanced in direct response to the outpouring of concern expressed by the graduate students and leading undergraduates. It was argument by exception, and it soon became common knowledge that Adams, Hartman, More, and Guerin were employing this tactic. The claim was that Stewart was "beyond" all but the outstanding students. When the oft-portrayed nondistinguished "average" students and those embracing alternative life-styles heard this claim, they denied it vehemently, thereby demonstrating the success Stewart had had with these and other students.

As expected, Adams and More attempted to delay and stonewall, but they continually betrayed the shifting ground upon which they operated. For example, when graduate students and outstanding undergraduates mounted a major criticism of the handling of Stewart's case, Stewart's opponents again began to focus on the claim that his effectiveness was limited to these few exceptional students, and not, as it was once described, "our kind of students." Once this claim became common knowledge, the students began to mobilize. With this turn of events, Adams and the other principals accused Stewart and some of his staunchest supporters, such as Masters, of aiding and abetting the students. Amazingly, at the same time that Adams, More, and Guerin were claiming that Stewart was unable to communicate with a wide spectrum of students, he was being viewed with suspicion as too "successful" at such communication.

Of the four—Adams, Hartman, More, and Guerin—Adams seemed to vacillate the most, frequently expressing his powerlessness in the situation. As a result, Stewart, Masters, and numerous students directed most of their actions at him. He was frequently caught in numerous contradictions, and even in his efforts to delay and stonewall, he seemed quite unsure of himself. Part of his problem may have been his propensity to personalize each circumstance. As Adams later revealed, for him the issues centered on whether he was a good person, and as far as he could determine, he was; those who resisted him, if not altogether bad, were misguided. He seemed oblivious to the fact that two of his own protégés, Nicholas Hartman and William Nielson, the latter a nontenured assistant professor, had, at times, pursued their own career aspirations at his expense. Hartman, Adams' successor to the chair at the end of the 1973-74 academic year, though generally well liked, got the appointment under unusual circumstances. For his part, Nielson regularly opposed Adams' administration of departmental affairs—except to Adams or in departmental meetings. As would later be known, Nielson had a hand in keeping the issues surrounding Stewart's career at Baldwin stirred up. Because of Adams' general regard for Hartman and Nielson, Stewart surmised that they had helped

sustain Adams' sketchy, negative impressions of Stewart. Adams'
regard for Hartman and Nielson predated the Stewart controversy.
Hartman and Nielson had both received their Masters degrees at
Baldwin during Adams' tenure. They completed additional graduate work elsewhere before becoming members of the staff at Baldwin.
At the same time, Adams seemed to be insulated from negative commentary on others, particularly Nielson. Stewart, Masters, and
Aquabar generally agreed that, of all the department members,
Nielson had incurred the greatest general disfavor among students,
not only for his bearing but for his insensitivities to student-faculty
relationships. Still, no formal complaints had been made against
him—nor had any formal complaint been made against Stewart.
Clearly, favoritism was involved, but Stewart did not care to employ such an argument, for it was not a compelling one. Moreover,
he objected to its use because of his professional standards. He
therefore decided to battle in the open.

A GIFT FOR ALL FOOLS' DAY

Meanwhile, relations within the Department of Sociology between
Adams and Hartman, on the one side, and Masters, on the other,
became strained. When the process of consensus decision making
was scrapped, it was blamed on Masters' insistence that Stewart be
treated fairly and that the issues surrounding the case, particularly
the 1973 deliberation relating to the now disputed terminal contract, be clarified. In an effort to do just that, Masters urged Adams
to contact Aquabar, volunteering to pay for the transoceanic telephone call if necessary. Adams refused. It appeared that Adams'
purpose was to nullify the record of the previous year and to make
sure that the fourth senior staff member of the department could
not participate in the issue. Throughout February, the three senior
professors remained at loggerheads. Eventually, individual statements from all three regarding Stewart were sent to Dean More.

Dean More received the statements on March 6, 1974. Stewart's
later investigation of the files revealed the following. Masters
endorsed Stewart, based on what he understood to be the agreement of the previous year: that Stewart's contract would be renewed
if he completed the doctorate in the time specified in the contract,

January 1, 1974. To reaffirm the significance of the previous year's deliberations in which Stewart was given an outstanding departmental recommendation, Masters noted that since those deliberations, nothing of a discrediting nature had come to his attention. Hartman's statement was mixed. He praised Stewart for his industriousness and work with outstanding students but stated that Stewart did not fit into the evolving programs and "needs" of the department. (What these programs and needs were was not identified.) Hartman's statement reflected Dean More's December 1973 directive to Adams that departmental needs were to be considered in the recommendation of personnel. Mysteriously, Masters, now the second-ranking person in the department with the temporary departure of Aquabar, was never informed of the departmental "need" consideration, and, as later detailed, the question would not come up in the case of other reappointments in the spring. Finally, Adams expressed great indignation at Stewart's and Masters' efforts to clarify and understand the rationale for the special procedure being employed in Stewart's case. In his statement, he charged both Stewart and Masters with being "unprofessional." He repeated some of the old rumors that had surfaced in the 1973 deliberations and also hinted at some new concerns regarding Stewart's teaching and professional conduct, none of which he documented or clarified. He did, however, add that Stewart had some very strong support among students. In short, Adams simply could not make up his mind. The result was one for, one against, and one undecided.

Nearly two weeks after the dean received these statements, on March 20, he forwarded his decision. Because of Stewart's lack of support by a "substantial majority," Dean More recommended that Stewart's terminal contract not be withdrawn. The dean called Stewart on April 1 to tell him of the decision and suggested that he look for a position elsewhere.

THE SPECIAL REVIEW COMMITTEE AND
A PARTIAL VICTORY

In the United States the nontenured faculty member occupies a unique legal position. If dissatisfied with the decision to terminate, the burden of proof regarding unfairness, prejudice, or the lack of due consideration resides with the faculty member, providing, of course, an appeal procedure exists. Stewart's case was somewhat more complicated. As of April 1, 1974, he had no clear course of action. His efforts to obtain reasons for the negative determination in his case were thwarted by Dean More who argued that the 1974 decision centered simply on the issue of whether the terminal notice of the previous year should be withdrawn. He seemed to be arguing that such a decision did not come under institutional or AAUP guidelines. Although the dean had chastised Stewart for his resistance to the "special" procedures used in this case, Stewart's previous concerns now seemed more than vindicated.

Stewart had one possible avenue of appeal, President Ledgecross. Several months earlier, when Stewart's future at Baldwin seemed dim, Jerome Pleasance, representing a number of concerned students, had consulted with Ledgecross. Ledgecross had promised to look into the matter if the decision in Stewart's case was negative. Pleasance confirmed the substance of that meeting in a memorandum to President Ledgecross. After April 1, Stewart appealed to the president. As Ledgecross later indicated, he took Stewart's appeal to the University Tenure and Promotion Review Committee. But the committee would not handle Stewart's case, apparently because it was not within its jurisdiction. If Stewart's case was to remain in the confines of the university, some other means would have to be found. It would take several weeks before the president would come up with a solution to this impasse.

While President Ledgecross was struggling to devise an adequate procedure, Stewart and a growing coterie of allies were continually hearing rumors that Stewart was a poor teacher and had acted unprofessionally during the past year. Most of these rumors, couched in vague terms, were being echoed by Guerin and Adams. A number of concerned graduate students began checking on these rumors and undertook a more direct questioning of Guerin and Adams. Their worry, as was Stewart's, was that Guerin and Adams might simply be operating on false information. As their investigation proceeded, they began to suspect that much of this information could have been authored by only two persons, Vicky Worthington and Margaret Penn.

Worthington and Penn had been Stewart's graduate teaching assistants during the previous year (1972-73). Both were known to have been negative toward Stewart's teaching and to have been involved in consultations with Guerin, Adams, and other principals in Stewart's case. Hence, their involvement in departmental and university affairs was significantly different from that of Stewart's other six assistants. The exact dimensions of their complicity would not be known for several months, but these two young women were isolated as particularly influential in providing Guerin and Adams the support they needed in justifying the treatment Stewart was receiving.

The most troubling aspect of the rumors was that they were identical to the rumors that had surfaced a year earlier when extraordinary procedures had been mandated, resulting in the dispute over the meaning and significance of the ensuing contract. When Guerin and Adams were pressed, they began to hint at more sinister behavior, suggesting that Stewart was divisive and unprofessional. This was news to Stewart, but in the defensive position he and his allies found themselves in, all they could do was track down the source. Through persistent questioning of Guerin and Adams, Worthington and Penn remained prime suspects.

Stewart was baffled by these developments. He felt his general teaching demeanor was exemplary, and he was confident that he had followed departmental guidelines for academic excellence. His classes were demanding, but at the same time he was cognizant of student rights. Furthermore, on any recognized measure of teaching, he was confident that his scores were very competitive. Still, Guerin and Adams remained intransigent.

Countering the atmosphere of innuendo and suspicion surrounding Stewart, which was generated by Guerin, More, and Adams, was Stewart's strong, open student support. Thus, when he decided to appeal Dean More's ruling that his terminal contract not be withdrawn, President Ledgecross could not decline to act. Rebuffed by the University Tenure and Promotion Review Committee, Ledgecross proceeded to establish a special faculty committee to investigate and advise him on Stewart's case. The move was unprecedented at Baldwin and involved great risk, for in so acting, the university president had in effect agreed with the student body president that something was awry. Still, he had two other considerations with which to grapple: the faculty and his administrators, who were vigorously pursuing the case with the objective of removing Stewart from Baldwin. The organization of the university was operationally hierarchical, but in principle it was a faculty-governed institution. Inasmuch as the decision not to withdraw Stewart's terminal notice was based, as Dean More had put it, on the "lack of a substantial majority" supporting Stewart, Ledgecross had to be very careful as an administrator not to act hastily and mobilize the faculty against him.

Ledgecross appointed five faculty members from five of the university's schools to the Special Review Committee. It was headed by one of the most prestigious, hard-working faculty members on campus, Ewald Schmidt, a physical scientist. The committee, henceforth known on the campus as the Schmidt Committee, convened at the end of April, during the final examination period of the second semester, and began extensive deliberations. It was charged with determining if Stewart had been given due consideration.

Before the committee got down to work, a controversy erupted. Stewart, suspicious of secret deliberations, particularly after his experiences of the past year, began to argue for open public meetings. Administrators such as Dean More had already indicated to the committee that open meetings would be unacceptable because of the confidential nature of some of the testimony. It was argued that third person communications would be cited, and since this communication had been given in confidence, public disclosure would be inappropriate. Whether this argument was convincing is not known, but the committee did ultimately side with the More position. As some committee members later indicated, they took this step because they were uncertain of whether or not the administrators lined up against Stewart would cooperate in an open meeting. This admission suggested that the committee was uncertain of the nature and extent to which the faculty governed affairs at Baldwin.

After some preliminary discussion, a compromise was reached. The Stewarts, Dick and Jean, plus an AAUP observer, were permitted to sit in during the testimony, but the public was to be excluded. Because Dean More objected to this concession, it was suggested that the Stewarts and the AAUP observer could sit only if a witness did not invoke the right of confidentiality. Here the AAUP representative, George Markham, strenuously objected that such action was merely a smoke screen for a lack of substantive evidence (he was later proved correct). Markham's protest was turned back and the hearings began. A series of witnesses came before the committee.

If anything distinguished the witnesses appearing before the committee, it was their style and preparation. Stewart's adversaries, Vice-President Guerin, Dean More, Chairperson Adams (who would relinquish his position to Hartman at the end of the semester, which would occur during the hearings), and Nicholas Hartman, tended to show indifference to the committee, not unlike that shown to Stewart earlier when he had pressed for clarification and details. They spoke mostly in vague generalities, or they could not recall critical information, often being off on some dates by as much as two years. They continually used the phrase "It was my impression." Hartman faced a blistering interrogation; Adams was openly contradicted; and Dean More was caught by the committee in the outright misrepresentation of materials as he proceeded with his well-known "ritual of the file." (Leafing through the mound of material in Stewart's personnel file, he selectively read from some of the documents.) The portrait he drew was seriously at odds with the contents of the file or the documents he selected. He used negative phrases to describe Stewart, but when the total document was examined, it was found that the clear intent of the writer had been to praise Stewart. The committee duly noted this contradiction. This had been the dean's pattern throughout the protracted conflict. Students had reported to Stewart that in their conferences with the dean, he had done the same thing. Though the dean expressed concern over confidentiality before the Schmidt Committee, he had not shown such concern in his office when conferring with third parties such as outside faculty and students.

In contrast, Stewart and his supporters were well prepared and were eager to testify. They also were committed to revealing that Stewart had been misrepresented. Stewart, after finding out the ground rules of the committee, prepared and typed his statements and gave each committee member a copy. When he appeared before the committee, he summarized the contents and made himself available for questions. In all, he gave the committee seventy-seven manuscript pages and over fifty supporting documents. With few exceptions, the documents turned out to be the most reliable chronicle of events in the case. The committee regularly used them for reference. Aware that the burden of proof lay with him and that, if he were to decide later to wage a court battle, he must exhaust all institutional means, Stewart decided against legal counsel. He did not wish to compromise his case. Inasmuch as he wished to be employed at Baldwin, he did not want to further inflame an already aggravated situation. Finally, he desired to show a good faith commitment to the university and his colleagues, despite the differences. If he was to be true to his own intellectual lights, reason should prevail.

Stewart's concern in writing his statements was to establish an unambiguous record of events, something that until now he had been unable to establish. In addition, he took on the challenge with relish, for he considered it a test of his scholarly mettle. He was committed to finding out the truth and to prove that his original contentions about his contract had been correct and that the foundation of his opposition was based on unsubstantiated rumor and innuendo.

Those who testified in behalf of Stewart likewise gave precise information, and often, they too prepared written statements for the committee. Most impressive of all was the fact that numerous students remained to testify long after the second semester had come to an end. Masters, Stewart's faithful faculty supporter, also came, armed with an impressive file of dealings within the department. During the 1973-74 academic year, the department had made numerous decisions on other nontenured faculty, as well as renewals of persons on terminal contracts, without resorting to the procedures used in Stewart's case.

Eventually, the committee began to examine how Stewart's performance compared to that of others in the department. Comparative data on course enrollments, and the like had to be collected at the request of the committee; thus, it was clear to all that no comparative review had been done earlier. It became Stewart's job to point out the context for interpreting any data. For example, there had been changes in both the curriculum and departmental policy that affected enrollments. If, as Stewart's detractors had apparently argued before the committee, his course enrollments were problematic, some attention to these details was a must. From Stewart's perspective, this was what one expected from competent academic administrators. His expectations were again off the mark.

While there had been rumors that his enrollments were weak, Stewart remained confident that a comparative analysis would disprove that charge. At that time, the discipline was suffering a nationwide erosion in enrollment, particularly when courses were not tied to the requirements of other curricula. Thus, if his detractors were basing their comparative assessments on the framework of five years earlier, they were simply not aware of what had been happening in higher education. Hopefully, the committee would be able to ascertain the truth of the matter, while Adams, More, and Guerin, it seemed, had been content to let their "impressions" dominate their judgments. The Schmidt Committee found that Stewart's enrollment patterns compared favorably with those of other departmental members.

With regard to the rumor that Stewart had a "communications problem," this seemed to resolve itself within a week of testimony and questioning when a committee member exclaimed that he could understand Stewart perfectly! He questioned Stewart if the way he talked before the committee was the way he generally talked. The answer was, "Of course." Thus, another prop in the tissue of rumor and innuendo appeared to be brushed aside.

The committee returned to exploring old ground: Stewart's handling of the introductory course in the 1972-73 academic year, the one in which Worthington and Penn had been teaching assitants. This concern was disturbing in the sense that if the documents which supported his reemployment in the spring of 1973 review had meaning, then those deliberations had dealt with this matter. It seemed to be a matter now of double jeopardy.

As the committee's questions of his handling of the introductory course unfolded, the Stewarts became increasingly suspicious that Vicky Worthington and Margaret Penn had been the source of the rumors that had raised the initial questions in 1973 about Stewart's teaching and had possibly continued to be a source of negative evaluation. These two had demonstrated antagonism toward Stewart and were also viewed with favor by Adams, Guerin, and Hartman. In the fall of 1972, for instance, when Vicky Worthington was a teaching assistant to Stewart, she had become upset over his handling of the introductory course, since she, unlike Stewart, saw students as children in need of parental-like guidance, and she had sought solace from Hartman. During the same semester Margaret Penn had lectured before the introductory classes and, during her lecture, had chastised the students for being complacent and uncommitted. Chafing at this criticism, the students sought Penn out and, with her assistance, mobilized a program of action—one directed at removing a course requirement for that semester, a book review of *The Pentagon Papers*. The students petitioned, and Stewart was confronted by a mobilized constituency of several hundred students. He dealt with the situation by giving the students an opportunity to present their petition, advance their argument, hear his side, and then vote. Penn received no blame for her part. The vote went against Stewart, and this negative vote, mandated in part because of the late time in the semester, was not without mixed effects.

Stewart kept many of his suspicions to himself, even during the committee's deliberations, waiting to see if conclusive evidence could be found. Also, he was given an opportunity to respond to committee questions and closed door testimony during the deliberations. The committee questions based on closed door testimony resulted in Stewart's being continually requested to answer questions whose foundation was suspect, but he had no way of demonstrating their lack of foundation. There was no means of cross-examination or independent determination of truth. Stewart could only hope that the force of his presentation and input into the proceedings would stimulate the committee to dig more deeply into the merits of some of the claims being made against him. This hope was nurtured by the good faith he had to extend to the committee, even though his own predilection, after being judged within the department and administration, was for an adversary system.

The committee's hearings were beginning to wind down, and, on balance, Stewart felt confident. Given the material that had been presented and the type of questions he had been asked, it seemed that he had a credible case.

From the outset, Stewart had indicated that his real concern was for the truth. In the compromise over confidentiality, Chairperson

Schmidt assured him that if there were any critical problems or questions, he would be apprised of them. Near the end of the hearings a question about Stewart's professionalism came up. It was not clear what dimensions this question of professionalism took; however, Chairperson Schmidt indicated that Stewart was linked with divisive actions which had pitted graduate student against graduate student and that in their zealousness some of his student allies had actually intimidated fellow students.

Student body president Jerome Pleasance, because of his role in the Stewart case and Adams' and More's suggestion that he was suspect, was summoned to a private meeting by Professor Schmidt. What took place between them is not completely clear, but it appears that when someone, whose identity remained confidential, testified before the Schmidt Committee, Margaret Penn's name was linked to the charges of Stewart's unprofessional activity and some of his student supporters' extreme "misbehavior." Pleasance, a friend of Penn's who had visited her several months earlier regarding the Stewart case, was surprised that her name had come up, but willingly offered to contact her and, if possible, to arrange to have her return to the campus and testify. Schmidt supported the suggestion. At this time, Pleasance, like Stewart, expressed the view that Penn's negative views of Stewart were of an innocent nature and that they had been blown out of proportion by Adams, Guerin, and others.

Penn had completed her M.A. in sociology in 1973. Following the awarding of her degree, she stayed on to teach an introductory course in sociology at Baldwin that summer. At the time the Schmidt Committee was convening, she was living in an adjoining state, some distance from Baldwin. Pleasance accommodated Chairperson Schmidt and arranged for Penn to appear before the committee.

The details of Penn's testimony were not made public. She chose, as did several other witnesses hostile to Stewart, to address the committee in private. Per their original agreement, the committee subsequently informed Stewart of matters that might be critical and were taken in closed door testimony. From what Stewart could surmise, Penn had told of an encounter she had had with Jerome Pleasance several months earlier in the spring of 1974. Pleasance, it seemed, had warned her that if she had said anything discrediting about Stewart while she was a faculty member, she should now be precise about such claims or, if she chose, not comment. She had apparently asked Pleasance whether this was a threat, a charge Pleasance would deny. Nonetheless, the oft repeated claim that students were threatening students seems to have had its genesis in this episode, and the incident mushroomed into yet another example of what Stewart's detractors termed his unwholesome influence on students.

The road had pointed to Penn in the spring of 1974 when numerous graduate students, piecing together information they had from their meetings with Vice-President Guerin, discovered that only Vicky Worthington or Margaret Penn could be the source of Guerin's charge that Stewart had engaged in questionable professional conduct. Penn, it was discovered, had visited with the vice-president in the late summer of 1973 after teaching the introductory sociology course. Pleasance had investigated the information, which seemed critical given the increasing frequency with which Guerin and the chairperson had hinted at Stewart's serious professional flaws.

Prior to his early spring visit with Penn, Pleasance consulted with Stewart who informed Pleasance that he should be very careful in dealing with her, informing her of the implications of the visit with Guerin. If Stewart's difficulties could be traced to Penn's 1973 visit with Guerin, Penn was in a vulnerable position inasmuch as she was Stewart's colleague at the time of the meeting. Professional, if not legal, recourse could result if this episode was found to be critical in Stewart's case. Pleasance carried out Stewart's instructions. He clearly understood that if the event was decisive, a potential case of libel was possible, since Stewart might very well lose his job because of such testimony.

Penn's response was highly defensive, as was that of those to whom she reported Pleasance's warning of a law suit. For those eager to discredit Stewart and his allies, this development reinforced their belief of Stewart's unfitness. Hence, Pleasance's warning, which they construed was a "threat," gave support to Stewart's opponents.

The interpretation given the Penn-Pleasance episode was puzzling but it could never be fully and wholly expunged. Even the Schmidt Committee fell victim to the twisted logic, possibly because it seemed too incredible to consider that the whole case against Stewart had the quality of a house of cards. Like Stewart, the committee searched for some redeeming basis in the opposition to Stewart, and only this had, possibly, a plausible ring to it. In their final report to President Ledgecross, they referred to a "student's threat of another student." Only the Penn episode suggested any kind of threat or warning. Unfortunately, in passing this suspect statement on, two errors were compounded. First, the threat of legal suit does not constitute the same kind of intimidation as the threat of physical violence. Furthermore, a legal suit is a threat only when actually instituted. Such a suit was never filed. Second, the wording of the Schmidt Committee about a student threatening another student further contradicted fact, something which Stewart's detractors did with immunity. When Pleasance spoke to Penn, she was a former student and Stewart's ex-colleague. Thus, even the reviewing committee had been ensnared in non sequitors, which could very easily have been aided by the reports of Stewart's opponents.

From his first days at Baldwin, Stewart had been quite popular with most graduate students in the department. Aquabar also had a substantial following. Nielson, on the other hand, had less support among graduate students. Several students indicated that Nielson blamed this situation on Aquabar and Stewart rather than on his own failings. As a graduate student, Penn had been a frequent confidante of Nielson's. Had this negative attitude toward Stewart perhaps been transmitted from Nielson to Penn and then on to someone within the administration? Stewart and others suspected it might have, but here again they were unable to prove it.

Since the record of deliberations was not made public, it was very possible that misperceptions would remain intact or that, contrary to its promise, the Schmidt Committee could break its promise to inform Stewart of all critical issues appearing before it. It seems likely that some misperceptions did persist, especially with regard to the role of the students in the case. Few, if any faculty, no less administrators, had ever faced such incessant and determined investigations on the part of the students. The rationale was that even if their search for truth was meritorious, wasn't there something strange about students such as Pleasance who would behave in such an extraordinary fashion? It is possible that even some mem-

bers of the Schmidt Committee thought Stewart's influence unwholesome. Whatever its basis, the "threat of a legal suit" remained
a vivid item in the minds of many.

Throughout the long conflict, Guerin, More, Adams, and Hartman had maintained that there had been "numerous" student complaints against Stewart. They provided no documentation and in
amplification could only say that the number of such complaints
was "above average." What average meant was never specified.
The committee combed the files available to them but could find no
negative statements from students. Instead, they found many supporting statements, some of which Adams had encouraged in early
1973 when the deliberations over the much disputed 1973-74
contract had taken place. Other documents, such as university-
wide teaching evaluations, were as Stewart described them: very
good.

In Stewart's mind, most of the rumors which were aimed at discrediting him had been exposed before the committee as having little
or no foundation. Even the rumblings about his handling of the
introductory course seemed less than compelling, given the fact
that a new half-time position had been created to teach the course.
Henceforth, no full-time faculty member would be teaching the
course on an annual rotating basis as was the case through the
1972-73 academic year. Moreover, the negotiations for the position
had occurred the previous year, at about the same time the department was reexamining the recommendation for Stewart. The avail-
ability of the position, discussed at some length by Guerin and
Nicholas Hartman, was known to both Worthington and Penn,
even before it became common knowledge to the departmental
faculty. There was some suggestion that Worthington, who now
occupied the position, had spoken at some length with Guerin
during the previous year as to the desirability of hiring a person for
the course who, in her opinion, could relate better than Stewart to
the introductory students. If she had discredited Stewart for her
own benefit, her involvement in Stewart's case, which she admitted
was of a negative nature, could have constituted a conflict of interest.
This was not, however, explored by the Schmidt Committee.

The creation of the half-time position to handle the introductory
course was not the product of the current controversy alone. Addi-

tional funds had been made available to the department. Most of the faculty had disliked teaching it and some student complaints had come up each year no matter who taught it. Aquabar later recalled that numerous complaints had been voiced the years that Neilson and Adams had taught it. This matter was never clarified before the committee. However, an even darker side of departmental affairs was yet to be exposed.

Student testimony revealed that long before the current controversy, even before questions leading to the deliberations in 1972-73 regarding Stewart's 1973-74 contract had been entertained, several department members had actively dissuaded students from taking courses from Stewart and Aquabar. Such suggestions were more than disagreements between colleagues; they were active *undermining* of a colleague. Even more arresting was some of the justification for such counsel; in Stewart's case, he was to be watched because, as one faculty member reportedly said, he was a "neo-Marxist."

At its inception, the Schmidt Committee agreed that whatever recommendation it would make, at least four out of five members had to concur. This mechanism was designed to encourage compromise. After the hearings and additional meetings, the committee delivered its report and recommendation. In all instances of substance, Stewart was vindicated. His concerns and claims were found to have merit, but the committee's recommendation was another matter. It read:

It is the position of the Special Review Committee that the employment of Professor Stewart should not be terminated at this time. We recommend that Professor Stewart be given a one-year contract. The committee recommends that by offering Professor Stewart this contract, the university is in no way obligated to grant him tenure at the completion of the contract. In the ensuing academic year, the Department of Sociology, at their discretion, might possibly consider adopting our recommendations for evaluation of probationary faculty. If an equitable solution cannot be achieved, Professor Stewart should have the option of submitting his resignation at the end of 1974-75 academic year. It is also the position of the Special Review Committee that the appeal made by Professor Stewart does not warrant a reevaluation.

The Schmidt Committee had clearly overstepped its mandate. The members realized that to act simply on whether or not Stewart was given due consideration, which they seemed agreed he hadn't been, would result in a reenactment of the same type of judgment against Stewart which, apparently, they had not found compelling. As a result, they recommended new procedures for the evaluation of probationary faculty as well as procedural guidelines for what they termed the "small department problem." The committee agreed with Masters' earlier contention that Aquabar should have been consulted about his interpretation of that fateful 1973 contract.

Stewart was out of town interviewing for a job when the Schmidt Committee recommendation was rendered.

Although there had been strong sentiment on the committee to vindicate Stewart, at least two committee members had held out. As Ewald Schmidt explained, there was agreement that the procedure was faulty and if employed again would work to Stewart's detriment. On the other hand, there was the feeling that Stewart was "somewhat" at fault for developments because of his persistent challenge of the actions being taken against him. Although his claim that he was treated unfairly was held to have merit, his aggressive pursuit of his own interests was criticized. Although the committee had, by and large, exceeded its mandate and had decided in Stewart's favor, its compromise position seemed to hold the basis for further contentions. First, it was strange that Stewart's vigorous actions, which resulted in the creation of unprecedented procedures, were held suspect. From Stewart's perspective, these actions had been warranted when the "tenure-like" review regarding the withdrawal of his terminal notice revealed that Adams was sympathetic to Hartman's negative view of Stewart, that Masters' opinion was being dismissed out of hand, and that Adams did not intend to consult Aquabar regarding his clarification of earlier departmental deliberations, leading to the strange wording of Stewart's 1973-74 contract. Second, if Stewart's efforts to obtain fair treatment had spawned a wave of support for which he was seen as a major contributor, then potential issues of academic freedom and free speech seemed to be emerging. If a professor is criticized or condemned for his own legally permissible actions and advocacy, then questions of academic freedom and free speech become of paramount importance, at least to a person of Stewart's makeup. Still, it would be hasty to raise issue with a committee which had worked tirelessly under what were contentious conditions. Their efforts did reaffirm the more noble elements which Stewart had grown to cherish at Baldwin. Stewart was willing to await further actions, for what did he have to lose? He did not have a job and his prospects were far from encouraging.

Several days later, the Stewarts met with President Ledgecross. They learned that Ledgecross felt his committee had exceeded its mandate and had given him an unworkable recommendation. Ledgecross sensed that Stewart would probably challenge the idea of another terminal contract. Yet, if Ledgecross were to act uni-laterally in Stewart's support, he might face resistance by some administrators and faculty.

As the discussion proceeded, Ledgecross noted that he had been supplied all the materials from the committee and had been examin-ing them. Jean Stewart suggested that a mistake must have been made. The file the president was examining was not as large as Stewart's typed testimony and documents. When so informed, Ledgecross requested a copy of Stewart's materials and indicated he would study them and be in touch.

Ledgecross had Stewart's materials independently investigated and found that they were consistent and supportable. As a result of his own investigations and on the basis of the Schmidt Committee's report, he decided to give Stewart a regular contract for the 1974-75 academic year. Matters of reappointment and tenure—forthcoming decisions—would be left to the department. It was to be hoped that new procedures would be instituted by the time the next re-view took place.

Stewart's papers for his 1974-75 contract were processed, but Dean More refused to sign the appointment. Meanwhile, Stewart began to catch up on matters that had been left in disarray for some five months. The pain he had experienced during the battle did not recede quickly, but as the new academic year loomed ahead, some of the old enthusiasm returned.

BACK INTO THE LION'S DEN

The fall of 1974 came and many things returned to normal. Teaching was as exciting as ever for Stewart, and his research efforts began bearing fruit. Meanwhile, the university began to develop appropriate procedures for renewal, tenure, and promotion recommendations. The Sociology Department was involved in this activity.

The first test of the "new" procedures came in the fall when Stewart and William Nielson were, according to university rules, advanced for consideration for the rank of associate professor. Stewart was not optimistic. His publication record, though better than Hartman's and Nielson's, was, by his own admission, not impressive enough to warrant the rank of associate professor. Otherwise, especially since the convening of the Schmidt Committee and its findings, he was competitive in professional activities, teaching, and service to the community. While he might not get promoted, there was some satisfaction that with any type of equitable procedure, Nielson would also be denied. Nielson, it had been revealed before the Schmidt Committee, had been active in passing rumors of a negative nature regarding Stewart. His lack of publication and his lack of inspiring teaching, which seemed to be widely acknowledged, would result in some small measure of justice.

The departmental review committee voted not to recommend Stewart for promotion. The vote was two against and two abstentions. The reasons given were as follows:

1. He had only recently completed the Ph.D.
2. The candidate's teaching effectiveness was uncertain. Additional time was deemed necessary to be able to clearly establish a predictable record.
3. He had spent too little time on the graduate faculty to enable an evaluation of his contribution in this area.

It was the consensus of the committee that Stewart should be reconsidered the following year.

Stewart was informed of this decision and then received the news that Nielson had been recommended, a recommendation that was carried through and resulted in his promotion to associate professor.

Stewart reviewed the memorandum. As he surmised and found out later, both Adams and Hartman had abstained from voting, leaving the two outside members to cast votes. Masters did not participate because he was on leave.

Stewart examined the file that was placed before the promotion review committee and nowhere found any indication that he did not have a dependable record as a teacher. His evaluations plus his record supported this.

There was no question that Stewart had only recently received the Ph.D. So that could be a matter of policy, although it was ironic that one of the persons who had voted on him was a tenured associate professor without the Ph.D. Again, it seemed that some of the "higher" reasoning that had pervaded last spring's deliberations regarding his teaching was reappearing. And, too, it was disconcerting to see such a technical interpretation regarding the graduate faculty. All that could be judged was how long Stewart had been on the faculty because Stewart had otherwise been very active in assisting graduate students with their theses. In fact, during the height of the spring controversy, as was testified before the Schmidt Committee, Hartman had turned a graduate student over to Stewart so that he could advise her on her thesis. As Hartman informed the student, anything Stewart did was acceptable to him; he would defer to Stewart's judgment. Hartman would merely serve as the "paper" chairperson. This was not strange. Stewart had been instrumental with graduate student theses since his first year.

In a carefully worded memorandum dated February 10, 1976, Stewart wrote Chairperson Hartman. Explicitly indicating that he was not challenging the non-recommendation for promotion, he did note that the memorandum involved several items bearing on departmental policy. Based on the time an individual held the Ph.D. and the time a person was on the graduate faculty—determinant issues in Stewart's case—Stewart recommended that a policy statement be made so that reviews could be terminated if an individual did not have the requisite time qualifications. More critical to Stewart was the question of the lack of a dependable record in teaching effectiveness. Stewart indicated concern because, as he pointed out, this judgment, if left without qualification, could have a negative effect on his forthcoming tenure review. Teaching effectiveness at Baldwin, as at any major institution, was one of the central criteria in the tenure decision. So Stewart took the opportunity to read into his file a record of substantive exhibits that were available, including the Schmidt Committee report, which might result in a different assessment of the question. Stewart was worried that the subsequent tenure review could use the negative outcome of the promotions committee as an exhibit in making a negative determination. Given that the committee might be the same one that made the non-recommendation for promotion, Stewart needed some way to introduce the possibility that word of mouth information that was clearly being relied upon was of a questionable nature.

Hartman's response came in a testy February 17 memorandum to Dean More in which he referenced Stewart's February 10 memorandum which was attached. He noted that while Stewart's memorandum did not challenge the promotion committee's decision not to recommend him for promotion, it had raised issues that impugned the committee (the department's promotion review committee) and the department chairperson. While he said that he did not concede to the arguments, they did create or continue circumstances that in his opinion precluded any departmental tenure review from being regarded as legitimate or unbiased. Upon receipt of Hartman's memorandum, Stewart quickly wrote an apology to him and sent a copy to Dean More.

Before Stewart could assess his new situation, he was informed that Adams, like Hartman, had seriously misread his memorandum. Adams was telling other faculty that Stewart was advocating "automatic" promotions—which was a completely false statement. He was also saying that he had no recent information on Stewart's teaching effectiveness.

More important, Adams was suggesting an unprofessionalism in Stewart that was of far greater gravity than that charged earlier. Stewart proceeded to obtain witnesses and supporting documentation that this was what Adams was saying. This might also play a critical role because Adams served on the dean's committee which reviewed promotion and tenure decisions, the same committee that would serve as Stewart's first order review. (Fortunately, Adams withdrew from the committee when Stewart's case came up.)

The dean moved quickly on Hartman's request that he undertake Stewart's first order tenure review. The dean met with Stewart to outline the procedure wherein a committee of full professors of the Arts and Science faculty, of which Bart Adams was a member, would review his case. The dean was clearly not in Stewart's corner, for he expressed his dissatisfaction with President Ledgecross's decision to give him another contract, again emphasizing that he had not signed Stewart's reappointment papers. The meeting, far from cordial, left Stewart dejected. He believed that the dean was setting up his own committee to present affairs that were seriously at odds with what had already been established not only in early departmental deliberations during 1973, but through the vigorous work of the Schmidt Committee in 1974.

Ever since Stewart's reappointment in the fall of 1974, Dean More had been agitating against him and Ledgecross's action. He had attempted to mobilize college-wide support against Ledgecross's decision the previous fall, but had not been successful. Once during the year, when Stewart requested travel funds to go to a national meeting where he was to present a co-authored paper, the dean had turned down the request, publicly expressing doubt to others that Stewart could have contributed to such a paper.

Several weeks passed before Stewart met with the dean's committee of full professors. After he was there a short time, it was clear that this committee had not, and probably would not, avail itself of the extensive Schmidt Committee report. As a result, he faced a barrage of old, long-discredited rumors for the third successive year. The committee interviewed all of Stewart's departmental colleagues, including nontenured ones. As one recent addition to the department later confided, he told the committee that he had heard nothing negative about Stewart except the rumor that earlier he had had difficulty with the introductory course. This type of testimony must have been persuasive because Stewart was questioned at length on the matter. At one point, one of the committee members expressed disagreement with Stewart's teaching philosophy, indicating that in introductory courses students must be guided. Stewart responded that in such courses, the teacher is introducing adult subject matter to young adults and that the presumption that students are children is inappropriate for any university. The committee was not impressed by his viewpoint.

Again, Stewart found himself being asked extraordinary questions; candidates for tenure who were recommended by the department were never asked such questions. In addition to his teaching of the introductory course, the committee delved into his career objectives, his relationships with his colleagues, and the like. The committee seemed oblivious to the fact that much of the questioning except that on his career objectives and relationships with colleagues, covered old ground, that questions regarding his handling of the introductory course in 1972-73 were irrelevant since there was now a special half-time position to teach it, and that other members of the department disdained to teach the course, which Stewart did not. The committee's actions seemed to be in line with Dean More's views on the Stewart case, and in so doing it gave at least tacit support to a mode of operations at Baldwin which was not only rapidly becoming antiquated but also could not stand vigorous review.

Shortly after May 5, 1975, Stewart learned his fate; his 1975-76 contract was terminal. He had been denied tenure. Stewart requested an appeal and asked Dean More as well as the chairperson of the dean's reviewing committee the reasons for the terminal notice. Stewart, like President Ledgecross, was unsuccessful in this endeavor. The dean informed the president at one point that the reason for the non-recommendation was that a majority of the committee had not voted for Stewart.

Although he promised a review, this time President Ledgecross did not move quickly on Stewart's request. The political sentiment present a year earlier and centered in student body president Jerome Pleasance was now gone. When one of the major components in administrative decisions of a university is student power, the canny official plays a waiting game. Even more than the faculty, students are the university's transients. One need only stall a year or so, and the students have graduated or moved on. The result is that the whole complexion of campus politics changes. If Stewart decided to challenge the sociology faculty and administration of Baldwin this time, he would have to rebuild his forces almost entirely or go outside the campus. Aquabar, a likely ally, had resigned. Masters, the courageous voice for decency and fair play, was on leave. Preliminary negotiations with the local AAUP revealed that there was not enough interest to finding out what had happened in Stewart's case. And although the state National Education Association representative kept dogging President Ledgecross, his actions were far from vigorous.

NEW HORIZONS

Twice before Stewart had challenged the decision process and had won reprieves, but he found it difficult to work up the necessary enthusiasm for a third round. For two and one-half years, he had battled and had attempted to keep professionally active as well as involved in his teaching. The prospect of engaging in one more battle with the same shopworn cast of characters, with at best, similar results was wearisome. And, too, his old adviser, Paul Bellamy, who had carefully monitored all phases of his contest with Baldwin in the past, kept insisting that Stewart was expending too much valuable energy on fruitless endeavors. The suggestion was becoming persuasive. Thus, when the call from Waltham University for a job interview came, he accepted and spent a few days with its faculty and administrators. Suddenly, he realized that he had almost forgotten what it was like to move among academics who did not steal sidelong glances at one, who did not approach one with a forced or artificial smile or with eyes hard with appraising calculations, who did not carefully monitor each word as if it might unexpectedly appear in court. In contrast to the opportunistic organization men who were still at Baldwin currying favor with those in power, here were relatively independent professionals working and producing. The appeal of far horizons became overwhelming. He returned to Baldwin and began the painful process of severing his ties with a place, which for all its problems, and perhaps in part because of them, he had grown to love.

Hopefully, Waltham University would be a place where the exercise of intellect in all phases of the academic life would be appreciated. Stewart's efforts to perform his scholarly and teaching jobs in the midst of a prolonged political conflict at Baldwin had turned out to be "Stewart's Folly."

10 NORMAN S. GOLDNER

Due Process in
Higher Education

Gerald Franklyn grew up in Northside, a depressed area of Martinsburg. Upon completion of high school, he went to Falmouth University where he earned a B.A. in sociology and entered graduate school. He completed the M.A. with a distinguished Master's thesis and was awarded a fellowship at Midcentral University to begin his Ph.D. studies while his wife undertook graduate studies of her own. In 1965, with only the Ph.D. dissertation remaining to be completed, he accepted the very attractive position of assistant professor at Mordor University.

THE ACADEMIC MILIEU OF THE LATE 1960S

Franklyn was well aware of the major juggling act required of young scholars as they struggled to establish both teaching and research careers and to complete their dissertations. Meanwhile, the social problems of American society in the 1960s were deeply affecting the academic scene: the civil rights movement was reorienting Black-White relations in the urban ghettos; the Chicano and American Indian movements were getting under way; and the Vietnam War was having major repercussions on campus life. In addition, the academic atmosphere was changing with increased pressures toward specialization, democratization of academic departments, and genuine participation by students in their governance. The social sciences, particularly sociology, were drawn into the urban and minorities' problems of the wider society to a much greater extent than other academic departments.

Franklyn's dissertation went slowly, for with his high teaching standards he simply didn't have enough time. His participation in departmental and campus movements further consumed his already extended energies and time. During his first three years at Mordor, Franklyn received only yearly contracts. He was establishing a fine reputation in the department, however, for on December 5, 1966, he received a letter from his department chairperson, Dr. Benjamin Gollum, informing him that the tenured faculty of the department had unanimously recommended that his contract, which would expire on June 8, 1967, be renewed effective September 1968. If he completed the Ph.D. prior to September, he would be extended a three-year contract.

Upon completion of the Ph.D. in 1968, Franklyn did, in fact, receive a substantial raise in salary and was recommended by the tenured faculty and the current chairperson, Dr. Keith Lindbloom (who had replaced the retired Gollum), for promotion and tenure. Dean George Sauron, however, rejected the recommendations.

Had Franklyn been a bit more sophisticated, he would have understood that Dean Sauron's rejection was a major indication that trouble was brewing. Franklyn, however, was still euphoric over having completed the Ph.D. and over the possibility of tenure. At this time, he began to undertake major new responsibilities in departmental and university affairs while simultaneously implementing new research projects. Moreover, he entered areas of community service, such as acting as a consultant to the U.S. Department of Health, Education and Welfare in a noncompliance action brought against a suburban school system in a case of alleged de jure segregation. On one occasion, such an activity found Franklyn on opposite sides of a court action at which the associate dean, Francis Gothmog, was also called to testify.

Among the campus activities in which Franklyn was assuming a responsible role, two were of particular importance: (1) a contest had developed between a departmental and administrative clique which was seeking to consolidate and retain power, and a larger group which was seeking to divide sociology and anthropology into autonomous administrative units; (2) on the campus at large, a movement was under way to amend the college by-laws in a manner that would permit limited student representation on departmental committees and hence give the students some role in their own governance. The dean's opposition to this proposal was well known.

The change in departmental chairpersonship from Gollum to Lindbloom had been part of the clique's strategy to consolidate its position and to prevent the separation of sociology and anthropology. Former chairman Gollum and Dean Sauron had engineered the separation and as a result had provoked strong faculty protest. Franklyn had been among those who had questioned the procedure, an action that would make him Gollum's everlasting enemy. Furthermore, Franklyn had been the spokesman for the junior faculty at a meeting held with the dean to discuss their preference for separating the two disciplines. Although the meeting was outwardly cordial, Franklyn was never again to enjoy good relations with the dean.

When sociology was permitted to form an independent department, Franklyn became identified with the majority seeking greater participation in the selection of a new chairperson to replace Lindbloom. The dean and a small but powerful minority among the faculty were opposed both to the idea of a new chairperson and to the majority choice, Dr. Edward Flowers.

Although Franklyn was aware of the fact that his position on many departmental and university issues was opposite to that of the dean and a powerful faction within his own department, he continued to act with complete openness and to retain his respect for the dean and his opposing colleagues. He was oblivious to the fact that he was accumulating an irreversible stock of ill will.

In 1969, the Sociology Department once again recommended that Franklyn be granted promotion and tenure—and once again the dean denied the recommendation. Informally, it was reported that Franklyn had not published enough to warrant promotion. As a result he stepped up the intensity of his research efforts, only to be faced with the long time lag between the completion of work and its publication. By 1970, in a department that had become more democratized, the Rank and Tenure Committee once more recommended Franklyn for tenure but was split over the desirability of recommending him for promotion.

The majority point of view was that since this was Franklyn's sixth year (and by the tenure rules must either be granted tenure or be fired), the safest strategy was to ask only for tenure without raising the question of promotion. The minority view was that such a minimal strategy might backfire. In fact, in a later rationalization of his action, Dean Sauron seized upon the departmental recommendation for tenure only as an admission of Franklyn's weakness. The dean suggested that perhaps it reflected the department's recognition that Franklyn's vita did not meet the standards for promotion in a complex graduate offering department.

On May 13, 1971, Chairperson Flowers of the Sociology Department wrote Franklyn a letter informing him that his application for tenure in the College of Arts and Science had been rejected. However, he said he would recommend Franklyn for an additional year of teaching at Mordor. However, when Flowers made the customary appearance before the Rank and Tenure Committee, he unexpectedly encountered a serious accusation against Franklyn's personal and professional integrity. A member of the committee reported that Franklyn had misrepresented himself as a consultant in a suburban community involving an integration controversy in the public schools. The source of the information was not revealed on the basis of confidentiality.

It was this startling revelation, which attacked his personal and professional ethics, that forced Franklyn to challenge the negative action on his recommendation for tenure.

FACULTY STANDING AND THE
BASES FOR PERSONNEL DECISIONS

Franklyn's first shock as he began his challenge was his discovery that the university had no appeal process. He thereupon requested an appointment with the university attorney, only to discover that a faculty member had no legal "standing" in the institution relative to reviews of administrative decisions. *Standing*, he learned, was a legal term that defined who might ask the court to rule on the legality of an action. It was intended to help weed out frivolous actions which could glut court dockets. The university attorney showed Franklyn the university's constitution and the official proceedings of the Board of Governors which stated that only the department might petition in behalf of its rejected recommendation; a faculty member could not. It was at this point that Franklyn decided to retain outside legal counsel, an attorney named Henry Paul.

While Paul conducted an intensive investigation of his client's case, Chairperson Flowers initiated some valiant efforts to obtain fair treatment for Franklyn. It soon became apparent that the source of Franklyn's problems was an alliance between former Chairperson Gollum and Associate Dean Francis Gothmog. Franklyn had been experiencing small, but increasingly nasty, incidences of Gollum's hostility for quite some time. Now, it appeared that the charge of professional misconduct leveled at him from behind closed doors had been made by Gollum, presently a member of the Rank and Tenure Committee.

Gollum's "confidential source," as Flowers later learned, was Gothmog, who, coincidentally, was a long-time consultant to the school district HEW had named in its discrimination suit. Flowers then requested that he be allowed to reappear before the dean's committee. At this second meeting, Flowers told the committee of Franklyn's disclosure of the full facts, as he saw them, surrounding the alleged consultantship misrepresentation. The committee seemed shocked. It apparently had not been told that it was the associate dean who had held this matter to be crucial to the question of tenure for Franklyn. Flowers left the meeting with the feeling that there was some personal ill will between the dean and Franklyn.

The probability that Associate Dean Gothmog, through Gollum, had made a false accusation against Franklyn during the tenure proceedings—made the tenure denial the administration's problem. Now it was being forced to respond, for Franklyn's civil rights may have been violated. It was not long before the dean agreed to grant Franklyn a personal audience with the committee to reconsider the tenure decision. The dean stipulated that no lawyer or anyone else could accompany Franklyn, not even Flowers. Flowers was promised a later audience (which never took place).

Since no appeal was usually possible at Mordor until all regular administrative procedures had been exhausted, Franklyn kept his appointment. No record of the meeting was kept. He was asked to discuss his scholarship; he, in turn, asked the committee to list its reasons for having denied him tenure. His request was refused. Franklyn then discussed his general professional interests, and with that the meeting ended. Prior to the meeting, Franklyn's lawyer had asked the president of the university, John Nazgul, to disqualify Gollum as a committee participant on the basis of his previous hostile relationship with Franklyn and his allegation concerning Franklyn's professional misrepresentation in a federal hearing. In a communication sent to Franklyn's lawyer on October 28, 1971, President Nazgul replied that the committee would not disqualify anyone. However, any member of the committee could abstain from voting.

Gollum sat with the committee and announced that he would not vote, but he participated in the discussion and in the committee's deliberations. Once more a vote was cast against granting Franklyn tenure. Thus, while the committee gave the appearance of justice, it simultaneously permitted the exercise of nearly total administrative power. Franklyn produced documentation and personal testimony that Gollum had held strong, negative opinions of him even before the 1970 application for tenure. Flowers exposed Gollum's responsibility for a surreptitious attack on Franklyn's professional competence and moral credibility. Nevertheless, the request was denied. The illusion of fair proceedings had been maintained by Gollum's voluntary exercise of his "right" to abstain from voting.

In Gerald Franklyn's case as in most cases in American universities, the administration has absolute control over rule making. For example, should a faculty member fail to follow exactly the procedural requirements for tenure and promotion application, he is allowed no second chance to rectify the error. On the other hand, if the administration makes a procedural mistake, it need only repeat the process until it "gets it right." For example, in the past tenure was automatically given when a university failed to review a candidate according to AAUP guidelines. In recent years, however, many schools have gotten around this rule by simply adopting another rule that tenure may not be gained on the basis of a university error. No school has been known to pass a similar statute for the benefit of procedurally careless faculty. Thus, when Franklyn proposed to the president that the Rank and Tenure Committee's second decision be made binding upon the college, the president replied that the committee's decision would be advisory only. Because of the crucial nature of tenure and promotion decisions, he would not allow executive officers with responsibilities in this area to delegate this function to third parties. Consequently, he said, the decision of the committee would be reviewed in accordance with standard university policy.

How much clearer could it be that at Mordor University one was judged by one's peers to the extent that the judgment did not interfere with or threaten "executive" prerogative. Franklyn had received an unfavorable tenure action from the Tenure and Rank Committee, but was willing to allow this committee to reconsider that decision in a binding fashion. The administrative officers may or may not have thought that the committee would reverse itself, but it is doubtful whether that was even a serious consideration. Undoubtedly, their primary concern was to prevent a precedent from being established which might uphold the right of the faculty to be judged by other faculty in a definitive way. The structural and procedural power of the executive officers of the university over faculty interests is substantial, and awareness of their desire to maintain it is critical to an understanding of the university's handling of Gerald Franklyn's case.

Meanwhile, at the Department of Sociology, Franklyn's colleagues had taken the unprecedented action of petitioning the president to look into the Rank and Tenure Committee's persistent rejection of the department's recommendation for tenure.

The faculty of the Department of Sociology urges the president of the university, in accord with university policy regarding appeal, to review the December 7, 1971, decision of the [Arts and Science] administration regarding the tenure of Dr. Franklyn of this faculty, giving renewed recognition to the strong recommendations of the departmental faculty. The president will understand that as a faculty of the university, we are in a position to speak to the needs and goals of our discipline. We trust you understand that our recommendations are based upon scholarly integrity and our immediate responsibility for the conduct of the department.

Fifteen faculty members voted for the petition and only five against. In addition to being a statement of support for Franklyn, the petition served as an alert that a serious intent to share power was in process.

THE AD HOC REVIEW PANEL

One important effect of the year-long series of meetings, hearings, and communications which ensued between Franklyn and Mordor University was to alert the entire faculty to the fragile character of their rights. During this period, the country was moving into a period of recession, and university policies toward new faculty were growing more severe. At Mordor, a number of other faculty members had hired attorneys to challenge the legitimacy of treatment and the validity of judgments rendered by the university administration. Concerned members of the Board of Trustees pressured President Nazgul into setting up a procedure for dealing with the increasing number of challenges.

Eventually, Nazgul established an Ad Hoc Review Panel (AHRP) consisting of three impartial tenured faculty . . . from the University Hearing Committee Panel. The administration also chose a member of the law school to serve as an official adviser to the panel's non-adversary but formal review. The vice-president directed them to conduct a preliminary and "probable cause" investigation. The specific task of the group was "to advise the president as to whether or not considerations violating academic freedom and constitutional rights adversely and significantly contributed to a decision not to award tenure" (March 13, 1972). The panel was empowered to "advise" the president and not to make binding determinations.

The AHRP held several hearings in which it interviewed the dean, the associate dean, Chairperson Flowers, and Franklyn (who was allowed to observe while others testified). The AHRP spent most of its time on two allegations: first, had the misrepresentation charge heard by the Rank and Tenure Committee violated Franklyn's rights? Second, had Franklyn's scholarly activity been appropriately reviewed? The AHRP could find for Franklyn in one or both of these matters and yet conclude that neither had "adversely" and "significantly" contributed to the denial of tenure, and, in any case, the finding would be advisory only.

As at other universities, at Mordor three general dimensions of faculty competence were judged important in the awarding of tenure and promotion: teaching ability, service, and scholarship. On April 27, 1971, the dean had forwarded an explanation of the foundations of tenure and advancement policies to the president of Mordor:

Although scholarship is important and encouraged, promotion to the rank of associate professor is frequently recommended largely on the basis of good teaching and service. Promotion to the rank of professor usually requires evidence of significant scholarship, although in many cases here, too, promotion has been recommended on the basis of outstanding teaching and service. Moreover, since the Promotions Committee is advisory to the dean and the central administration, there have been occasions when I have made recommendations for individuals ranked somewhat lower but who I thought contributed outstandingly in areas less amenable to measurement.

Student evaluation of teaching performance has been used by many departments for many years, and, under the stimulus of the dean's office, this practice is increasing. . . . outstanding teachers are recognized, and I think it no accident that teaching evaluations, whether by peers or by students, are usually in excellent agreement on the best teachers. The same may be said of the worst teachers.

Such a formulation was of advantage to the dean in that it supplied an objective rationale for arbitrary decisions. With it, he could reward or punish anyone he chose, regardless of the judgments of the individual faculty member's peers. On the other hand, it meant that when the Ad Hoc Review Panel (AHRP) reviewed contested cases of tenure or promotion, such as Franklyn's, it would inevitably be forced to consider the extent to which the given individual's teaching, service, and scholarship had been accurately and fairly appraised by the departmental Rank and Tenure Committee, the college's Rank and Tenure Committee, and the dean's office. It also meant, of course, that the AHRP's deliberations could become a battleground in a final effort to defend or destroy the given faculty member. It is thus of special interest to follow the AHRP's review of Franklyn's record in these respects.

The AHRP Review of Franklyn's Teaching

When the dean was required to justify tenure denial in Franklyn's case, he wrote in a letter to the vice-president of the university:

. . . we expect all of our faculty to be devoted to good teaching, which is necessary but by itself is not usually a sufficient criterion for tenure. Unfortunately, as you know, departments and individual references are not sufficiently critical in evaluating teaching. Practically every recommendation we receive rates teaching performance from "good" to "superlative." Franklyn appears to be a dedicated and devoted teacher (January 31, 1971).

In his statement of 1970, however, the dean had stated that outstanding teaching merited tenure and that a teacher's colleagues and students were valid and reliable judges of teaching performance. Now, on January 31, 1971, he assured the vice-president that good teaching was *not* "a sufficient criterion for tenure."

This issue of teaching excellence proved more resistant to manipulation because Franklyn's colleagues and two different department chairpersons, among others, had praised his classroom performance. In 1966, Chairperson Lindbloom wrote that both he and his colleagues generally considered Franklyn a fine instructor and that he had excellent rapport with students and was regarded as a popular, but very competent, instructor.

In 1968, Chairperson Flowers, in his recommendation to the college, wrote that in both his university classroom and in his televised courses, Franklyn was widely perceived by his colleagues and by the public to be an extraordinarily capable teacher. Flowers reemphasized Franklyn's teaching strengths in his memorandum of January 12, 1970, to the vice-president in which he said Franklyn was cited in the Student Course Evaluation Study of 1966-67 to be the faculty member in the Department of Sociology with the highest number of student recommendations.

In his statement to the vice-president justifying the denial of tenure, the dean acknowledged that Franklyn appeared to be a dedicated and devoted teacher but added that the consensus of the Rank and Tenure Committee was that, while Franklyn was somewhat better than average, he was quite below their best group of teachers (January 31, 1972).

The AHRP Review of Franklyn's Service

Regarding Franklyn's service, Associate Dean Gothmog prepared an unsigned document (dated December 22, 1969) for the use of the Rank and Tenure Committee purporting to analyze the evidence submitted by the department in support of its tenure recommendation. He termed practically all of Franklyn's consultant activities low level, "overload," paid activities involving very elementary training of community aides. With regard to his consultation service to HEW in connection with a civil rights case, he said he had first-hand information that Franklyn was rejected by the federal district court as an expert witness on the basis that he did not possess the qualifications he claimed. As for Franklyn's role as an instructor of paraprofessionals for the public schools, he said that all indications were that this was a very low level service for which Franklyn was paid a fee. Finally, the training Franklyn provided while on the staff of an employment institute jointly conducted by the State employment service and Mordor University was also termed very low level.

This interpretation of Franklyn's service record followed him throughout the AHRP deliberations. The AHRP was also presented a chronology (unsigned), dated September 28, 1971. After listing his degrees and the dates they were received, the chronology cited twenty items dating from September 1965 to May 1971. Fourteen of these items concerned remuneration for services rendered the university, such as extension courses and special institutes, and salary increases. The intent of this chronology was to portray Franklyn's services as almost exclusively motivated by fees.

The associate dean established the following criteria for "worthy" service:

1. A consultant or other service which is remunerated is not a service. The implicit assumption is that faculty should take vows of poverty. Payment for services rendered amounts to a demerit on a faculty member's record. (Catch 22: organizations which seek skilled services are willing to pay for them, but that becomes prima facie evidence to the associate dean that the service is valueless by administrative criteria.)
2. Low level service represents a false claim for community service. (Thus, training paraprofessionals to work in public schools and state employ-

ment agents to deal sensitively with various ethnic and racial groups is presumably low level because of the socioeconomic levels of those being trained and/or those that they will serve.)

3. For a service to be relevant to tenure, it must contribute to the faculty member's development as a professional. (That such a criterion might be construed as self, rather than community, service did not seem to occur to the associate dean. Must someone who gives of his skills to others develop his professional skills too before it constitutes a bona fide service?)

Both the Rank and Tenure Committee and the AHRP questioned Franklyn on these matters. In response, he provided each with a complete list of his community services. His document revealed that fourteen of his services were *uncompensated*; four were accompanied by honorariums (less than $50); and four were compensated ($50 or more). The other charges, Franklyn argued, were based on bogus criteria.

Appearing before the AHRP on May 15, 1972, the dean was questioned about how Franklyn's community service had been treated by the Rank and Tenure Committee. Whereas in his position paper of April 27, 1969, he had said service was an important criterion for granting tenure, now he said that it shouldn't be given much weight. Besides, he stated, Franklyn's service had not been of a high professional level. Futhermore, it was his judgment that if, for example, Franklyn had said he was on an HEW board reviewing grant proposals, or had he been involved with a large grant or contract, that would be of a very high professional caliber. Franklyn's work was useful, but not sufficiently important to merit his attaining tenure.

The AHRP Review of Franklyn's Scholarship

Having neutralized Franklyn's teaching record and having dismissed his community service as insignificant, the Rank and Tenure Committee next considered his scholarship. While Franklyn had had six articles published at the time of the committee's deliberations, the dean brought only two to its attention. The AHRP chastised the dean for being aware that Franklyn had had several other articles, in addition to the two, accepted, and not bringing this fact to the panel's attention.

THE BEGINNING OF THE END

In summer 1972, the Ad Hoc Review Panel presented its final report to the president. First, with regard to his scholarship, it noted that a reasonable effort to seek all available information was not made. While this failure did not reflect any bad faith, or even negligence, on the part of the dean or the Rank and Tenure Committee, still Franklyn should have been consulted in regard to those of his publications he deemed most representative of his ability. Second, the charge that Franklyn had misrepresented his credentials as an expert witness in the HEW suit was dismissed on the grounds that the supervising attorney at HEW who proffered Franklyn as an expert witness in the case strongly denied that Franklyn had misled him at any time. Furthermore, the AHRP maintained that copies of the transcript of Franklyn's testimony tended to confirm the claims put forward by the supervising attorney. The committee also reported that the proceedings surrounding Franklyn's denial of tenure did not rise to the level of fair procedure consonant with academic freedom.

The committee noted one further matter for consideration which resulted from its investigations. It said that it appeared that the dean's office had taken a strongly negative view of Franklyn's academic qualifications, and that it seemed highly unlikely that a further consideration of the matter by the dean's office would be an adequate remedy for Franklyn. In veiw of the apparently close relationship between the dean's office and the Rank and Tenure Committee, it deemed it equally doubtful that that committee as presently constituted would be the appropriate body to conduct any reconsideration that might occur.

The AHRP decisions thus not only supported Franklyn's substantive allegations, but also went beyond them in suggesting that neither the dean nor his committee could be trusted to be any more procedurally correct in the future than they had been in the past. Furthermore, it appeared to confirm Franklyn's contention that personal animosities on the part of the dean and former Chairperson Gollum had influenced the denial of tenure.

THE COUP DE GRACE

Given the conclusions of the AHRP, the president could hardly return the matter to the dean and his committee. On the other hand, the university did not take this opportunity to award Franklyn tenure. Three months later, President Nazgul informed him that he, the president, would select three sociologists to make a confidential evaluation of Franklyn's scholarship. A retired faculty member, already selected, would investigate his teaching, service to the university, "contributions to the public," and "other appropriate criteria." This individual would also report "confidentially" to the president who assumed the right to conduct "further investigations and interviews" as he deemed appropriate.

Franklyn was now in a quandary: he was in debt for legal fees, he was emotionally exhausted by the appeal, and now he was faced with a "remedy" that contained no due process guarantees whatever. He consulted with his lawyer, following which Attorney Paul wrote the president's attorney (on September 12, 1972) that interim disposition as outlined by the president was not consistent with the letter or spirit of their preliminary meetings in which the procedures to which they subjected themselves were agreed upon. If the president, he continued, seriously proposed to consult both within and without the institution regarding Franklyn's competence without giving Paul an opportunity to participate in the selection and examination of those experts, he would be compounding the same deficiency in due process previously found by the Ad Hoc Committee.

Based on the committee's findings with reference to Franklyn's participation in the HEW case, Paul believed his chances of success in federal court would be substantial. Paul therefore advised that, prior to filing in the federal court, he would deem it appropriate to appeal the president's current process to the Board of Governors. Before exercising either of these options, however, he requested an opportunity to meet with the president to discuss the matter.

Paul and Nazgul did indeed meet. Nazgul assured him of his intention to find positively for tenure, or, should some complication arise, to inform Paul and his client of the problem and give them sufficient time to file suit if that was to be their option.

Franklyn was greatly relieved that the president seemed to be seeking a gracious way in which to award him tenure, for, privately, he had decided that legal action against the university was, at least for him, ill-advised. This decision was wiser than he realized at the time, for no court could have awarded him tenure; the court would simply have ordered that due process be observed. Moreover, Franklyn would have been compromised had he chosen the legal avenue. Many universities, regardless of the outcome of the suit, would probably be very reluctant to hire a teacher who had sued for a grievance with a university.

The dénouement, when it came, was abrupt indeed. On December 8, 1972, he received the following message from President Nazgul: "It is with personal regret that I must now inform you that on the basis of advice I have received and my own review, I have concluded that I cannot recommend you for favorable consideration for a tenured professorial appointment."

And so it ended—almost two years after the original denial of tenure. The struggle need not have ended even then. The Board of Governors could have been asked to overrule its administration, and next, the state and federal courts could have been petitioned. But even if Franklyn's lawyer had handled the case and possible appeals at cost (as he offered to do), a decision costing as much as $20,000 and five years of litigation awaited him. It was a path of certain prolonged pain and uncertain rewards. Franklyn felt that he did not have the right to subject his family to the psychological and economic hardship of such a struggle, and so he turned his back on Mordor University and relocated at another university.

There are moments when he recalls not only all the old villainy but also the rare gestures of gallantry and grace: Chairman Edward Flowers who placed his position on the line for principle and for people he believed in and who resigned from Mordor shortly after tenure was finally denied to Franklyn; Vice-President Vincent Jones who was dismissed as a betrayer of the administration for seeking to establish a fair review committee and similar "indiscretions"; Attorney Henry Paul who labored tirelessly sharing highs and lows alike; friends Martin (who seemed instinctively to guess what would happen at every turn) and Ron (who never failed of encouragement, help, and friendly counsel); those colleagues who voluntarily came forward and exposed themselves to reprisals out of a sense of decency and outrage at injustice; and finally, his wife and in-laws who strengthened his resolve by never losing theirs.

Once upon a time, Gerald Franklyn believed that an institution of higher learning was truly an ivory tower, a gleaming bastion of reason, principle, and honor, but that was before he experienced the pain of dashed illusions and broken dreams. Today, the respect, admiration, and love he so freely gave to the university goes out to those friends and allies who demonstrated their belief in him and in the value of his struggle. Although he lost his own case, Gerald Franklyn's hard-fought contest has focused attention on the tenuous nature of the rights of junior faculty and has strengthened the safeguards to due process for those who followed. This has caused Franklyn to retain his basic faith that universities and other institutions of higher education in America can, with proper vigilance, be made to serve their students and faculties more humanistically.

PART II.

Consequences of the Tenure Crisis

One of the striking features of the case studies in this volume centers on the question of the adequacy of procedures used to make critical personnel decisions. Despite the claims for the United States' rational-legal system, this system does not always seem to be in operation in higher education. Sometimes procedures become little more than what a powerful person says they are. At other times they are undertaken haphazardly or are very narrowly interpreted.

Complicating the problem of procedures is the fact that many institutions of higher learning employ a mix of rational-legal and archaic procedures. At the immediate level, such as within a department, informal norms predominate. The ancient common-places of academic life appear: colleagueship and some remnants of an independent, but closed, community of scholars. In practice, of course, these norms can mask conflicts resulting from personal ambition, jealousy, and general suspicion. In such circumstances, the nontenured must be very careful. Meanwhile, at the administration level, concerns over adequate funding, conflicts between competing departments and programs, and the like are faced. The complex missions and ambitions of faculty have frequently resulted in an expansion of the administrative sector of the college or university.[1] Given the proliferation of professional objectives, along with the general decline in demand for college-educated persons, critical decisions must be made.[2]

While the administration may be the cause for some of the dramatic personnel decisions, very often faculty are intimately tied to the decision-making process. Faculty do not constitute a united front. Some may resist the intrusions of administrators, while others may willingly not only capitulate to changing policies, but, as is true of any bureaucracy, also imaginatively invoke some of their own. For the nontenured caught in these circumstances, the experience is disorienting, if not disheartening.

For over half a century, various faculty groups and associations have attempted to provide vehicles of redress for all faculty, tenured and nontenured. They have sought to increase the legal standing of faculty persons, closely monitor areas in which academic freedom may be violated, and generally make procedures more open and accessible. Their results have been mixed. Some policies have been developed to protect the rights of at least some faculty. However, faculty generally have not given such efforts united support.

Even if a professional faculty organization sides with a faculty person who has a grievance, there is no guarantee that a response will be forthcoming. Financial demands, legal standing, the importance of the case — all these factors determine whether a case shall be pursued. And in the case of nontenured faculty, the areas of concern are proscribed inasmuch as such persons do not have extensive legal standing in the courts.

Nontenured faculty, those most likely to be candidates for the hidden professoriate, are employed on a probationary basis, which means they can be dismissed providing they are given proper notice in due time. The time varies depending upon length of service. This, however, cannot continue indefinitely. If an individual has not been notified by the sixth year of employment, it is generally understood that tenure is awarded. Tenure simply means that dismissal must proceed according to certain procedures and according to certain claims. In recent years, probationary faculty have been extended some rights previously reserved for the tenured. For instance, they may obtain reasons for their dismissal, and, in some instances, they can mount appeals to reverse decisions if inadequate consideration was given them. These, of course, are the official goals and procedures; the actual circumstances may be radically different.

"The Professional Organization to the Rescue" (Chapter 11) by Fran French is a case study of a faculty person whose probationary status extended beyond the sixth year, who was dismissed, and who subsequently appealed to a professional faculty organization. French describes the variety of obstacles encountered in such a case, even if there is general agreement on the merits of the case.

There are several reasons why professional organizations of academicians cannot be a cure-all for aggrieved academics. First, they have limited resources. While the demands on them are increasing, their memberships are often declining. Second, regardless of their central mission, they have a tendency to operate much as those organizations they oppose, in this case university administrations. Hence, a professional organization pursuing faculty interests is made up of an administrative cadre similar to that of a professor's own university administration, wherein matters of budget and routine are commonplace. Unusual circumstances are as much a problem for the professional organization as for the college or university administration. Thus, the aggrieved faculty member faces a battle on two fronts: one with the home institution and the other with the professional organization charged with the defense. The politics in the professional organization are intricate and, as Chapter 11 illustrates, can sometimes be humorous.

It is not just the hidden professoriate which has forced the creation of procedures for review and redress. In Chapter 9, for example, the president of Baldwin University undertook an experiment in academic review procedures in the case of Richard Stewart. The rudiments of a review procedure were also in evidence in the case of Gerald Franklyn (Chapter 10, "Due Process in Higher Education"). In both instances, however, the review procedure either was hastily constructed or the independence of the reviewing body was compromised.

Chapter 12, "Judicial Committees and the Tenure Crisis," shows how a major institution, Maitland University, sought to develop procedures to handle the cases of faculty who wished to appeal negative decisions. Such procedures can have both positive and negative consequences. On the positive side, clearer and more direct action to assist the faculty can be taken through such procedures. Hence, they can help overturn administrators' as well as colleagues' judgments against a professor when such decisions are found to be merely impressionistic and without foundation in fact. On the negative side, the possibility that litigation may ensue directly from the engagement in these procedures can result in the university or college cultivating legal expertise in these matters, making deliberations confusing and burdensome. Furthermore, by keeping many of the technical details of the review process in mind, a faculty member pursuing a career may incur numerous liabilities, such as being viewed as a "poor" colleague if plans and actions for the contingency of an appeal are vigorously pursued. On the other hand, being ignorant of the procedures as, it seems, many of the appellants in Chapter 12 were, results in much redundancy and is highly time consuming for faculty who render service to such committees without additional compensation.

Had review procedures such as those found at Maitland University been operative in the cases described in Chapter 7 ("The Rules Keep Changing Every Day"), there is a great likelihood that the women affected would have been evaluated comparatively and would not have been dismissed for reasons based on their sexual status. In the case of Clyde Matuse (Chapter 8, "The Trials in a Little *Gemeinschaft*"), such procedures could have measurably reduced the capricious judgments of Matuse's immediate superior. The existence of adequate review procedures for Richard Stewart (Chapter 9, "Stewart's Folly") would have required that adequate comparative measures of judgment be employed. Further, it would have avoided the successive defining and redefining of procedures which worked to Stewart's detriment. And in the case of Gerald Franklyn, viable procedures would have reduced the effect of the animosity of certain key administrators, thereby muting their impact on decisions affecting his career.

The above suggests what should happen if procedures exist and are followed. Even with established procedures, however, some roadblocks remain. These may radically affect the course and direction of higher education in the coming years. Any time procedures are introduced, there is a tendency to employ them in the narrowest fashion. Currently, this tendency is in evidence in many institutions in which teaching is being reemphasized. The measurement of teaching is reduced to the tabulated results of widely administered surveys. This form of consumer preference, not unlike that exhibited at the supermarket or record shop, can significantly alter the character and quality of education. The professor, especially the nontenured one, who wants to score well may find that his or her ability as a huckster is far more critical than the exercise of an independent, critical intellect.

Even if procedures exist, there will always remain the problem of getting standing. How does one get a review? This requires painstaking and time-consuming preparation, which may not be worthwhile for many or may be so engrossing that many other responsibilities are sacrificed.

Finally, any procedure instituted to serve others requires the participation of knowledgeable, conscientious individuals who are capable of withstanding the immense pressure mounted by contesting interests. Not all faculty come to such assignments with equal fervor or experience. In many instances, the procedures are well beyond them inasmuch as many are trained in disciplines in which organizational procedures are secondary or nonexistent. It is to these persons that an aggrieved faculty member must appeal. And always stalking any proceedings is ambition. Numerous faculty see themselves rising up in the organization, which can only mean that administration is their ultimate goal.

While the conditions giving rise to the hidden professoriate have been stressed in this volume, there are other important problems. Less perceptible, but of growing concern, is the direction many educational efforts are taking. In his examination of professional education, Edgar Schein comments that "professions have a less clear concept of what standards and ethics should govern client relationships."[3] The experiences of the students in Chapters 4, 5, and 6 highlight ambiguities within graduate and legal education. As the concern expands to clients in the community at large, one senses that a general type of anomie is afflicting many segments of higher education. Despite recent perceptions by faculty that their power has increased,[4] there is a growing sentiment in higher educational ranks that is shifting toward unionism.[5] This comes at a time when there are notable instances of decline in the diversity of higher education.[6] Unionization might serve those faculty now destined for the hidden professoriate, but a lingering concern of some is whether the labor-management model is compatible with the noble images of university life. Indeed, unionization might provide new opportunities for many creative faculty, but the immediate prospects are not encouraging.

Conflicts in higher education are not a wholly new phenomenon. Some of the changing faces of American higher education can be traced in the long teaching career of one person: Joseph S. Pilgrim in Chapter 13 ("Authoritarianism and Permissiveness in American Higher Education") presents his memoir of experiences in higher education spanning more than a half century. His own orientations, while distinct and unique, give a glimpse of the unfolding developments in higher education. His experiences in the last years of his career elucidate the growing controversy over professionalism versus unionism.

Pilgrim's experiences serve as reminders that procedures formulated as a result of controversy may well have their own imperfections. Without constant vigilance, many human beings can be victimized. The growth of the hidden professoriate and the agonies attending it testify to the lack of such vigilance. While some may have justly deserved their fate, many others became embroiled in conflicts that took an immense toll of resources, talent, and above all, the dream that higher education could be a noble pursuit.

NOTES

1. Joseph Ben-David, *American Higher Education* (New York: McGraw-Hill, 1972), p. 15.

2. Edgar H. Schein, *Professional Education* (New York: McGraw-Hill, 1972), p. 31.

3. Ibid.

4. Edward Gross and Paul V. Grambsch, *Changes in University Organization, 1964-1971* (New York: McGraw-Hill, 1974).

5. Everett Carll Ladd, Jr., and Seymour Martin Lipset, *Professors, Unions, and American Higher Education* (Berkeley, Calif.: Carnegie Commission on Higher Education, 1973).

6. C. Robert Pace, *The Demise of Diversity?* (Berkeley, Calif.: Carnegie Commission on Higher Education, 1974).

11 FRAN FRENCH

The Professional Organization to the Rescue: A Real-Life Academic Drama

PROLOGUE

You are a woman professor in a technical field. You have taught at Deep South University (DSU) for ten years, been praised by your students, been given generous merit raises, and have even received a written commendation from your department head. You have donated time for tutoring, accepted heavy teaching loads, and performed extra administrative tasks, such as coordinating the department's freshman program. You don't have tenure and you don't have the Ph.D. You have no fears, however, for you know that your university adheres to the Principles on Academic Freedom and Tenure of the prestigious Faculty Professional Organization (FPO).

ACT I

On a bright day the mail arrives. In it is a one-sentence letter informing you that at the end of the coming academic year, your services at DSU will no longer be needed. It must be a mistake. Even if "they" are trying to get rid of you, a quick check of the FPO's Principles on Academic Freedom and Tenure reassures you—full-time continuous employment for a minimum of seven years brings de facto tenure. Relax.

ACT II

You know the procedure: send copies of all relevant documents to the Faculty Professional Organization. It will defend you. After all, a principle has been violated.

Letters go back and forth between the national office of the FPO and your administration. The local chapter's Committee on Tenure deliberates and meets with administrators to point out what is obviously an error, but the year passes and, though you cannot believe it, you are out of a job.

Belief arrives as you look for another job. Belief is your companion as you pick up your unemployment check. Hope is with you too, for the national office of the FPO has "taken the case." If DSU's administration doesn't reinstate you, the university will most likely be censured! Meanwhile, strongly worded letters go back and forth between the FPO and the DSU administration. It is clear that the FPO doesn't give quarter when matters of principle are at issue.

Two years and much ado later, you are ready for a confrontation— not with the DSU administration, but with the FPO. The national office of the FPO has made what looks suspiciously like a "deal"— the national office will not pursue your case toward censure. The DSU administration has made an offer which, translated into plain English, reads: "Get off our backs about this woman professor and we promise we won't do this kind of thing again."

ACT III

You are now an observer at the national meeting of the FPO, and you're watching the delegate your local chapter has sent to plead your case. She is having an audience with a representative of the national office.

REPRESENTATIVE: "We're sorry your chapter is upset about this, but you must realize that we don't defend people; we defend principles."

DSU DELEGATE: "A principle has been violated. Has the Deep South case been turned over to the national Committee on Tenure?"

REPRESENTATIVE: "We can't send every rinky-dink case that comes along to the national committee."

DSU DELEGATE: "I will speak from the floor at the general meeting, I will challenge this decision and let the entire membership know how this case has been mishandled."

REPRESENTATIVE: "You will not be recognized, or you will be ruled out of order. It would be a serious mistake."

At the general meeting of the FPO, your delegate attempts to gain recognition from the president. The chairperson of the national women's committee offers to give the delegate time to speak if the president refuses. An FPO representative learns of this offer and arranges for the president to recognize your delegate during the discussion period following the national committee report. Discussion is an agenda item, presumably designed for just such exigencies. "But," the FPO representative warns the delegate, "you will be ruled out of order."

At the general meeting, the DSU delegate seats herself on the aisle near one of the microphones. After the national committee concludes its report, the president does not call for discussion, but goes on to the next item on the agenda. The DSU delegate rises and speaks into the microphone, reminding the president that discussion should follow the national comittee's report.

The delegate is given three minutes to present the case, which is now four years old and has created correspondence filling five folders. She concludes: "Has the national committee considered the Deep South case? If so, why was there no report, and if not, can the DSU chapter expect a report at the next annual meeting?"

PRESIDENT: "Perhaps the chairperson of the national committee would like to answer that?"

CHAIRPERSON OF THE
NATIONAL COMMITTEE: (audible mumble)

DSU DELEGATE: "I don't think the chairperson has addressed himself to my questions."

PRESIDENT: "I can only suggest that you may, if it is willing, and you insist, and it agrees, if it can, that you might, just possibly perhaps, turn this matter over to the Complaint Committee. Of course, it doesn't want to take the matter, then you know, it just won't take it."

Your delegate returns to her seat. Soon she is tapped on the shoulder. Another delegate is pushing a handbill at her saying, "I am assisting the homosexuals who, along with many heterosexuals and bisexuals, are introducing a resolution making discrimination on the basis of marital status or sexual preference a censurable act. If it comes to a proportional vote, how many votes do you have?"

DSU DELEGATE: "Only about eighty."

ASSISTANT TO THE
HOMOSEXUALS: "Not many; still, if you will support us, we may be able to help you."

DELEGATE (thinking fast): "My chapter hasn't given me instructions on this, but I am certain that Deep South wholeheartedly supports homosexuality."

ASSISTANT TO THE
HOMOSEXUALS: "And we can count on all your votes?"

DELEGATE: "Absolutely."

ASSISTANT TO THE
HOMOSEXUALS: "I will speak to some acquaintances in the Consolidation of Collective Bargaining Chapters in your behalf. They may be able to help pressure the FPO into reopening the Deep South case."

Moments later, there is another tap on the delegate's shoulder. It is the chairperson of the national women's committee. If the Complaint Committee has not agreed to take the DSU case by the time her report is due, she will give time to the DSU delegate to speak again. In the meantime, she will attempt to convince the Complaint Committee of the merits of the DSU chapter's case.

The DSU delegate's shoulder is ready and has not long to wait. This tap is a delegate from a union chapter. "You know," he says, "we all have been through the same things you're going through. Even though we have gone to collective bargaining, we still have trouble with our academic freedom and tenure cases. If you will just look at the budget of the FPO for the coming year you'll understand why. Six years ago, tenure matters got almost over half of the yearly budget; now they get only about 21 percent. Six years ago, collective bargaining got nothing, whereas it now is scheduled for about 32 percent. They just don't have enough staff or money to handle all of the tenure cases that come up. But we're on your side and we'll see that they reconsider your case, or we'll bring the matter up on the floor." He leaves to apply pressure; the women and the homosexuals also exit.

Tap. This time it is two people who say they are members of the Executive Council of the FPO and they, too, will speak to the Complaint Committee, or, they swear, they will bring the matter up tomorrow when the Executive Council meets in executive session and behind closed doors with very few people present.

Shortly thereafter, the DSU delegate is summoned to the lobby to speak to a member of the Complaint Committee. The member explains that the chairperson of the committee is not present, but she is sort of certain that the committee will be happy to consider the DSU case. However, no one who is now on the committee has ever served before, so the members have no idea of what to do. Even so, your delegate is assured, the committee will proceed with haste.

EPILOGUE

Many months after the national meeting of the FPO, you have written and described the story of your termination many more times. Your files of relevant documents have been recopied, redistributed, reexplained. You have a part-time job with a small community college at less than half your former salary at Deep South, and you are seldom reminded that, as an adjunct instructor— you will never get tenure.

12 CONSTANCE A. SULLIVAN

Judicial Committees and the Tenure Crisis: The Experience at Maitland University

In the late 1930s, Maitland University formally recognized and accepted the principle of academic tenure by adopting a tenure code. Within several years, a Judicial Committee composed of faculty members was made a part of the system of devices protective of the individual faculty member's rights, the provision of which corresponded to what seemed a firm tradition of faculty governance at the university. An active local chapter of the AAUP kept tabs on the university's treatment of rights and prerogatives, intervening by spoken or written word if necessary.

The appeals structure lay dormant, relatively unused, for years. Complaints came in spurts, in times of crisis, which permitted a small, five-member committee to exist with slow turnover of membership. While the appeals procedures, formalized in the 1950s, provided for both legal and faculty advisers to a petitioner, hearings were for the most part informal and always confidential, with emphasis on mediation of the conflict before hearings were held. Tenured faculty brought few problems to the committee, as few attempts were made to remove a tenured professor for whatever reason in those years. A sudden brief flurry of appeals during the

McCarthy period of the early 1950s was caused by a rash of dismissals of nontenured faculty. With hearings, most were reinstated.

The Judicial Committee experienced a period of inactivity through the late 1950s and most of the 1960s. Particularly in the post-Sputnik era of great expansion in higher education, money was available, more faculty were hired, tenure was relatively easy to acquire (indeed, almost automatic if the professor performed adequately), and faculty mobility was the order of the day as colleges and universities vied for teachers and researchers. Given the economics of higher education, a job loss then was not disastrous, and in more than a few cases, less than excellence in teaching and publication got people over the tenure hurdle.

The university became more politicized in the 1960s as teach-ins and marches increased participation in social protest; greater awareness of racial and sexual discrimination and new respect for, and knowledge of, rights accompanied changes in state and federal laws. Students voiced demands for institutional reforms, notably in curriculum and grading systems, and, insisting on a larger role in university affairs, were included in committees on every level. Teaching quality was the object of some complaints; course evaluations by students were stressed and good teachers were given prizes and recognition.

EVENTS REACTIVATE THE COMMITTEE

Who knows what might have come of all this without the new economic circumstances of the late 1960s? Suddenly, with the money crunch of the late Vietnam war years came retrenchment. Maitland University instituted systematic and intensive review of programs and budgets, causing some units to be cut back severely.[1] When a faculty member died, retired, resigned, or was not renewed, a department or unit frequently lost that budgeted item to central administration, the money being reallocated by administrative discretion either to that same unit or another. New positions were granted parsimoniously to departments, and only after lengthy and specific justification and review by newly created committees. Jobs were harder to find, and achieving indefinite tenure became not only less than automatic, but also difficult. Renewal and tenure decisions were accomplished with increasing care, and emphasis was ever more clearly placed on documented proof of performance.[2]

Problems of retrenchment may have contributed to the reactivization of the appeals process at Maitland University in 1969-70. Within the space of eighteen months, three nontenured faculty cases were heard by the five-man Judicial Committee. The university's legal counsel in these cases, aware of the nebulous state of nontenured faculty appeals in federal courts across the country, argued against the right of nontenured professors and instructors to appeal. Encouraged by the local AAUP chapter, however, the Judicial Committee chose to honor the tradition of due process and heard the appeals. In the two successful appeals, the committee found significant infringements of the individual's academic freedom or of his or her constitutional rights and ruled that errors of fact had contributed to the arbitrary nature of one decision to terminate an appointment. The unsuccessful appeal hinged on the issue of "collegiality," a somewhat imprecise term that covers anything that could be interpreted as interfering with the academic freedom of others or with the unit's proper functioning.[3]

Most significantly, these cases resulted in the administration's awareness of weaknesses in its procedures regarding the status of academic personnel. Central administration agreed with the recommendations of the Judicial Committee, whose function was held in some regard at that time, and reinstated one faculty member, paid a year's salary to another, and assumed the legal expenses of one successful petitioner.[4] In addition, on various levels of internal governance the following manifestations of an urge to reform began to appear.

THE UNIVERSITY RESPONDS

1. At the beginning of 1971, with several appeals still pending, the vice-president for academic administration issued a memorandum to all provosts, deans, directors, and department heads that attempted to clarify procedures and criteria to be used in making recommendations concerning the status of individual faculty members. It still stands as the statement of guidelines but was updated in 1975 by a new administration.[5] The 1971 document's first paragraph explains its purpose:

Departments will shortly be making recommendations concerning promotion, granting of indefinite tenure and termination or reappointment of probationary members of the faculty. It is desirable that these recommendations be made on the basis of well-understood criteria and procedures. Some departments have become involved in review procedures, often both embarrassing and time-consuming, following from complaints by members of the faculty affected by their recommendations. In order to assist departments as much as possible to avoid such difficulties, I have consulted with the chairmen of the University Committee on Tenure, the Senate Judicial Committee, and the Committee on Academic Freedom of the (local) chapter, American Association of University Professors, about the formulation of criteria and procedures which would satisfy minimum standards of due process in reaching departmental decisions upon these questions. This memorandum reflects their advice and guidance.[6]

In the clarification of procedures, several paragraphs are devoted to who is entitled to vote, how to report the voting, how to prepare the materials to be considered in personnel evaluations, the faculty member's submission of relevant materials to his personnel file, the necessity of a meeting with discussion of the materials in each case, voting procedures, recording votes taken, the chairperson's summary of reasons expressed by faculty for their votes, and preservation of ballots and the chairperson's summary. A long discussion gives the rationale for not providing reasons for nonreappointment to a probationary faculty member:

Section Z of the [tenure code] provides that it is not necessary to give a probationary member of the faculty who is not to be reappointed a statement of the reasons for his nonreappointment. This is because such action carries no necessary implication of dissatisfaction with the individual's work or conduct. A decision not to reappoint such a probationary member of the faculty may rest not upon inadequate work or unacceptable conduct, but upon other factors, such as budgetary limitations or departmental personnel priorities or options which reflect no discredit upon the individual who is not reappointed. For example, an individual whose work and conduct is acceptable may not be reappointed because the department thinks it can attract someone better qualified to fulfill the department's objectives.

To give no reasons for the recommendation not to reappoint may avoid embarrassment to the individual affected by making it unnecessary for him either to relate matters discreditable to him or to conceal them at the risk that others might disclose them. However, if the individual affected requests a statement of the reasons for the recommendation made, he should be informed of this provision of Section Z of the [tenure code] and the reasons for it. If he persists in requesting a statement, the chairman shall furnish him with a written statement of the reasons for the departmental recommendation.

The memorandum ends with a detailed statement of proper and improper criteria used in decisions regarding academic personnel. The 1975 version is quite different:

The provision in Section Z of the [tenure code] that it is not necessary to give a probationary member of the faculty who is not to be reappointed a statement of the reasons for his or her nonreappointment seems to be superseded by requirements of law whenever the individual desires disclosure. The individual has the right under [state law] to see and obtain copies of anything in his or her personnel file and to have the meaning of any papers in it explained. In the event that the individual should challenge the departmental recommendation, or action taken in consequence of it, either before the Senate Judicial Committee or by legal action, due process would entitle the complainant to disclosure of the reasons for nonreappointment in order to enable him or her to show whether there were any grounds inconsistent with academic freedom or with legal standards. In those cases in which nonreappointment does not rest upon any judgment of the individual's work or conduct that is discreditable but upon such grounds as budgetary considerations or departmental academic or personnel priorities or options, it seems preferable to communicate the reasons as a regular departmental practice. There may continue to be occasional situations in which the individual does not desire disclosure of the grounds for nonreappointment because they are discreditable and nondisclosure may enable the individual to avoid embarrassment, e.g., in seeking other employment. The department, however, ought to consider whether the circumstances are such that it can properly afford such protection consistently with fairness to other employers. It therefore appears that in nearly all circumstances it should be departmental practice to notify probationers who are not reappointed of the reasons for nonreappointment. The chairman shall also inform them of their procedural rights in this situation.

Both the 1971 and the 1975 documents show the influence of Judicial Committee cases: the first, by its very existence and the careful delineation (for the first time) of proper procedures; the second, by the omissions and additions made in areas both of procedures and criteria to be used in evaluating an individual. Among the most outstanding were the omission of consultation with the AAUP,[7] clarification of the manner in which a dossier is gathered prior to evaluation, what it should include, and voting procedures on the departmental level. (The individual may now, in response to new laws, see everything that the dossier contains, before the voting.) Also included are the need for annual review of the status of probationary faculty members (which would prompt the yearly counseling that caused problems in appeals cases, for its absence), the statement that a nonreappointed faculty member must be given reasons for that recommendation without his repeated insistence that they be given, new stress on impermissible criteria, and a statement that there is no automatic right to reappointment.[8]

2. Tenure and Promotion Review Committees already existed in some units of the university by 1971. Generally, they are appointed by the dean or director of a college or school to assist him or her in personnel decisions, and in some cases committee membership is not publicized. This has led to accusations, fair or not, that deans use these committees to support their discretionary reversals of departmental recommendations, particularly in the vague areas of purported tenure quotas and administrative attempts to strengthen or weaken departments that are, respectively, necessary to the college or school but perceived as professionally substandard or unnecessary in a time of financial difficulty and doomed to eventual elimination. These review committees have formulated no rules of procedure, and their recommendations or advice to the deans are generally confidential. This area has been one of the most vulnerable to charges of administrative manipulation toward centralization of control.

Grievance Committees, also established on nearly all levels in the 1970s, handle appeals from both students and faculty in matters that do not involve the tenure code. A ruling by a department's Grievance Committee may be appealed to the college committee, and subsequently to the University Committee on Academic Freedom and Responsibility. Part of the rationale for the creation of this alternate grievance system was to alleviate the Judicial Committee's heavy load.

3. In conjunction with, and perhaps as a result of some cases heard by the Judicial Committee, revisions of the tenure code were undertaken in 1971. When the process of revision was suspended by the unionization dispute in mid-1973, the faculty Senate had approved a provisional document that reflected the painful experiences of recent years, specifying more clearly the right to appeal, the procedures for appointments and review, and even the university's assumption of legal costs to a successful petitioner in Judicial Committee cases. A lengthy document, it would also have made tenure more difficult to acquire by stating that near unanimity of the votes of a unit would be necessary for a recommendation that someone be granted indefinite tenure. Maitland University still operates under the preceding tenure code, however unclear some believe it to be because of a perceived lack of specificity.[9]

4. Modifications of the Rules of Procedure for the Judicial Committee, as well as an enlargement of its membership, were made in 1971-72. From five members, all white males with tenured positions, the committee was expanded to thirteen, and the university's president appointed significant percentages from three groups traditionally underrepresented, if not unrepresented, on the committee: minorities, women, and nontenured faculty.[10]

The need for a larger committee stemmed from the number of appeals to be heard, and the rules modifications reflected the experience of hearings in the early years of the 1970s. Three-person hearing panels were established, and their findings were discussed by the whole committee before they reached the final stage. The panel's conclusions were seldom challenged by the larger committee, which did not hear the evidence directly. Rules of procedure grew more formal and very significantly legalistic, owing both to the influence of several law professors on the committee and to the university's desire to follow as closely as possible the legal profession's current understanding of the requirements of due process. Hearings were to be recorded on tape and to be kept in archives. In addition, specifications were amplified with regard to such formal aspects as prehearing conferences, disclosure and exchange of documents to all parties, time limits in the various steps in the process, establishment of the burden of proof, and the committee's reporting duties. The principle of confidentiality hung heavy over these rules, and its broaching caused no small tensions in several cases in the early 1970s. The committee has made smaller revisions, mostly of language, from time to time, but essentially the rules of procedure are detailed, lengthy, and legalistic, yet not difficult to read.

The Judicial Committee is the only university-wide, appointed faculty committee with such a carefully wrought document to guide its work. The seriousness of its task, the fear of lawsuits against committee members (several have been initiated; even more were threatened), and the pressure of having attorneys on both sides of the table led to this amplification. The committee is considered a quasi-legal entity with a duty to provide due process of appeal; it is the major "internal remedy" to be exhausted by an aggrieved faculty member before an appeal is made in court. Nevertheless, its role is only that of reporting findings of fact and making recommendations to the president; it does not issue "rulings."

5. In the administrative review of recommendations by departments, many procedural errors are found, as a result of which recommendations are sent back to the colleges or the departments for changes. This return for review or correction involves technical aspects of recommendations, such as improper appointments (temporary appointments, for example, where the tenure code does not permit them) and improper voting procedures or documentation. Such checking has prevented some potential faculty grievances by forcing corrections before the decisions are made final.

THE NATURE OF THE COMMITTEE'S WORK

Multiple appeals, primarily from temporary or nontenured faculty, occupied the Judicial Committee's time in the past six years. Several cases were brought by faculty who loudly protested the confidentiality, or secrecy, of the entire appeals process in public and campus newspapers and in rallies. One case went to federal court without a Judicial Committee hearing, when the committee refused to hold open hearings. Support committees for another faculty member raised money in public appeals and applied intensive pressure on a new administration by means of media exposure of the issues as they saw them, and by private conferences with the president to force his resolution of the grievance without Judicial Committee hearings. However, the committee was active, and the university community knew of its existence, and that it worked in closed sessions and made no public report of the cases it heard.

The appeals created problems for the university as well as for the individuals who brought them. The time taken from that which could be devoted to other efforts by administrators, faculty members, and staff was enormous and increasingly an irritant to all concerned.[11] Legal costs to the university in appeals increased greatly, from close to $28,000 in 1971 to $172,000 in 1975.[12] The university suffered from bad public relations when internal problems became known, particularly as the public grew more sensitive to what was perceived as the institution's mistreatment of good teachers and "the little guy." Bad relations with the state legislatures always worry the administration, and the partial airing of faculty disputes did not help to better them. The appeals also contributed to a general deflation of faculty morale in the university as professors and students were angered at what appeared to be injustices to other professors, especially if they were popular teachers. The faculty feared for themselves as the tenure system came under fire and as published results of research, rather than good teaching, became the primary consideration in promotion and tenure decisions. More and more the cult became impatient at the hearing process, the time involved, and the Judicial Committee's insistence that professors reveal confidential recommendations and their reasons for voting "aye" or "nay" in personnel decisions. By 1974, the Judicial Committee faced a problem of noncooperation by some faculty members who refused to testify in hearings or otherwise have anything to do with a committee process that might question their actions or opinions. Because it lacks subpoena power, the committee was forced to terminate a hearing when several professors refused to reveal confidential letters about one petitioner who, in his turn, refused to proceed without them. The committee spent much time in persuading other faculty members to cooperate in the hearings. On the whole, the university as an institution was viewed as an unassailable monolith that crushed the hapless and lonely individual.

The individuals who brought the appeals also had large problems. The process is slow, although much faster than any court appeal, and it is made slower by the presence of attorneys with their emphasis on multiple documents.[13] Many faculty members have complained of the complicated procedures. Money to pay legal fees has always represented an obstacle for the petitioner. And sadly, far too few university instructors seemed to know the regulations applicable to their faculty status. Many had not read carefully their notices of appointment, which state salary, term, and nature of appointment, and few had any acquaintance with the tenure code, not to speak of the Judicial Committee rules of procedure. Perhaps some of this ignorance can be blamed on the university's failure to publish repeated memoranda and reminders to them about procedures and rights. On the other hand, the individuals too often showed an irresponsible degree of inattention to the documents and regulations available to them, until, of course, their status was threatened and they thought to appeal.

This ignorance was complicated by unfamiliarity with university regulations and procedures on the part of the lawyers who represented the petitioners. Trained for the courtroom and civil or criminal law, these frequently young and inexperienced attorneys did not have prior access to, or knowledge of, internal policy or precedents either for the university or the Judicial Committee. This put them at a significant disadvantage in the hearings. The university, on the other hand, has retained the same highly paid lawyer to represent its side in almost all cases heard by the committee in the past few years. He has access not only to the resources of his large and prestigious law firm, but also to all university documents, including all internal reports from judicial Committee hearings, in addition to hearings he knows from having participated in them. He knows the committee procedures and university regulations so well that his superiority over the petitioner's counsel (which he enhances by the psychological impact of overpreparation) is a major disadvantage to the petitioner.

Among the negative effects of bringing an appeal is the increased precariousness of relationships between the petitioner and his or her departmental colleagues, made worse by the tensions of the appeal process. Departments have been known to split into opposing camps over the issues, and the aggrieved faculty member unavoidably gains the reputation of a mediocre sorehead, a troublemaker, one who either won't or doesn't know how to play the game. In a job search following either a successful or an unsuccessful appeal, the petitioner will also carry that stigma and will be judged more for having made an appeal at all than for his or her qualifications.

Of the many appeals made from 1971 to 1976, most were unsuccessful. Some potential cases were mediated and resolved before the hearings. Some were judged by the committee to be "untimely," the faculty member having brought the appeal too late—either through individual misreading of regulations that specify time limits, or through incorrect advice by administrators at the lower levels. The Judicial Committee did hear some technically "untimely" appeals, particularly when a dean or other administrator gave the person the wrong advice about how and when and where to appeal. One case was resolved by the president without a hearing.

Of the appeals that actually reached the hearing stage, and because of the university's attempts to broadcast regulations more thoroughly and to check all personnel recommendations for errors in procedure, most were not clear-cut cases of extremes of good or bad performance on either side. They were "murky," in the sense that no overwhelming abuse of an individual by a department was proved, nor did the individuals claim to be the most outstanding talents in their fields. All the appeals made on the whole or partial basis of racial or sexual discrimination were unsuccessful; in cases where discrimination is not exaggerated and overt, it is very difficult to prove.

The several successful appeals, which may not have looked like "successful" appeals to all concerned, were won because failures of due process had marred the recommendations not to promote or reappoint. Several people received the limited redress of a one- or two-year special appointment, with reconsideration by their units, or a year's severance salary. Tenured faculty members with salary grievances reviewed by the Judicial Committee were successful in achieving higher salary and back pay, but one tenured professor who appealed his dismissal for cause (that cause being non-feasance) did not succeed and subsequently took his case to court.

GUIDING PRINCIPLES

Limits of space and the still confidential nature of individual case findings preclude giving their details, but from these most recent appeals one can derive certain principles sustained repeatedly by the Judicial Committee. They provide an insight into what the committee regards as its proper function and an idea of current rights, responsibilities, and prerogatives of faculty and administration at Maitland.

1. Academic freedom and constitutional rights, most importantly those of free speech, association, and due process, are the nearest to sacrosanct of the principles at issue in recent cases. The university may neither abrogate these rights nor contradict any provision of the tenure code. Neither may an individual. This obviates any decisions made on "arbitrary or capricious" bases or mistakes of fact. Of course, the right to privacy has also been upheld, most significantly in the committee's refusal to reveal the contents of a personnel file belonging to a faculty colleague of a petitioner. A comparison of files was requested in at least two cases, where the petitioner's complaint was of unequal treatment of comparable people. The committee's decisions were consistent in stating that except in instances where a prima facie case of racial or sexual discrimination could be made or where the nonlitigant faculty member volunteered his or her file to the petitioner, the contents of a confidential personnel file were not to be used as evidence in someone else's complaint.

2. That guiding principle corresponds to another: administrative "discretion" in deciding between apparent equals. Deans, for example, may contradict the recommendations of departments and distinguish between seemingly similar individuals in their own recommendations to the next administrative level, choosing to promote some and not others. This "discretion" is broad and constitutional (within university regulations), and applies to areas such as program cutbacks, budgetary recommendations, and decisions to move to improve certain weak departments. It has caused greatest explicit protest, however, in regard to personnel decisions, and even the buffer zone between departmental and college-level recommendations that Tenure and Promotion Review Committees provide has not diminished the sense of unfairness this "discretion" provokes.

3. The Judicial Committee, composed as it is of faculty members from many disciplines, will not, if such can be avoided, rehear what is called "the merits" of a decision, or second guess a unit's evaluation of a professor's scholarship or teaching. In practice, this principle is nearly impossible to live by, and the panels of the committee have, in fact, slipped over the fine line between checking

procedural due process and evaluating the work of an individual. One tenured faculty member with a salary grievance maintained that his scholarship had been undervalued by his department because of its decision that his area of expertise was not within the department's preferred program. The committee's recommendation to the administration that he be given a larger salary hinged on apparently procedural errors, but it was their reexamination of that individual's professional work that caused them to find that the procedures were unfair. Another panel determined that a professor had not been unfairly denied promotion after lengthy perusal of lists of publications and teaching evaluations, in both of which areas they saw enough weakness to prove that the administration's decision had not been arbitrary. The Judicial Committee seems to have made repeated attempts to separate the issue of the relative worth of a person's research and teaching from the area of correct procedures, where it would prefer to concentrate its attention because failures of due process are more readily discernible.

4. With specific regard to nontenured faculty cases, the committee has relied heavily on the technical provisions of the tenure code, where the nature of, and reasons permissible for, different appointments are stated. In this it has recognized the university's right to make temporary appointments, even for more than seven consecutive years, if that temporary status is legitimate by reason of temporary funding, graduate student status, or as otherwise provided in the code, and if the faculty appointee has been duly notified of that status. Problems in this area have led both to appeals and to the administration's subsequent policy decision not to make temporary appointments for more than seven years.

5. The Judicial Committee has not yet recognized a case of de facto tenure, partly because of technical confusion in the cases brought before it and partly because of its reluctance to recommend that tenure be granted by the administration over the negative recommendation of a department. This principle of the peer group's right to decide has been a much debated one within the committee. However, even in difficult cases, where a panel has concluded that a department-level decision was not fair, its recommendations have not gone beyond the granting of an extra year or two on special appointment with reconsideration of the individual's status

within that time. This reluctance to second guess or overrule a department corresponds to the committee's reluctance to evaluate, as a committee, individual scholarship or research.

6. Committee findings in appeals brought by probationary and temporary faculty reflected its opinion that faculty members have the responsibility to know the conditions of their appointments and the provisions of the tenure code. They should also be professionally aware, in the sense that they should not dedicate their efforts to committee service or administrative assignments when what will be most important to their promotion or reappointment is the quality and the quantity of their published research. Regarding one assistant professor who had devoted three years of his probationary period to revamping a major program in his unit and acting as its director, the committee found that even without the yearly counseling his department should have given him about his progress, he himself should have foreseen the effect such heavy teaching-related duties would have on his research. In the last analysis, he had been judged for promotion on the basis of his publications, and they were not strong enough. In this instance, the committee upheld a unit's right to shift the weight of the criteria for evaluation and stated that the individual must be alert to such shifts and act accordingly in his best interests.

RESIDUAL PROBLEMS

Some people perceived a need for a legal adviser to the Judicial Committee, or at least for members with legal training. New members, particularly, find the presence of attorneys for the parties a complicating factor in hearings, and an intimidating one as well. Attorneys for both parties tend to view the committee as their adversary; arguments are directed sometimes as much against committee rulings as against the opposing counsel's arguments. Many faculty petitioners currently do not retain a lawyer to represent them, in which case the university's side is not presented by legal counsel either. With faculty advisers rather than lawyers, the tone of the hearings has been less severely legalistic.

The Judicial Committee recently made an attempt to release anonymous resumés of the past eight years of cases to assist potential petitioners in understanding precedents and the bases of past cases. This initiative has been effectively thwarted by the refusal of those past petitioners who are members of one of the contending groups in the unionization drive to permit release of anonymous summaries without full release of the findings in each case.

Discussions within the committee show its near-readiness to hold open hearings. This responds to a certain "bad press" the committee has suffered, resulting from partial and inaccurate statements offered publicly by interested parties; committee members, bound by the rule of confidentiality, have not been able to answer or correct any distortions of their activities and findings. The main obstacles to the contemplated open hearings involve potential public embarrassment to the petitioner and other faculty (a lot of "dirty linen" is exposed in hearings) and the possible refusal of the faculty to testify in public sessions. Willing to open its proceedings, the Judicial Committee worries that the entire appeals process might be stopped if the faculty refuses to cooperate.

Currently, most faculty members of Maitland University at least pause to consider an appeal of decisions that negatively affect their job status, while not all of them actually go through with the appeal. The Judicial Committee has a profile in the university community, however much it may be viewed with skepticism or cynicism. The appeals structure is established, and it functions. The university as an institution has responded to weaknesses as revealed in successive appeals, but this situation could easily change. If central administrators lose either faith in faculty committee recommendations or patience with the long and costly process of appeals of its decisions, the authenticity of this structure and function will evaporate.

Signs of this happening have already appeared: administrators have questioned the legitimacy of the Judicial Committee's readiness to hear all appeals brought before it, advising the committee to hear only those appeals with precedent-setting features. In response, the committee has kept referring to the tenure code, where the right to appeal is guaranteed to all faculty. This is also its response to civil court rulings in the past two or three years that would deny right of appeal to nontenured teachers. Distrust of the committee's operations and disagreement with its findings on the part of petitioners, and occasionally of the administration, have caused re-argument of certain appeals before the president and again, before the Board of Trustees. This weakening of confidence in the committee's function and, indeed, disdain for its findings indicate, perhaps, that the future will be different at Maitland University. Intensification of academic job market problems, further attacks on academic tenure, or the consequences of faculty unionization, all could modify or eliminate the appeals apparatus as it has existed at this institution to the present.

NOTES

1. More often than not, the constant threat of budgetary and programmatic cuts was worse than retrenchment itself.

2. The administration also had issued a directive that prohibited appointment of graduate students as full-time tenure-track instructors; ingrowth had developed in some departments because faculty who could hold on to a full-time position into an eighth year frequently "slipped" into tenure without evaluation by a department.

3. This subjective category of "collegiality" continues to provide the promotion standards' most convenient loophole.

4. That reimbursement is unique to date.

5. Revisions could not be substantive, merely clarification and changes imposed by new state or federal laws after 1973. A state ruling on collective bargaining units was challenged by the administration at that time, and a cease-and-desist order prohibiting any alteration of the faculty's conditions of employment has not yet been lifted.

6. The 1975 revision adds: "This memorandum . . . is explanatory in nature. It may occasionally express a widespread institutional practice that reflects a standard higher than that required by the law or the [tenure code]. In such cases departments are free to follow practices consistent with due process, law, and the [tenure code] when these are specified in college constitutions approved by the (Trustees)."

7. The AAUP could not be consulted after 1973 if all other potential faculty unions were not consulted equally. See note 5.

8. This document in some part summarizes other internal memoranda concerning appointment procedures sent between 1973 and 1975.

9. Discussions of the proposed revisions of the code influenced the amplifications of the 1975 guidelines on personnel, which anticipated provisions yet to be enacted.

10. Under new administration, and perhaps partly as a result of the overwork of these minorities in university committees, this trend has been

reversed. With one exception, the Judicial Committee's membership is currently composed of tenured faculty, and from a high point in 1975, when women and minorities formed one-half of its membership, the committee looks increasingly white and male.

11. A typical hearing takes two full days. Some have taken as many as five days, plus the time for prehearing arrangements and conferences, and for discussion and preparation of the written findings.

12. These figures were provided by the administration in response to a question put to the president during a faculty Senate meeting in the spring of 1976.

13. In one case that had generated a mountain of legal briefs and memoranda, a panel requested the attorneys to desist from further one-upmanship and to refrain from issuing more repetitive paper arguments. Lawyers, of course, are paid by the hour; faculty time for petitioners, witnesses, and committee members is not reimbursed.

13 JOSEPH S. PILGRIM

Authoritarianism and Permissiveness in American Higher Education: A Memoir

In 1920, I arrived in the United States as an immigrant from Central Europe. My decision as to what career to pursue in this new land was determined by the mentality of a generation raised under the influence of the traditional Germanic cultural heritage—a heritage now largely defunct as a consequence of first Fascist and later Communist totalitarianism—which was still dominant in Central Europe.

Central to the Germanic cultural heritage prior to World War I was the role played by an intellectual and artistic elite. With the secularization of religion that accompanied the rise of the nation-state, this artistic and intellectual elite acquired a status that at earlier periods had largely been monopolized by the clergy. Individuals who managed to gain access to its circles were potentially welcome in the courts of kings and princes and were relied upon to carry out major tasks of administration. They came to serve as advisers and staff assistants in all major social enterprises. With further development of the nation-state, this elite took the lead in the supply of the technical, scientific, and cultural skills essential to Western civilization. Members of privileged strata have always tended to consolidate their gains and to transform them into hereditary prerogatives descending automatically to their children. The intellectuals and artists of every society, however, have resisted this conversion into ascriptive properties. In every society where talents and abilities are valued, intellectual and artistic circles are to some extent open. There is simply no guarantee that the sons and daughters of intellectuals and artists will inherit their parents' abilities. While the intellectual and cultural elites in various countries dominated by the German cultural heritage were partially closed and relatively limited, young persons of unusual ability, regardless of humble origin, could potentially gain access to the ranks of the intelligentsia.

For reasons I do not even now fully understand, from the first moment that I began to reflect on a potential career, the role of the university professor had the most powerful appeal to me. No figure was more attractive to me than the charismatic *Herr Doktor* who moved as easily in national politics as in education. His natural home was the university where he was a star among brilliant satellites (the *Dozents*). At times he moved from education into the highest ranks of national politics, as illustrated by the careers of President Thomas G. Masaryk and Foreign Minister Eduard Beneš of Czechoslovakia, both of whom were professors of sociology. Above all, I was impressed that a small number of carefully selected and promising students could run the gauntlet of stiff periodic examinations and join the magical circle of these luminaries.

I do not recall ever wavering in my conviction that I was destined for the intellectual life, and in the more open society of the new world, I dedicated myself to becoming a university professor.

Earning the Ph.D. proved to be difficult economically but not intellectually. I supported myself during my studies by such diverse activities as digging dandelions, washing windows, performing janitorial services, and serving as a waiter and even as a motion picture extra. My studies, up to and including the doctorate, were facilitated in some measure by my European background. In most fields in which I worked, I knew more than my professors which, at times, is not saying much. For example, one of my Ph.D. advisers only held an A.B. degree. The highest academic rank he attained in his entire career was an honorary M.A. degree.

I spent part of my teaching career in small junior colleges and eventually moved to the university level. For a time I served as head of the departments of sociology and political science. In retrospect, my experience in teaching was exhausting and most disappointing; all in all, it quite approximated Thoreau's description, the "life of quiet desperation." Paradoxically, in a formal sense I realized all of my youthful ambitions: I became a professor but the experience turned out to be surprisingly empty. As I reflect on the entire experience, I am most impressed by the irreconcilable gap in American academic life between ideological pretenses and practical realities, between the noisy advertisement, the Madison Avenue claims for the American educational system, and the facts of life.

To be sure, not all teaching experiences in American higher education are as unsatisfactory as, on balance, mine have been, but many thousands have been and continue to be at least as disappointing. Part of the reason is that the image of American higher education as democratic is only a partial truth. In hundreds of institutions, many "democratic" traditions are replaced by authoritarianism, on the one hand, and by permissiveness or license, on the other—a permissiveness that easily passes over into anarchism and the rule of cliques. In either case, the American dream tends to yield before a grim and disappointing reality that is all too seldom documented in American higher education. In what follows I will outline my personal experience with both of these deviant models of American higher education.

THE AUTHORITARIAN MODEL

The authoritarian model of the American university may be illustrated by Utopian University, a private college located in the metropolitan area of Oceanport. Under the pragmatic direction of a president chosen by the trustees, Utopian University pursued its long-range goals in sometimes astonishing day-to-day expediencies.

In the view of the president and trustees, "bigger was better." They were moved by a mighty passion for size. In the idiom of the president, "we are not tradition breakers, but tradition makers," with the aim of making our institution "the fastest growing one in the region." To accomplish this aim meant the addition of more and more buildings to the physical plant and to justify this expansion meant an increase in the student body as fast as possible. While loudly proclaiming that "under no circumstances shall we lower our high standards," the president and the trustees pursued a purely quantitative standard of success.

Since student tuition fees were steep, innumerable scholarships, fellowships, and grants were necessary to supplement student finances. At the same time, there were numerous devices to get back whatever money had been paid out in student financial inducements. For example, all out of town students were forced to live in the ever-growing number of dormitories and to eat in the campus dining room. In an attempt to circumvent Utopian University's dormitory and dining regulations, the students resorted to endless expedients, some of the students giving spurious local addresses.

Utopian University's enrollment was derived not only from students in the local area who were unable to gain entry into more reputable institutions, but also from the outside. In addition to giving numerous financial exemptions, the institution employed a traveling corps of public relations experts to recruit students.

Meanwhile, the faculty was under constant pressure to contribute to the general university fund and to maintain student morale. A special duty of the dean of student personnel was to check into all cases of failing students. Dossiers were kept on professors who earned reputations for severe grading. When students complained of low or failing grades, the offending professor was called in for interrogation. At such times, he or she discovered that the dean was in the habit of periodically inviting students to his home to check up on the behavior of his teaching staff.

Sooner or later, any professor who resisted the pressures for easy grading and who, out of some misguided notions of integrity and of the value of maintaining standards, assigned grades on the basis of merit was pressured into resigning. Utopian University had no tenure and no basis for expectations of job continuity other than the provision in the Faculty Handbook that after five years of consecutive service a professor "might expect" reappointment. Faculty

turnover rates were high, and those who survived endured an atmosphere of threats and psychological intimidation.

From time to time, faculty members were chastised by the president, whose presence was continuously felt everywhere. The president's weekly meetings with deans, executive assistants, and executive secretaries continually supplied him with ammunition against
the teaching staff. The administrators were under pressure and won
Brownie points for reporting real or alleged incidents of how a
professor mishandled his classes, how he behaved in all situations,
what he may have said upon any given occasion. The system made
the teachers and administrators deadly enemies. It was the practice
to call in the victim of what was often pure and malicious gossip
and confront him with an evaluation, never, presumably, made by
the president but by the anonymous collective judgment of the
Council of Deans.

There was special trauma each spring when, not only every
faculty member, but even the deans were informed on the basis of
their dossiers for the year whether the regular faculty increase was
justified in the particular individual's case. In anticipation of the
spring executions, as some faculty members described the annual
review, individuals anxiously reviewed the year's events to anticipate whether they could expect a salary increase, or even a decrease.
On such occasions, some faculty members were preemptorily dismissed. Those unhappy about such treatment were reassured that
Utopian University was not desirous of a faculty interested only in
money, but in a faculty that was happy there.

These authoritarian procedures were skillfully transformed into
an institutional operation which consolidated authority at the top
of the hierarchy while locating responsibility at the bottom. As a
department chairperson, for example, I reported my evaluation of
the teaching staff I supervised *only* after a session with the dean. At
these sessions, we arrived at *his* decision which I then was required
to sign as *my* recommendation. Orders as to what was to be done
with respect to particular individuals thus came from above, while
all appointments and dismissals were executed as if, theoretically,
they had been made by the heads of the departments. As a result, in
the sociology and political science departments persons with ques-

tionable degrees were hired as well as persons with minor degrees (B.A.'s and M.A.'s rather than Ph.D.'s) in related fields.

Although salaries were poor and, particularly in the evening division, minimal, persons at times were found who were willing to return all or part of their fees to the University Fund. As chairperson of the sociology and political science departments, I occasionally found myself with new faculty members we did not need, but who had been hired for extraneous, including racial, reasons. The sole qualification of some faculty members was that they lived in the area and were "cheap."

Financial pressures generated by the expansion plans of the president and the trustees dominated every phase of faculty behavior. Fee-paying students had to be appeased and patronized at all costs. One spring we even had to spend a day in a section of the city assigned to each of us, knocking on doors and begging for contributions. At the time I was hired, I was informed that I would be eligible for a sabbatical leave in my seventh year. As time passed, I discovered that the sabbatical was in the eighth year and, was, for only half a year, and that the plan of study had to be approved by the Council of Deans. Even this limited sabbatical proved to be illusory, for there was no ongoing institutional support for it. If anyone requested one, it was conditional upon the voluntary assumption of his teaching duties by his departmental associates, adding his teaching duties to their already overburdened schedules. Who dared put his associates to such stress? My first sabbatical came under these restrictive conditions.

The continuous draining of all available funds into building programs produced periodic difficulties from accreditation agencies. It was not possible to hire cheap but incompetent staff without also harming the quality of instruction. For a time, two divisions of Utopian University were under suspension as a result of investigations by accreditation committees which revealed that the instruction was being offered by non-qualified personnel. Utopian University's library was strongly criticized for a lack of basic requirements amounting to around 375,000 volumes. The official justification for its small-size library was that in view of the library resources of the city and surrounding areas, Utopian University had more than met the minimum requirements of an adequate library.

Another practice by Utopian University which came under severe censure of the accrediting agencies was the license permitted to departments with the largest numbers of registered students. For example, during the burgeoning demand for teachers in the 1950s, the Department of Education expanded imperialistically in all directions. Courses which in their brochures and on paper belonged to education were actually taught in other departments. Courses in science, political science, sociology, and history, for example, were listed as Education and Science, Family Education and the like. On one occasion, I had a severe altercation with the dean of education when I discovered that he was certifying students in sociology even though they had taken no sociology at all. His reply was that sociology was a "required elective" subject. Hence, by listing sociology under the rubric Social Science Education, if a student had taken any courses at all in social science, the dean claimed the privilege of certifying him as a specialist in sociology.

Among the practices engaged in to secure enrollments justifying ever-expanding building programs was the device of paying student tuitions. This practice continues to this day within the framework of the Open Admissions policy. Inasmuch as such enrollment buildup practices tended to recruit students who were not particularly interested in higher education, these students tended to drop out even with the relaxed grading policies of the teaching staff. Presumably it made no sense to go to such extraordinary lengths to jam students through the top only to have them leak out of the bottom of Utopian University's educational barrel. The council of Deans arose to this emergency with the New Start concept.

Failing students were called into the dean's office and informed that they would be permitted to re-register and start studying again, thereby wiping out their previous unsatisfactory records. Moreover, they were informed that if they did well in their new start, as a bonus they would receive full credit for failed courses taken during the earlier period. Students were sometimes granted a number of such New Starts. Meanwhile, the faculty was advised to spend more time on these delinquents, for such time would figure as a consideration in the deliberations over whether or not a given faculty member would qualify for a yearly salary increase.

It is hardly surprising that in the desperate attempt to maintain enrollments at all costs, weak or unhappy students were transferred from department to department and awarded credit for courses they had failed.

Finally, among the problems faced by the faculty, which arose from the complex of factors associated with the financing and enrollment practices of Utopian University, was the burden of carrying on "constructive activities" in the community. In my own field, for example, any frank discussion of current affairs ran the risk of counter-reactions from political partisans (if you pleased the Democrats, you enraged the Republicans and vice versa), religious zealots, fanatics in several assorted variations, do-gooders, pressure groups (such as the American Legion), and the like.

It was unthinkable that the administrators of Utopian University would defend in the name of academic freedom the rights of its teaching staff when criticized even by the most partisan of community groups. Quite the contrary, on one occasion, the Council of Deans, represented by the president, was called into emergency session to demand an offending professor's account for what he did or did not say. I was blessed with two such experiences. In one case, a group supporting the United Nations complained that our classes had criticized that august body. The administration arranged for a special public meeting at which we, the professors, had to testify to our "love of" and our intention to work for the United Nations. In the second case, I had lectured to a college club in town on geopolitics. Someone in the audience was so naïve that he thought I had lectured upon "Jew-O Politics." One would assume that this innocently humorous misunderstanding would simply have been ignored. However, the president called me to his office and severely chastised me for giving a false impression of Utopian University to the local community.

After teaching under these conditions for eighteen years, I was happy to retire from this academic confinement camp. In retrospect, it seems an eon in purgatory. It is difficult for me to understand today how I ever managed to put up with it, but then we tend to forget the dreadful pressures that were on the teacher in the small American college in the 1930s when there was no tenure and the world was involved in a massive depression. The viewpoints of those who began teaching in this period were fixed long into the time of the affluent society.

INTERLUDE

After having served as head of two departments for eighteen years, I was receiving a salary of only $8,700 and was being kept at that figure. At the same time, the university was paying around $12,000 for newly hired and inexperienced instructors and assistant professors. When I protested the inequity, I was reminded that as I as about ready to retire, I might consider it now. This prompted me to inform the administration that I could not continue serving as the chairperson of two departments for a mere $150 a year. (This was what the administration computed as my pay over and beyond my salary as a teacher for service as the head of two departments.) Not only were chairpersons poorly paid, but they were required to be on call for twelve months a year service and were obligated to hire substitutes out of their own pocket when taking vacations. I was informed that if I did't like my job, I should quit.

After some rather bitter confrontations occasioned by this ob- servation, a representative of the president informed me that he had visited a number of my friends in the area and had asked them to set up a fund for appointing me a research professor. Finally, I was offered a second sabbatical which was overdue. It was to cover an entire year with full pay and did not directly burden other de- partmental faculty. This offer, however, was not without strings. This sabbatical, incidentally, was several years overdue. In return I was asked to promise to keep quiet about "what was going on," since another accreditation inspection team was scheduled to examine the institution during the year. I was required to put my promise into writing.

As I approached the mandatory age of retirement at Utopian University, an announcement of this forthcoming event quite unex- pectedly brought eighteen invitations from various colleges and universities to serve as visiting professor or to organize new de- partments. While I was considering these offers, I was informed of an opening in the city university system. I was introduced to the acting president by friends, interviewed, and hired on the spot. To my astonishment, I was offered the starting salary of a full pro- fessor; it was nearly triple my salary at Utopian.

After long bitter years under the authoritarian atmosphere that so often dominates American private colleges, it suddenly appeared that the American dream was a reality after all.

THE PERMISSIVE MODEL

Only a person who has lived through authoritarian oppression can appreciate the euphoria with which I joined Cosmopolitan University of the city university system. How different it all was: here academic affairs were in the hands of academic colleagues, and not the administration. Openness, frankness, and democracy were the rule. I was not even distressed by the information that each semester I was to be evaluated by the tenured professors of the department. The department chairperson was fond of me and often asked me to lecture in his classes. At this stage, I still experienced the joyous open camaraderie of peers.

However, by my second year at Cosmopolitan, I had begun to be aware of another type of perversion of the democratic educational system of the American university. Utopian University preserved the formal features of democracy while it actually operated as an oppressive form of authoritarianism in which the president tyrannized the entire university. In contrast, at Cosmopolitan University, while power was indeed in the hands of the tenured faculty, in many of the larger departments it was not being exercised in the form of a responsible democracy, but rather was fragmented and deployed in the vicious politics of contending cliques.

Cosmopolitan University was in fact riven by contending factions. The major point of contest was the P & B (Personnel and Budget) Committee. I was thrust into the center of clique rivalry by the fact that as a full professor my vote counted heavily in partisan politics. I soon learned that the current chairperson of the department had managed to beat out another aspiring faculty member in the contest for the chairpersonship. His rival was scheduled to return from a sabbatical and was determined to depose him.

The disaffected professor immediately visited me upon his return to the campus and offered me the chairpersonship. When he learned that I was not interested, he requested that I support his own candidacy. I refused to commit myself to him, as a result of which he became a deadly enemy. I felt, after all, loyalty to the current chairperson, who had always treated me with warmth and decency. I wished only to remain neutral in the contest. While I had the rank of full professor, I was not tenured. It seemed inappropriate for me to enter the clique conflicts when they would have to pass judgment on me. In the end my neutrality was probably responsible for helping the disaffected professor win the chairpersonship. At the election meeting for a new chairperson which I declined to attend, he won by a majority of a single vote. Had I been there and voted against him the council would have been deadlocked. Later, the new chairperson made my life miserable; his reasoning seemed to be that since I was not at the meeting I did not vote for him.

At Cosmopolitan University, power was concentrated in the division P & B committees. In my division, the P & B Committee consisted of tenured professors (or in many cases full but nontenured professors) elected for three years. By majority vote, P & B committees recommended appointment or dismissal of nontenured faculty; decided the hours courses were to be given by the staff; approved or disapproved of courses; recommended promotions; and decided on leaves of absence and sabbaticals. Legally, these functions belong to the administration, but in fact, the P & B committees had full practical control over them.

During my stay at Cosmopolitan, we had a serious strike which eventually required police intervention. The strike was conducted by radical students and was headed by a group of professors. They were protesting the administration's refusal to rehire an instructor newly hired by the faculty P & B (composed of the chairpersons of various departments) and its refusal to hire a popular instructor who had substituted one semester for a professor on leave of absence.

The P & B system forced every member of the department to engage in full-time departmental politics. Anyone who wished to be retained, promoted, or assigned reasonable hours of teaching had to court the favor of the P & B Committee. Sooner or later, everyone, including the department head—if for no other reason than self-preservation—was drawn into the power struggles of the department. The result was chronic internecine political struggle, both open and hidden, carried on by factional combinations that continually formed and dissolved. Deals were made and betrayed. The chairperson had to worry about keeping not only his departmental P & B Committee in line, but the faculty P & B Committee as well.

The new chairperson quickly demonstrated his power to his supporters and over his opponents. He ensured conformity by assigning his friends to evaluate nontenured individuals. Favorable evaluations depended on the degree to which the individual concerned cooperated with the ruling elite. While a formal evaluating report was submitted on such items as colleagueship and teaching abilities of the evaluated individual, the real foundations of the evaluation never entered such reports.

In the first semester of his appointment, the new chairperson evaluated my teaching by visiting one of my classes in person. In the second semester, however, as observer he sent a young twenty-six year old, who had just had received tenure and who had never taught anywhere else. The chairperson's committee voted not to renew my contract.

When I appealed the recommendation to the faculty P & B Committee, I had to appear personally in my defense and answer such accusations as I upset most students with my "queer" ideas; I tried to attract students sexually; my writings were disgraceful; and I was an anti-Semite.

Ultimately, I was saved only by a split of the department into two separate and independent factions, which resulted in the election of a new chairperson and his committee which unanimously favored my retention. On appeal of this new committee, the recommendation of my dismissal by the previous committee was reversed.

Before the division of the department went into effect, however, the antagonized chairperson did all he could to destroy me. For the fall semester he assigned me to teach courses at 8:00 A.M. and 5:00 P.M., five days a week—this, despite the fact that all other department assignments were limited to four times a week, and courses were assigned in a limited time period (early or late morning or early or late afternoon) to conserve an individual's time. I appealed to the dean of instruction to check into my case for possible harassment, but the chairperson defended his action by citing the regulations of the Board of Education giving to each department sole responsibility for its assignments and hours of each class. Only with the election of the new chairperson was my teaching schedule amended.

The new department head lasted only two years, although he had been elected for three. He had been elected by persons excluded from power under the previous regime and hence determined to revenge themselves for past injustices and to take advantage of power now that they had it. Savage new political struggles had gotten under way even before his election.

REFLECTIONS ON THE MODELS

If the traditional objectives of education are the transmission of culture, socialization of the individual, and the provision of vocational and professional skills, then it must be said that both the authoritarian and permissive models of American higher education are largely failures.

Despite all the Madison Avenue fluff and despite all the fine slogans concerning open admissions, equal opportunity, and the like, educational experiments all too often tend to backfire and to become ends in themselves and new arenas for contests of power. For all their bizarre appearance, the minority of students who participated in the counter-cultural revolts of the 1960s, the flower children, peaceniks, beatniks, and the like had a point when they accused the universities of being self-centered and of distorting the true ends of education. And yet the counter-cultural revolt, too, backfired. And if any generalization has any validity, it would be that in both the authoritarian and permissive models, excellence is the first quality to be sacrificed.

The miserly wages paid by the authoritarian institution and the overpayment (the highest in the United States) in the permissive institutions both lead to the alienation of the faculty from educational aims. Those who are underpaid, terrorized, and constantly reminded as to how fortunate they are to have their jobs eventually abandon all educational idealism and seek merely to survive. Those who are overpaid tend to conceive of their jobs in terms of financial reward; they tend to do only the minimum teaching since most of their energies are devoted to political maneuverings to attain better paying executive positions (especially once tenure is achieved). They therefore view their educational task as a necessary evil interfering with their fundamental interests.

Both models lead to poor selections of new faculty and to inadequate teaching methods. In the authoritarian example, in order to save money there is pressure to select cheap, even unqualified, instructors and to keep their salaries down by constant threats of dismissal. In the permissive system, the low caliber of the new instructors can be attributed to another factor. The P & B system forces the members to select "safe" applicants, and, certainly, no one who might be or is better qualified than the P & B members. In both cases, real motives are concealed by smoke screens: "We get the best that we can pay"; the search for new faculty must be nationwide and even global; chances must be given to minorities and even outstanding foreign scholars. If the pressure from the critics or the trustees or the Board of Education is great, appointments are postponed until the last day and made arbitrarily at the last moment, since "the classes have to be covered." (We do not dare to discuss here the role racism and religion has in this process.)

Those hired in both models typically do not have their Ph.Ds (or even the newly devised substitute degrees, such as Doctor of Education); some have only their B.A. degrees. The administration's pressure on such aspirants to acquire higher degrees nearly always becomes ineffective, once the instructor has tenure. (In-depth research should provide concrete evidence that not a single tenured professor has ever been dismissed for not acquiring the Ph.D. after being tenured "for life.")

Even more serious consequences result form hiring poorly qualified instructors. In both models, faculty members justify their failure to obtain advanced degrees by devoting their energies to "politicking," public and committee functions, running various organizations on the campus, and giving public lectures off campus. In short, they can claim they have no time to take advanced degree courses. Especially in the case of the permissive model, teaching becomes a sideline activity, if not an actual nuisance. A favorite teaching technique is to "lecture" by reading passages from a textbook not known to the students or copying passages from various encyclopediae while giving the impression that they are the products of original research. Married instructors frequently miss classes due to the "sickness of my children"; others miss classes without reporting them to the administration; and some disappear for weeks on "educational tours" while their classes are being "taken care of" by willing chairpersons. To salvage their popularity, such non-instructors may allow their students unlimited absences, give only one or two examinations each semester, and even permit their students to write up their final examinations at home.

Such practitioners of advanced methods of teaching usually receive high evaluations by most students, especially those who attend classes only once in a while, who do not write term papers, and who are as addicted as their instructors to the art of "discussion." There is no easier or surer route to popularity than conducting classes by discussion, especially about current topics, and by demanding no preparation or factual information. Everyone in class has his own opinions about the moral, political, and aesthetic aspects of any current problem. Since the less they know about a problem, the more their emotionalism, such discussions give the participants a sense of their self-importance. As for the professor, such classes require only minimal preparation.

Another popular technique is to hold class by arranging visits to the local museums, jails, police stations, ghettoes, or theaters, and then having the students write up their impressions. Such trips avoid the bother of attending classes. The open admissions students are a class of their own. I found nearly all of them to be hopeless students, for to be of value courses in social science require at least some knowledge of history, contemporary events, and the basic theories of society (a *terra incognita* for these unfortunates). I was asked such questions as "What is Zionism?" "You are constantly mentioning Stalin; who is he?" The administration tried to alleviate this situation by suggesting that we hold special briefing sessions during our office hours for such students. Since there was no check on these office hours, they simply were not held.

In summary, it is apparent that in both models the original aims of education, tested by centuries, are being perverted or denied validity, that the educational machinery is being operated more for the sake of ruling cliques than for students, and that politics pervades all higher educational processes. While it is true that, since Max Weber, we have come to acknowledge that politics penetrates all forms of social life, in the case of American education, there is a definite hiatus between the ideological claims of the educational system and its accomplishments. It is also true that no system is without its "circulation of elites" (as taught by Pareto and others). The only difference between the elite of the authoritarian model discussed here is that it was headed by a small elite and its courses determined by a single strong man (and often his wife); in the case of the permissive model, the diffusion of power in the P & B committees intensified the power struggle, since the competition was focused on many individuals rather than on a single noncharismatic personality.

Above all, the unchallenged belief in the promises of both models, that "education for everybody will solve all problems," may be seen as one of the great illusions of our age. It allows the rise and prominence of "educators," who are selling the idea to an uncritical public that the operations from which they derive so many personal benefits are inseparable from the cause of a tested and valuable education.

BARBARA JEAN WILKE

Bibliography: Selected Concerns in Higher Education, 1969 to the Present

This bibliography is devoted to some of the pressing concerns in higher education that have an effect on the prospect and fate of the hidden professoriate. In researching the literature, several things are readily apparent in reviewing the various sections of the bibliography:

—While there is a general agreement that a crisis in higher education exists, the nature of the problem and its solutions remain areas of intense debate (I).

—Many debates on the legitimacy of higher education center on the economic payoffs of the post-secondary degree (II).

—Knowledge of the graduate student experience is quite limited (III).

—The prospect of a steady-state or incipient decline in the economics of higher education finds administrators increasingly urged to employ more businesslike techniques (IV).

—While the immediate prospects for higher education are not encouraging, the intellectual significance of this fact has not been extensively probed (V).

—Issues of due process have taken on greater significance as the prospects of non-renewal for nontenured faculty have increased (VI).

—One response to the current crisis in higher education has been increased interest in collective bargaining for the faculty. The issue has been widely debated and discussed in journals addressed to college and university administrators (VII).

—Cross-cutting the current controversies of higher education and the faculty are concerns over equal opportunity and affirmative action (VIII). During the 1970s, more attention has been directed at women faculty (X) than other minority faculty (IX).

I. THE CRISES IN HIGHER EDUCATION—GENERAL

Altbach, P., et al. *Academic Supermarkets: A Critical Case Study of a Multiversity.* San Francisco: Jossey-Bass, 1971.

_____. *University Reform.* Cambridge, Mass.: Schenkman, 1974.

"American Higher Education: Toward an Uncertain Future." Volumes I and II. Symposium. *Daedalus* 103, no. 4 (Fall 1974) and 105, no. 1 (Winter 1975).

Aptheker, Bettina. *The Academic Rebellion in the United States.* Secaucus, N.J.: Citadel, 1972.

Astin, A. W., et al. *The Power of Protest: A National Study of Student and Faculty Disruptions with Implications for the Future.* San Francisco: Jossey-Bass, 1975.

_____. *Academic Gamesmanship: Student-Oriented Change in Higher Education.* New York: Praeger, 1976.

Axelrod, J., et al. *Search for Relevance: The Campus in Crisis.* San Francisco: Jossey-Bass, 1969.

Ballotti, G., and S. R. Graubard (eds.). *The Embattled University.* Daedalus Library Series. San Diego and New York: George Braziller, n.d.

Banker, P. *Higher Education in Transition.* Naperville, Ill.: American Society Press, 1975.

Ben-David, J. *Trends in American Higher Education.* Chicago: University of Chicago Press, 1974.

Berke, J. S., et al. *The New Era of State Education Politics.* Philadelphia: Ballinger, 1976.

Birnbaum, N. "The Carnegie Commission. The Politics of the Future." *Change* 5 (November 1973): 28-32, 34-7.

Bloom, A. "The Future of the University." *Daedalus* 103, no. 4 (Fall 1974): 58-66.

Bowen, H. R. "Higher Education: A Growth Industry?" *Educational Record* 55, no. 3 (Summer 1974): 147-58.

Carnegie Commission on Higher Education. *Invisible Colleges: A Profile of Small Private Colleges with Limited Resources.* A. Astin and C. Lee (eds.). New York: McGraw-Hill, 1972.

_____. *New Depression in Higher Education: A Study of the Financial Conditions at 41 Colleges and Universities.* New York: McGraw-Hill, 1971.

_____. *A Statistical Portrait of Higher Education.* S. E. Harris (ed.). New York: McGraw-Hill, 1972.

_____. *The Purposes and the Performance of Higher Education in the U.S. Approaching the Year 2000.* New York: McGraw-Hill, 1973.

_____. *Teachers and Students: Aspects of American Higher Education.* M. Tron (ed.). New York: McGraw-Hill, 1975.

Carnegie Council on Policy Studies in Higher Education. *The Federal Role in Postsecondary Education: Unfinished Business, 1975-80.* San Francisco: Jossey-Bass, 1975.

Carnegie Foundation for the Advancement of Teaching. *More Than Survival: Prospects for Higher Education in a Period of Uncertainty.* San Francisco: Jossey-Bass, 1975.

_____. *The States and Higher Education, A Proved Past and Vital Future.* San Francisco: Jossey-Bass, 1976.

Carnoy, M. *Schooling in a Corporate Society.* New York: David McKay, 1975.

Chambers, M. M. "Panic in Higher Education." *Educational Forum* 38, no. 1 (November 1973): 7-12.

_____. *Higher Education and State Governments, 1970-1975.* Danville, Ill.: Interstate, 1974.

Cheek, K. V., Jr. "Impact of National Trends in Higher Education." *NASPA Journal* 13, no. 1 (Summer 1975): 25-32.

Cohn, S. M. *Eclipse of Excellence.* Washington, D.C.: Public Affairs Press, 1973.

Dennis, L. J. "I Learn You: Accountability at the Academy." *Liberal Education* 61, no. 3 (October 1975): 319-21.

Diamond, R. M. "Academic Redesign in Education: A Matter of Survival." *Audiovisual Instruction* 19, no. 3 (December 1974): 6-8.

Digest of Reports of the Carnegie Commission on Higher Education, A. New York: McGraw-Hill, 1974.

Duffy, J. "Depression, Recovery and Higher Education." *AAUP Bulletin* 13, no. 4 (December 1974): 365-6.

Dugger, R. *Our Invaded Universities: Form, Reform and New Starts.* New York: Norton, 1974.

Eurich, A. C. (ed.). *Nineteen Eighty: The Shape of the Future in American Higher Education.* New York: Delacorte Press, n.d.

Fashing, J., and S. Deutsch. *Academics in Retreat: The Politics of Educational Innovation.* Albuquerque, N.M.: University of New Mexico Press, 1971.

Fincher, C. "The Paradox and Counterpoint of Public Expectations for Higher Education." *Educational Record* 55, no. 2 (Spring 1974): 101-9.

Fortunato, R. T. "Seventies: Decade for Decisions, Revisited." *Journal of the College and University Personnel Association* 26, no. 3 (July 1975): 1-3.

Francis, R. *Crumbling Walls.* Cambridge, Mass.: Schenkman, 1970.

Glenny, L. "Pressures on Higher Education." *College and University Journal*, no. 4 (September 1973): 5-9.

_____. "The Unsteady State: Personnel Impact." *Journal of the College and University Personnel Association* 26, no. 1 (January/February 1975): 1-7.

Harcleroad, F. F. (ed.). *Issues of the Seventies: The Future of Higher Education.* San Francisco: Jossey-Bass, 1970.

Heim, A. *Teaching and Learning in Higher Education.* Atlantic Highlands, N.J.: Humanities Press, 1976.

Henderson, A. D., and J. G. Henderson. *Higher Education in America: Problems, Priorities and Prospects.* San Francisco: Jossey-Bass, 1974.

Henry, D. D. "Accountability: To Whom, for What, by What Means?" *Educational Record* 53, no. 4 (Fall 1972): 287-92.

Herman, W. R. "The University as a National Asset." *Change* 8, no. 5 (June 1976): 31-7.

Holmes, R. M. *Academic Mysteryhouse: The Men, the Campus, and Their New Search for Meaning.* Nashville, Tenn.: Abingdon Press, 1970.

Jamison, D. T., et al. *Education as an Industry.* New York: National Bureau of Economic Research, 1976.

Kerr, Clark, et al. "Follow-up/The Carnegie Report." *Center Magazine* no. 6 (November/December 1973): 46-55.

Landini, R., and P. Douglas (eds.). *Quality in Higher Education in Times of Financial Stress.* Proceedings of the Pacific Northwest Conference on Higher Education. Corvallis, Oreg.: Oregon State University, 1976.

Lineberry, W. P. (ed.). *American Colleges: The Uncertain Future.* Bronx, N.Y.: H. W. Wilson, 1975.

Lyons, M., and J. Lyons. "Power and the University—A Perspective on the Current Crisis." *Sociology of Education* 46, no. 3 (Summer 1973): 299-314.

McCully, G. "Multiversity and University." *Journal of Higher Education* 44, no. 7 (October 1973): 514-31.

McIntyre, J. P. "Legacy of the 60s and the Challenge of the 70s." *Peabody Journal of Education* 52, no. 1 (October 1974): 43-7.

McMurrin, S. M. "Purposes and Problems in Higher Education." *AAUP Bulletin* 60, no. 1 (Spring 1974): 5-7.

Martin, D. (ed.). *Anarchy and Culture: The Problem of the Contemporary University*. Irvington-on-Hudson, N.Y.: Columbia University Press, 1969.

Martin, W. B. *Conformity: Standards and Change in Higher Education*. San Francisco: Jossey-Bass, 1969.

_____. "The Ethical Crisis in Education." *Change* 6, no. 5 (June 1974): 28-33.

Martorana, S. V., and E. Kuhns. *Managing Academic Change: Interactive Forces and Leadership in High Education*. San Francisco: Jossey-Bass, 1975.

Mayer, M. "Everything Is Shrinking in Higher Education." *Fortune* 90, no. 3 (September 1974): 121-5, 190, 192-4, 196, 198.

Mayhew, L. B. "The Steady Seventies." *Journal of Higher Education* 45, no. 3 (March 1974): 163-73.

Millet, J. D. *Politics and Higher Education*. University, Ala.: University of Alabama Press, 1974.

Nisbet, R. "The Decline of Academic Nationalism." *Change* 6, no. 6 (July/ August 1974): 26-31.

_____. "Social Diversity and Higher Education." *Intellect* 105, no. 1 (October 1974): 14.

Noel, B., and A. F. Fontana. "The University as a System with Competing Constituents." *Journal of Conflict Resolution* 18, no. 4 (December 1974): 595-614.

Parker, F. "After Student Protest, What University Reforms?" *Journal of Educational Thought* 3, no. 3 (December 1969): 133-40.

Parsons, T. and G. Platt. *The American University*. Cambridge, Mass.: Harvard University Press, 1973.

Paul, R. J., and R. D. Schooler. "Generation Conflict in Academia." *Personnel Journal* 50, no. 1 (January 1971): 22-7.

Seabury, P. *Universities in the Western World*. Riverside, N.J.: Free Press, 1976.

Shils, E. "Sources of Change in the Character and Function of Universities." *Universities Quarterly* 28, no. 2 (Summer 1974): 310-17.

_____. "The Academic Ethos Under Strain." *Minerva* 13, no. 1 (Spring 1975): 1-37.

Stewart, D. M. *The Politics of Higher Education and Public Policy: A Study of the American Council on Education.* Philadelphia: Ballinger, 1976.

Suchodolski, B. "The Future of Higher Education." *Higher Education* 3, no. 3 (August 1974): 331-40.

Thistlethwaite, D. L. "The Impact of the Episodes of May, 1970 upon American University Students." *Research in Higher Education* 1, no. 3 (1973): 225-43.

Timm, N. H. "A New Method of Measuring States' Higher Education Burden." *Journal of Higher Education* 42, no. 1 (January 1971): 27-33.

Ulam, A. *Fall of the American University.* La Salle, Ill.: Open Court, 1973.

Useem, E. L., and M. Useem (eds.). *The Education Establishment.* Englewood Cliffs, N.J.: Prentice-Hall, 1974.

Van Alstine, C. "Economic Costs of Federally Mandated Social Programs in Higher Education." *Journal of the College and University Personnel Association* 27, no. 1 (April 1976): 16-22.

Weinstein, W. L. "Social Purposes in Search of Higher Education, or Higher Education in Search of Social Purposes?" *Higher Education* 4, no. 4 (November 1975): 409-28.

II. THE CRISES IN HIGHER EDUCATION: INPUTS, OUTPUTS, AND PAYOFFS

Berendzen, R. "Population Changes and Higher Education." *Educational Record* 55, no. 2 (Spring 1974): 110-14.

Bird, C. "Case Against College." *Journal of the National Association of Record* 55, no. 2 '(Spring 1974): 110-14.

Carnegie Commission on Higher Education. *Higher Education and Earnings: College as Investment and a Screening Device.* P. Taubman and T. Wales (eds.). New York: McGraw-Hill, 1974.

_____. *Higher Education and the Labor Market.* M. S. Gordon (ed.). New York: McGraw-Hill, 1974.

Carnoy, M. "Political Consequences of Manpower Formation." *Comparative Education Review* 19, no. 1 (February 1975): 115-28.

Dore, R. P. "Human Capital Theory, the Diversity of Society and the Problem of Quality of Education." *Higher Education* 4, no. 1 (February 1976): 79-102.

Freeman, R. B. "Overinvestment in College Training?" *Journal of Human Resources* 10, no. 3 (Summer 1975): 287-310.

_____, and J. H. Holloman. "The Declining Value of College Going." *Change* 7, no. 7 (September 1975): 24-31.

Hartnett, R. T. *Accountability in Higher Education: A Consideration of Some of the Problems of Assessing College Impacts.* Princeton, N.J.: College Entrance Examination Board, 1971.

"Higher Education, Human Resources and the National Economy." Addresses and Discussion Papers from the 60th Annual Meeting of the Association of American Colleges. *Liberal Education* 60, no. 1 (March 1974): 5-110; 1-200 (Supplement).

Howe, H., II. "The Value of College: A Non Economist's View." *Educational Record* 57, no. 1 (Winter 1976): 5-12.

Jackson, G. A., and G. B. Weathersby. "Individual Demand for Higher Education: A Review and Analysis of Recent Empirical Studies." *Journal of Higher Education* 46, no. 6 (November/December 1975): 623-52.

Larkin, P., and J. Teeple. "Education Must Anticipate Shifts in U.S. Goals." *College and University* 47, no. 1 (Fall 1969): 83-4.

_____. "The Challenge of Higher Education of National Manpower Priorities." *Journal of Higher Education* 41, no. 3 (March 1970): 195-203.

Mills, O. (ed.). *Universal Higher Education: Costs, Benefits, Options.* Washington, D.C.: American Council on Education, 1972.

Raymond, R., and M. Sesnowitz. "The Returns to Investments in Higher Education: Some New Evidence." *Journal of Human Resources* 10, no. 2 (Spring 1975): 139-53.

Renshaw, E. F. "Are We Overestimating the Returns from College Education?" *School Review* 80, no. 3 (May 1972): 459-75.

Schultz, T. W. (ed). *Investment in Education: The Equity-Efficiency Quandary.* Chicago, Ill.: University of Chicago Press, 1972.

Sewell, W. H., and R. M Hauser. *Education, Occupation and Earning: Achievement in the Early Career.* San Francisco: Jossey-Bass, 1973.

Stewart, L. "Unemployment of College Graduates with High Degrees: Time for Action." *Vocational Guidance Quarterly* 21, no. 2 (December 1972): 103-8.

Taubman, P., and T. Wales. *Higher Education and Earnings: College As an Investment and a Screening Device.* New York: National Bureau of Economic Research, 1974.

Thompson, R. B. "Population Trends: Effect on School/College Enrollments." *College Store Journal* 42, no. 5 (August/September 1975): 12-15.

III. GRADUATE STUDENTS AND GRADUATE EDUCATION

"Boom Over in Professional Schools." *Chronicle of Higher Education* 13, no. 2 (September 13, 1976): 4.

Breneman, D. W. "Predicting the Response of Graduate Education to No Growth." *New Directions for Institutional Research* 2, no. 2 (Summer 1975): 77-87.

Carnegie Commission on Higher Education. *Escape from the Doll's House:*

Women in Graduate and Professional School Education. S. D. Felman (ed.). New York: McGraw-Hill, 1974.

Davison, N.J. "Professional Orientation for Doctoral Candidates in the Humanities." *Modern Language Journal* 57, no. 6 (November/ December 1973): 412-15.

Dresch, S. P. "Research, Graduate Education and the University." *Educational Record* 55, no. 3 (Summer 1974): 171-6.

Eble, K. E. "Graduate Students and the Job Market." *Current Issues in Higher Education* 28 (1973): 49-55.

Field, H. S. "Graduate Students' Satisfaction with Graduate Education: Intrinsic Versus Extrinsic Factors." *Journal of Experimental Education* 43, no. 1 (Winter 1974): 8-15.

Heiss, A. M. *Challenges to Graduate Schools.* San Francisco: Jossey-Bass, 1970.

Holmstrom, E. I. "Plight of the Woman Doctoral Student." *American Educational Research Journal* 11, no. 1 (Winter 1974): 1-17.

Jako, K. L. "Let's Abolish the Ph.D. Orals." *Change* 6, no. 7 (September 1974): 8-9, 64.

Katz, J., and R. T. Hartnett (eds.). *Scholars in the Making: The Development of Graduate and Professional Students.* Philadelphia: Ballinger, 1976.

Kidd, Charles V. "Graduate Education: The New Debate." *Change* 6, no. 4 (May 1974): 43-50.

Kline, L. W. "Changing Expectations in the Doctorate." *School and Society* 99 (Fall 1971): 93-4.

Martindale, D. *The Romance of a Profession: A Case History in the Sociology of Sociology.* St. Paul, Minn.: Windflower Publishing, 1976.

Mayhew, L. B., and P. J. Fork. *Reform in Graduate and Professional Education.* San Francisco: Jossey-Bass, 1974.

Millett, J. D. "Public Interest in Graduate Education." *Educational Record* 55, no. 2 (Spring 1974): 79-86.

Mitchell, S. B., and R. T. Alciatore. "Women Doctoral Recipients Evaluate Their Training." *Educational Forum* 34, no. 4 (May 1970): 533-9.

National Board on Graduate Education. *Graduate Schools Adjustments to the New Depression in Higher Education.* Washington, D.C.: National Academy of Sciences, 1975.

————. *Minority Group Participation in Graduate Education.* Washington, D.C.: National Academy of Sciences, 1976.

National Research Council. *Invisible University: Postdoctoral Education in the United States.* Washington, D.C.: National Academy of Sciences, 1969.

Sales, E. "The Doctoral Student Experience: A Preliminary Study." *Journal of Education for Social Work* 11, no. 2 (September 1975): 102-8.

Taylor, A. R. "Graduate School Experience: Excerpts from Essays by Graduate Students." *Personnel and Guidance Journal* 54, no. 1 (September 1975): 34-9.

University, Government and the Foreign Graduate Student. Princeton, N.J.: College Entrance Examination Board, 1969.

Weisinger, H. "Consumerism, Manpower Management, and Graduate Education." *Journal of Higher Education* 46, no. 5 (September 1975): 585-99.

IV. RESOURCE ALLOCATION: THE ADMINISTRATORS' CONCERNS

Andrew, L. D., and L. Robertson. "PPBS in Higher Education: A Case Study." *Educational Record* 54, no. 1 (Winter 1973): 60-7.

Balderston, F. E. "Cost Analysis in Higher Education." *California Management Review* 17, no. 1 (Fall 1974): 93-107.

Bowen, H. R. "Manpower Management and Higher Education." *Educational Record* 54, no. 1 (Winter 1973): 5-14.

Carey, W. D. "Policy-Making in a Negotiating Society." *Journal of Medical Education* 51, no. 1 (January 1976): 14-18.

Cleveland, H. "The Costs of 'Openness'." *AGB Reports* 17, no. 5 (March/April 1975): 7-10.

Dressel, P. L. *Handbook of Academic Evaluation: Assessing Institutional Effectiveness, Student Progress, and Professional Performance for Decision Making Higher Education.* San Francisco: Jossey-Bass, 1974.

Dyer, J. S. "The Use of PPBS in a Public System of Higher Education: 'Is It Cost-Effective'?" *Academy of Management Journal* 13, no. 3 (September 1970): 285-99.

Hakala, D. R. "Resource Allocation Problems of Reduced Growth in College Enrollments." *Journal of the College and University Personnel Association* 25, no. 2 (December 1973): 40-3.

Hoenack, S. A., and A. L. Norman. "Incentives and Resource Allocation in Universities." *Journal of Higher Education* 45, no. 1 (January 1974): 21-37.

Ives, F. A. "Curbing the Crunch on Higher Education." *Journal of the College and University Personnel Association* 25, no. 4 (October 1974): 72-5.

Keene, C. M. "Administration of Systemwide Faculty and Staff Affairs." *Public Administration Review* 30, no. 2 (March/April 1970): 113-17.

Kenny, Philip W. "Reflections on Educational Capitalism." *College and University* 51, no. 1 (Fall 1975): 44-8.

Kerr, C. "Administration in an Era of Change and Conflict." *Educational Record* 54, no. 1 (Winter 1973): 38-46.

Lupton, A. H., J. Augenblick, and J. Heyison. "The Financial State of Higher Education." *Change* 8, no. 8 (September 21-26, 1976): 28-35.

Mills, J. L. "Court Decisions and Financing." *Community and Junior College Journal* 43, no. 4 (December/January 1972-73): 14-15.

Morgan, A. W. "Flexibility for Whom: The Case of Forced Savings in Budgeting for Higher Education." *Educational Record* 56, no. 1 (Winter 1975): 42-7.

Smith, C. S. "Resource Allocation in Education." *Journal of Educational Administration* 9, no. 2 (October 1971): 135-50.

Van Fleet, D. D., and B. D. Stone, Jr. "Progression Curves in Salary Administration for Colleges and Universities." *Journal of the College and University Personnel Association* 26, no. 3 (July 1975): 20-7.

Weiss, E. H. "Apples, Oranges and College Administration." *College Management* 8, no. 9 (November/December 1973): 26-7.

V. THE FACULTY: THEIR SITUATION AND PROSPECTS

Allen, A. D., Jr. "Organizing the Eggheads: Professors and Collective Bargaining." *Labor Law Journal* 23, no. 10 (October 1972): 606-17.

Atwood, L. E., and S. Crain. "Changes in Faculty Attitudes Toward University Role and Governance." *Journal of Experimental Education* 41, no. 4 (Summer 1973): 1-9.

Anderson, C., and J. Murray (eds.). *The Professors.* Cambridge, Mass.: Schenkman, 1971.

Bayer, A. E. "College Faculties: 'Le Plus ça Change . . .'" *Change* 6, no. 2 (March 1974): 49-50, 63.

———. "Faculty Composition, Institutional Structure and Students' College Environment." *Journal of Higher Education* 46, no. 5 (September 1975): 549-65.

Bezdel, R. H. "Whither the Market for College Faculty." *College and University* 49, no. 1 (Fall 1973): 77-100.

Bornheimer, D. G., et al. *Faculty in Higher Education.* Danville, Ill.: Interstate, 1973.

Budig, G. A., and C. R. Decker. "Assistant Professors Disillusioned by Tenure Believe Unionization Offers Better Protection." *Phi Delta Kappan* 55, no. 2 (October 1973): 143-4.

Buswell, J. O. "Publish or Perish?" *College and University* 23, no. 1 (Autumn 1975): 219.

Carnegie Commission on Higher Education. *The Divided Academy: Professors and Politics.* E. Ladd (ed.). New York: McGraw-Hill, 1975.

Carnegie Commission on Higher Education. *Ph.D.'s and the Academic Labor Market.* A. M. Cartter (ed.). New York: McGraw-Hill, 1976.

Cartter, A. M. "Faculty Manpower Planning." *Current Issues in Higher Education* 25 (1970): 231-9.

_____, and J. M. McDowell. "Changing Employment Patterns and Faculty Demographics." *New Directions for Institutional Research* 2, no. 2 (Summer 1975): 49-75.

Entine, A., and A. Zambrano (eds.). *A Guide to Career Alternatives for Academics.* New Rochelle, N.Y.: Change Magazine, 1976.

Feuille, P., and J. Blandin. "Faculty Job Satisfaction and Bargaining Sentiments: A Case Study." *Academy of Management Journal* 17, no. 4 (December 1974): 678-92.

_____. "University Faculty and Attitudinal Militancy Toward the Employment Relationship." *Sociology of Education* 49, no. 2 (April 1976): 139-45.

_____. "Determinants of Attitudinal Militancy Among University Faculty." *Educational Administration Quarterly* 12, no. 1 (Winter 1976): 54-66.

Fox, D. L. "Academe in the Marketplace." *College and University* 45, no. 1 (Fall 1969): 77-81.

Golatz, H. J. "Restive Faculty." *Educational Forum* 37, no. 4 (May 1973): 453-8.

Golozor, E. "Coming of Age in Academe or How I Finally Stopped Flitting Around from School to School, from Department to Department, Settled Down and Got a Ph.D. Seven Years After I was Supposed to, Got Shipped to Africa and Was Never Heard of Again, and Got Shipped Home and Was Never Heard of Again Again." *Change* 7, no. 5 (June 1975): 39-43.

Gusfield, J. "American Professors: The Decline of a Cultural Elite." *School Review* 83, no. 4 (August 1975): 595-616.

Hargens, L. L. "Patterns of Mobility of New Ph.D.'s Among American Academic Institutions." *Sociology of Education* 42, no. 1 (January 1969): 18-37.

Karns, L. T. "Potential Professors: Sought or Not?" *Improving College and University Teaching* 18, no. 3 (Summer 1970): 210-2.

Kelly, R., and B. D. Hart. "Role Preferences of Faculty in Different Age Groups and Academic Disciplines." *Sociology of Education* 44, no. 3 (Summer 1971): 351-7.

King, M. "Anxieties of University Teachers." *Universities Quarterly* 28 (Winter 1973): 69-83.

Ladd, E. C., and S. M. Lipset. *Professors, Unions and American Higher*

Education. Washington, D.C.: American Enterprise Institute for Public Policy Research, 1973.

Lewis, L. *Scaling the Ivory Tower: Merit and Its Limits in Academic Careers.* Baltimore, Md.: Johns Hopkins University Press, 1975.

Lindemann, L. W. "Five Most Cited Reasons for Faculty Unionization." *Intellect* 102, no. 2 (November 1973): 85-8.

Livesey, H. *The Professors.* New York: Charterhouse Books, 1975.

Lozier, G. G. "Changing Attitudes Toward the Use of Strikes in Higher Education." *Journal of the College and University Personnel Association* 25, no. 2 (April 1974): 41-8.

McGee, R. *Academic Janus: The Private College and Its Faculty.* San Francisco: Jossey-Bass, 1971.

Martindale, D. *The Romance of a Profession: A Case History in the Sociology of Sociology.* St. Paul, Minn.: Windflower Publishing, 1976.

Nixon, H. L. "Faculty Support of University Authority." *Administrative Science Quarterly* 20, no. 1 (March 1975): 114-23.

Rivlin, H. N. "College's Responsibility to Its Faculty." *Teachers College Record* 75, no. 3 (February 1974): 327-32.

Roszak, T. (ed.). *The Dissenting Academy.* New York: Vintage Books, 1968[1967].

Shull, Fremont A. "The Changing Campus Community: The Faculty." *Journal of the College and University Personnel Association* 20, no. 1 (November 1968): 30-6.

VI. TENURE, NON-RENEWAL, DUE PROCESS, AND RELATED CONCERNS

Allshouse, M. F. "New Academic Slalom: Mission, Personnel Planning, Financial Exigency, Due Process." *Liberal Education* 61, no. 3 (October 1975): 349-68.

Arns, R. G. "Has Tenure Gotten Out of Hand?" *Journal of Physical Education and Recreation* 46, no. 3 (October 1975): 36-8.

Benewitz, M. C., and T. Mannix. "Grievance Procedure in Higher Education Contracts." *Community and Junior College Journal* 44, no. 4 (December/January 1974): 22-4.

Bonanno, J. "Academic Due Process in Colleges." *Educational Form* 40, no. 2 (January 1976): 185-97.

Brubacher, J. "The Impact of the Courts on Higher Education." *Journal of Law and Education* 2, no. 2 (April 1973): 267-82.

Canavan, F. "The Process That Is Due." *Journal of Higher Education* 44, no. 2 (February 1973): 114-23.

Carr, R. K. "Uneasy Future of Academic Tenure." *Educational Record* 53, no. 2 (Spring 1972): 119-27.

Chait, R., and A. T. Ford. "Affirmative Action, Tenure and Unionization." *Current Issues in Higher Education* 29 (1974): 123-30.

Commission on Academic Tenure in Higher Education. *Faculty Tenure: A Report and Recommendations.* Keast, W. R. (ed.). San Francisco: Jossey-Bass, 1973.

Cormican, J. D. "Dean Man (or Woman) in Academe." *AAUP Bulletin* 61, no. 1 (April 1975): 39-48.

Crase, D. "Tenure Crisis: Implications for Higher Education Faculty." *Physical Educator* 32, no. 3 (October 1975): 115-20.

Crase, D. R., and D. Crase. "New Tenure and Promotion Guidelines Produce Growth Pains." *Peabody Journal of Education* 54, no. 1 (October 1976): 56-9.

Devaughn, J. E. "Termination and Due Process—A Comment." *Journal of Law and Education* 2, no. 2 (April 1973): 305-11.

Dill, D. D. "Tenure Quotas: Their Impact and an Alternative." *Liberal Education* 60, no. 4 (December 1974): 467-77.

"Due Process and Tenure in Institutions of Higher Education." *Today's Education* 61, no. 4 (December 1972): 60-2.

Eddy, E. D., and R. L. Morrill. "Living with Tenure Without Quotas." *Liberal Education* 61, no. 3 (October 1975): 399-417.

Furniss, W. T. "Giving Reasons for Nonrenewal of Faculty Contracts." *Educational Record* 52, no. 4 (Fall 1971): 328-37.

———. "Steady-State Staffing: Issues for 1974." *Educational Record* 55, no. 2 (Spring 1974): 87-95.

———. "Retrenchment, Layoff and Termination." *Educational Record* 55, no. 3 (Summer 1974): 159-70.

Gillis, J. W. "Academic Staff Reductions in Response to Financial Exigency." *Liberal Education* 57, no. 3 (October 1971): 364-77.

Griffin, D. W. "If Not Tenure, What?" *Journal of the National Association of Admissions Counselors* 20, no. 1 (July 1975): 26-9.

Hackerman, N. "Uses and Abuses of Tenure." *Journal of Medical Education* 50, no. 3 (March 1975): 252-6.

"Halloween Special: Hobgoblins and Witches: Professors Denied Academic Tenure for Political Reasons." *Saturday Review* 53 (November 21, 1970).

Hamblin, W. H. "Mandatory Retirement and Dismissal in Institutions of Higher Learning." *Journal of the College and University Personnel Association* 27, no. 2 (April 1976): 1-15.

Hechinger, F. M. "Loss of Tenure: Return of a Nightmare." *Saturday Review* 2 (May 31, 1975): 49-51.

Hildebrand, M. "How to Recommend Promotion for a Mediocre Teacher Without Actually Lying." *Journal of Higher Education* 43, no. 1 (January 1972): 44-62.

Hoppins, D.S.P. "Analysis of Faculty Appointment, Promotion and Retirement Policies." *Higher Education* 3, no. 4 (November 1974): 397-418.

House, E. R. "The Politics of Evaluation in Higher Education." *Journal of Higher Education* 55, no. 8 (November 1974): 618-27.

Hughes, R. E. "How to Solve the Tenure Problem: Departmental or College Professorship." *College Management* 9, no. 1 (January 1974): 7ff.

Jackson, F. H., and R. S. Wilson. "Toward a New System of Academic Tenure." *Educational Record* 52, no. 4 (Fall 1971): 338-42.

Johnson, H. C., Jr. "Court, Craft, and Competence: A Reexamination of 'Teacher Evaluation' Procedures." *Phi Delta Kappan* 57, no. 9 (May 1976): 606-11.

Joughin, L. (ed.). *Academic Freedom and Tenure: A Handbook of the American Association of University Professors.* Madison, Wis.: University of Wisconsin Press, 1969.

Keck, D. J. "Tenure: Who Needs It?" *Phi Delta Kappan* 54, no. 2 (October 1972): 124-7.

LaNoue, G. R. "Tenure and Title VII." *Journal of College and University Law* 1, no. 3 (Spring 1974).

Lewis, L. S. "Academic Freedom: A New Threat?" *Journal of Higher Education* 44, no. 7 (October 1973): 548-61.

Lockard, J. "Tenure Controversy." *Journal of General Education* 25, no. 3 (July 1973): 121-35.

Lombardi, J. "When Faculties Are Reduced: Community Colleges." *Change* 6, no. 10 (December/January 1974-75): 55-6.

Luecke, J. "Alternative to Quotas: A Model for Controlling Tenure Proportions." *Journal of Higher Education* 45 (May 1974): 273-84.

Lunine, M. J. "Alternative to Tenure." *Current Issues of Higher Education* 29 (1974): 142-5.

McDonald, J. G. "Faculty Tenure as a Put Option: An Economic Interpretation." *Social Science Quarterly* 55, no. 2 (September 1974): 362-71.

McHugh, W. F. "Faculty Unions and Tenure." *Journal of College and University Law* 1, no. 1 (February 1973): 46-73.

Maier, R. H., and J. W. Kolka, "Retrenchment—A Primer." *Liberal Education* 59, no. 4 (December 1973): 433-41.

Malpass, L. F. "Dividing Up the Tenure Pie." *College and University Business* 57, no. 8 (August 1974): 33-5.

Manard, A. P. "May Tenure Rights of Faculty Be Bargained Away?" *Journal of College and University Law* 2, no. 3 (Spring 1975): 256-68.

Mann, W. R. "Is the Tenure Controversy a Red Herring?" *Journal of Higher Education* 44, no. 3 (October 1973): 85-94.

Metzler, J. H., and D. J. Brandon. "Tenure and Faculty Collective Bargaining Seem Certain to Lead to Binding Arbitration." *College Management* 9, no. 3 (March 1974): 4.

Miller, J. P. "Tenure: Bulwark of Academic Freedom and Brake on Change." *Educational Record* 51, no. 3 (Summer 1970): 241-5.

Morris, A. M. "Flexibility and the Tenured Academic." *Higher Education Review* 6, no. 2 (Spring 1974): 3-25.

Nisbet, R. "The Future of Tenure." *Change* 5, no. 2 (April 1973): 36-40.

"On the Imposition of Tenure Quotas." *AAUP Bulletin* 59, no. 2 (June 1973): 185-7.

Schier, R. F. "Problem of Lumpenprofessoriat," *AAUP Bulletin* 56, no. 4 (December 1970): 361-5.

Shultz, W. O. "Nontenured Faculty: Current Legal and Practical Problems in Connection with Nonrenewal of Such Appointments." *Journal of College and University Law* 1, no. 1 (February 1973): 74-83.

Simpson, W. A. "Tenure: A Perspective of Past, Present and Future." *Educational Record* 56, no. 1 (Winter 1975): 48-54.

Sinowitz, B. E. "Fighting Reductions in Forces." *Today's Education* 64, no. 4 (March 1975): 32.

Smith, B. L., et al. *Tenure Debate.* San Francisco: Jossey-Bass, 1973.

Smith, V. H. "Modest Proposal for Improving Promotion and Tenure Procedures." *Phi Delta Kappan* 52 (December 1970): 256.

Sprenger, J. M., and R. E. Schultz. "Staff Reduction Policies." *College Management* 9, no. 5 (May 1974): 22-3.

"Statement on Professors and Political Activity." *AAUP Bulletin* 55, no. 3 (September 1969): 388-9.

Teacher's Day in Court: Review of 1969, The. National Education Association, Research Report 1970-R8, 1970, 57 pp.

"Teachers Defend Tenure." *Intellect* 102, no. 2 (November 1973): 72-3.

"Tenure: Status and Prognoses." Symposium. M. Lieberman (ed.). *Phi Delta Kappan* 56, no. 7 (March 1975): 450-60.

"Termination of Faculty Appointments Because of Financial Exigency, Discontinuance of a Program or Department or Medical Reasons." *AAUP Bulletin* 61, no. 4 (December 1975): 329-31.

Tucker, J. C. "Financial Exigency—Rights, Responsibilities, and Recent Decisions." *Journal of College and University Law* 2, no. 2 (Winter 1974-75): 103-13.

Van Alstyne, W. "Tenure and Collective Bargaining." *Current Issues in Higher Education* 26 (1971): 210-17.

_____. "The Supreme Court Speaks to the Untenured: A Comment on Board of Regents v. Roth and Perry v. Sinderman."

West, Richard R. "Tenure Quotas and Financial Flexibility in Colleges and Universities." *Educational Record* 55, no. 2 (Spring 1974): 96-100.

Yearbook of School Law, The. Topeka, Kan.: National Organization on Legal Problems of Education, 1972.

_____. Topeka, Kan.: National Organization on Legal Problems of Education, 1973.

VII. ISSUES AND RESPONSES TO RETRENCHMENT: COLLECTIVE BARGAINING AND GOVERNANCE

Allen, A. D., Jr. "Organizing the Eggheads: Professors and Collective Bargaining." *Labor Law Journal* 23, no. 10 (October 1972): 606-17.

Angell, G. W. "Suggested Responses to the Impact of Academic Collective Bargaining on University Costs and Structures." *Journal of the College and University Personnel Association* 27, no. 1 (January 1976): 39-44.

Atwood, L. E., and S. Crais. "Change in Faculty Attitudes Toward University Roles and Governance." *Journal of Experimental Education* 41, no. 4 (Summer 1973): 1-9.

Baldridge, J. V. (ed.). *Academic Governance: Research on Institutional Politics and Decision-making.* Berkeley, Calif.: McCutchan Publishing, 1971.

_____, and F. R. Kemerer. "Academic Senates and Faculty Collective Bargaining." *Journal of Higher Education* 47, no. 4 (July/August 1976): 391-411.

Begin, J. P., and J. Chernick. "Collective Bargaining Agreements in Colleges and Universities: Grievance and Job Allocation Provisions." *Journal of the College and University Personnel Association* 22 (May 1971): 52-63.

_____. "Faculty Bargaining in 1973: A Loss of Momentum." *Journal of College and University Personnel Association* 5, no. 2 (April 1974): 74-81.

Boyd, W. B. "Collective Bargaining in Academe: Causes and Consequences." *Liberal Education* 57, no. 3 (October 1971): 306-18.

Brown, R. S., and I. Kugler. "Collective Bargaining for the Faculty." *Liberal Education* 56, no. 1 (March 1970): 26-9.

Bucklew, N. S. "Administering a Faculty Agreement." *Journal of the College and University Personnel Association* 22 (May 1971): 46-51.

_____. "Collective Bargaining and Policymaking." *Current Issues in Higher Education* 29 (1974): 136-41.

Carnegie Commission on Higher Education. *Faculty Bargaining, Change and Conflict.* J. W. Gabain (ed.). New York: McGraw-Hill, 1975.

Chait, R., and A. T. Ford. "Affirmative Action, Tenure and Unionization." *Current Issues in Higher Education* 29 (1974): 123-30.

Chamberlain, P. C. "Collective Bargaining and Legal Influences in Higher Education." *Viewpoints* 52, no. 5 (September 1976): 51-63.

Coleman, D. R. "Evolution of Collective Bargaining as It Relates to Higher Education in America." *Journal of the College and University Personnel Association* 23 (March 1972): 40-66.

"Collective Bargaining: A Symposium." *Community and Junior College Journal* 44, no. 5 (December 1973): 12-31.

"Collective Bargaining: Symposium." *Journal of the College and University Personnel Association* 25, no. 2 (April 1974): 1-103.

"Collective Bargaining Goes to College." *Pennsylvania School Journal* 121, no. 1 (September 1972): 6-13.

"Collective Bargaining in Postsecondary Institutions: Panel Discussion." *Compact* 6, no. 4 (August 1972): 30.

Crossland, F. E. "Will the Academy Survive Unionization?" *Change* 8, no. 1 (February 1976): 38-42.

Danoy, N. B. "Affirmative Action in Labor Contracts: Some Implications for College and University Personnel." *Civil Rights Digest* 5, no. 3 (October 1972): 41-5.

Dement, J. "Collective Bargaining: A New Myth and Ritual for Academe." *Peabody Journal of Education* 50, no. 1 (October 1972): 3-7.

Duryea, E. D., and R. S. Fisk. *Faculty Unions and Collective Bargaining.* San Francisco: Jossey-Bass, 1973.

Edmonson, W. F. "Arbitration: Resolving Conflict in Higher Education." *Personnel Administrator* 19, no. 6 (September 1974): 32-4.

Enarson, H. L. "Tinkering with University Government." *Educational Record* 54, no. 1 (Winter 1973): 47-50.

Ferguson, Tracy H. "Collective Bargaining in Universities and Colleges." *Journal of the College and University Personnel Association* 20, no. 1 (November 1968): 1-23.

Finkin, M. W. "Collective Bargaining and University Government." *AAUP Bulletin* 57, no. 2 (January 1971): 149-62.

Fratkin, S. "Collective Bargaining and Affirmative Action." *Journal of the College and University Personnel Association* 26, no. 3 (July 1975): 53-62.

Goodwin, H. I., and J. Andes. "Contract Trends in Higher Education Collective Bargaining: 1972." *Journal of Collective Negotiations in the Public Sector* 1, no. 4 (Fall 1972): 299-307.

Graham, H. E., A. V. Sinicropi, and P. A. Veglahn. "The Extent of Collec-
tive Bargaining in Higher Education—A Pilot Study." *Journal of the
College and University Personnel Association* 24, no. 3 (May 1973):
45-59.
Hanley, L. W. "Issues and Models for Collective Bargaining in Higher
Education." *Liberal Education* 57, no. 1 (March 1971): 5-14.
Hedgepeth, R. C. "Consequences of Collective Bargaining in Higher Educa-
tion." *Journal of Higher Education* 45, no. 6 (November 1974): 691-705.
Hill, F. "Unions Fight Quotas and Periodic Reassessments: U.S. Campuses."
The Times [London] Literary Supplement, No. 3060 (January 18,
1974), p. 16.
Howe, R. A. "Collective Bargaining and Accreditation in Higher Education:
An Examiner's Point of View." *North Central Association Quarterly*
47, no. 4 (Winter 1973): 270-4.
Ianni, L. "Critical State of Collective Bargaining in Higher Education."
Intellect 102, no. 5 (February 1974): 294-6.
Jascourt, H. D., et al. "Faculty Collective Bargaining in Higher Education."
Journal of Law and Education 3, no. 3 (July 1974): 409-55.
Johnson, K. P. "Faculty Collective Bargaining in Public Higher Education."
Educational Record 57, no. 1 (Winter 1976): 34-44.
Katz, E. "Faculty Stakes in Collective Bargaining: Expectations and Reali-
ties." *New Directions for Higher Education* 2, no. 1 (Spring 1974): 27.
Kemerer, F. R., and J. V. Baldridge. *Unions on Campus: A National Study
of the Consequences of Faculty Bargaining*   San Francisco: Jossey-
Bass, 1975.
_____. "The Impact of Faculty Unions on Governance," *Change* 7, no. 10
(December/January 1975-76): 50-1.
Kienart, P., and R. B. Peterson. "Bargaining Alternatives for University
Faculty." *Journal of Collective Negotiations in the Public Sector* 2,
no. 4 (Fall 1973): 433-44.
Kirk, R. "Academic Freedom and the 'Agency Shop'." *Education* 94, no. 3
(February/March 1974): 194-9.
Ladd, E. C., Jr., and S. M. Lipset. "Unionizing the Professoriate." *Change*
5, no. 6 (Summer 1973): 38-44.
_____. *Professors, Unions and American Higher Education*. Washington,
D.C.: American Enterprise Institute for Public Policy Research, 1973.
Leslie, D. W., and R. P. Satryb. "Collective Bargaining and the Manage-
ment of Conflict: Proposed Research Directions." *Journal of the
College and University Personnel Association* 25, no. 2 (April 1974):
12-22.
Lieberman, M. "The Future of Collective Negotiations." *Phi Delta Kappan*
53, no. 4 (December 1971): 214-6.

————. "Impact of Proposed Public Employee Bargaining on State Legislation on Mandatory Subject of Bargaining." *Journal of Collective Negotiations in the Public Sector* 4, no. 2 (1975): 133-65.

Lindeman, L. W. "Five Most Cited Reasons for Faculty Unionization." *Intellect* 102, no. 2 (November 1973): 85-8.

Lipset, S. M. "Faculty Unions and Collegiality." *Change* 7, no. 2 (March 1975): 39-41.

Lozier, G. G. "Changing Attitudes Toward the Use of Strikes in Higher Education." *Journal of the College and University Personnel Association* 25, no. 2 (April 1974): 41-8.

Lussier, V. L. "Faculty Bargaining Associations; National Objectives Versus Campus Contracts." *Journal of Higher Education* 46, no. 5 (September 1975): 507-18.

McHugh, W. F. "National Labor Relations Board Goes to College." *College and University Business* 49 (July 1970): 44.

————. "Faculty Unions and Tenure." *Journal of College and University Law* 1, no. 1 (February 1973): 46-73.

Mannix, Thomas. "Community College Grievance Procedures: A Review of Contract Content in Ninety-Four Colleges." *Journal of the College and University Personnel Association* 25, no. 2 (April 1974): 22-40.

Metzler, J. H., and D. J. Brandon. "Tenure and Faculty Collective Bargaining Seems Certain to Lead to Binding Arbitration." *College Management* 9, no. 3 (March 1974): 4.

Mortimer, K. P., and G. G. Lozier. "Faculty Workloads and Collective Bargaining." *New Direction for Institutional Research* 1, no. 2 (Summer 1974): 49-64.

————, and M. D. Johnson. "Faculty Collective Bargaining in Public Higher Education." *Educational Record* 57, no. 1 (Winter 1976): 34-44.

Nixon, H. L. "Faculty Support of Traditional Labor Tactics on Campus." *Sociology of Education* 48, no. 3 (Summer 1975): 276-86.

Ping, C. J. "On Learning to Live with Collective Bargaining." *Journal of Higher Education* 44, no. 2 (February 1973): 102-13.

————. "Unionization and Institutional Planning." *Educational Record* 54, no. 2 (Spring 1973): 100-6.

Ramsey, M.A., and F. W. Lutz. "Cargo Cult in the Isles of Higher Education." *Journal of the College and University Personnel Association* 26, no. 1 (January 1975): 26-33.

Richardson, R. C., Jr. "Governance and Change—Junior Colleges." *Journal of Higher Education* 44, no. 4 (April 1973): 299-308.

Sadler, B. "Women on the Campus and Collective Bargaining: It Doesn't Have to Hurt to Be a Woman in Labor." *Journal of the College and University Personnel Association* 25, no. 2 (April 1974): 82-9.

Schmeller, K. R. "Collective Bargaining and Women in Higher Education." *College and University Journal* 12, no. 3 (May 1973): 34-6.

"Teacher Unions Press for Bargaining Laws." *Chronicle of Higher Education* 14, no. 3 (March 14, 1977): 1.

Van Alstyne, W. W. "Tenure and Collective Bargaining." *Current Issues in Higher Education* 26 (1971): 210-7.

Weeks, K. M. "Handbook on Collective Bargaining." *Journal of the College and University Personnel Association* 25, no. 2 (April 1974): 1-3.

Zeller, B., et al. "Faculty Collective Bargaining: The End of Professionalism—On the Road to Effective Education?" *Change* 7, no. 2 (March 1975): 48-50.

VIII. EQUAL OPPORTUNITY AND AFFIRMATIVE ACTION: THE FACULTY

"Academic Institutions and Affirmative Action Programs." *Intellect* 102, no. 6 (March 1974): 346.

Cass, J. "Affirmative Action in the Academy." *Saturday Review* (Education) 2 (February 8, 1975): 45.

Boring, P. Z. "Antibias Regulation of Universities: A Biased View?" *AAUP Bulletin* 61, no. 3 (October 1975): 252-5.

Carnegie Commission on Higher Education. *Antibias Regulation of Universities: Faculty Problems and Their Solutions.* New York: McGraw-Hill, n.d.

Chait, R., and A. T. Ford. "Affirmative Action, Tenure and Unionization." *Current Issues in Higher Education* 29 (1974): 123-30.

Danoy, N. B. "Affirmative Action in Labor Contracts: Some Implications for College and University Personnel." *Civil Rights Digest* 5, no. 3 (October 1972): 41-5.

Elwood, A., and R. L. McKeen. "Affirmative Action and Hiring Practices in Higher Education." *Research in Higher Education* 3, no. 4 (December 1975): 359-64.

Garcia, R. L. "Affirmative Action Hiring: Some Perceptions." *Journal of Higher Education* 45, no. 3 (May 1974): 268-72.

Gittell, M. "The Illusion of Affirmative Action." *Change* 7, no. 8 (October 1975): 39-43.

Goldstein, J. M. "Affirmative Action: Equal Employment Rights for Women in Academia." *Teachers College Record* 74 (February 1973): 395-422.

Gould, K. H. "Goals and Timetables vs. Quotas: Nondiscrimination or Reverse Discrimination." *Journal of the National Association for Women Deans, Administrators and Counselors* 40, no. 1 (Fall 1976): 3-6.

Hirl, F. "Unions Fight Quotas and Periodic Reassessments: U.S. Campuses." *The Times [London] Education Supplement*, No. 3060 (January 18, 1974), p. 16.

Hook, S., and M. Todorovich. "The Tyranny of Reverse Discrimination." *Change* 7, no. 10 (December/January 1975-76): 75-6.

Lester, R. A. "The Fallacies of Numerical Goals." *Educational Record* 57, no. 1 (Winter 1976): 58-64.

Loggins, Philip R. "Calculating Staff Affirmative Action Goals and Time-tables." *Journal of the College and University Personnel Association* 24, no. 4 (September 1973): 64-77.

Nickel, J. W. "Preferential Policies in Hiring and Admissions: A Juris-prudential Approach." *Columbia Law Review* 75, no. 3 (April 1975): 534-58.

Nordvall, R. C. "Affirmative Action Implementation: Rightness and Self-Righteousness." *Journal of the College and University Personnel Association* 25, no. 3 (July/August 1974): 21-6.

Ornstein, A. C. "Return of Racial Quotas." *Educational Forum* 40, no. 1 (November 1975): 94ff.

_____. "Two Views of Affirmative Action." *Phi Delta Kappan* 57, no. 11 (December 1975): 242-50.

Potlinger, J. S. "Administering a Solution: Goals Versus Quotas." *Journal of the College and University Personnel Association* 26, no. 1 (January/February 1975): 21-5.

Roberts, S. "Equality of Opportunity in Higher Education: Impact of Contract Compliance and the Equal Rights Amendment." *Liberal Education* 59, no. 2 (May 1973): 202-16.

Shea, B. M. "Two Year Colleges and Inequality." *Integrated Education* 13, no. 1 (January 1975): 38-43.

"Some Thoughts About Affirmative Action: Symposium." *Journal of the College and University Personnel Association* 26, no. 4 (October 1975): 1-48.

Stienback, S. E. "Equal Employment Opportunity on Campus: Issues in 1974." *Journal of the College and University Personnel Association* 25, no. 3 (July/August 1974): 1-7.

Travis, T. G. "Affirmative Action on Campus: How Firm the Foundation?" *Journal of the National Association for Women Deans, Administrators and Counselors* 39, no. 2 (Winter 1976): 50-7.

IX. MINORITY EDUCATORS—WOMEN

Astin, H. A., and A. E. Bayer. "Sex Discrimination in Academe." *Educational Record* 53, no. 2 (Spring 1972): 101-18.

Centra, J. H. "Women with Doctorates." *Change* 7, no. 1 (February 1975): 48-66.

Carnegie Commission on Higher Education. *Opportunities of Women in Higher Education.* New York: McGraw-Hill, 1973.

Chambers, E. L. "Achieving Equity for Women in Higher Education, Graduate Enrollment and Faculty Status." *Journal of Higher Education* 43, no. 3 (October 1972): 517-24.

"Committee on University Women." *College and University Business* 49 (July 1970): 22.

Cottle, T. J. "College Women." *Liberal Education* 60, no. 4 (December 1974): 514-20.

Dinnerman, B. "Sex Discrimination in Academia." *Journal of Higher Education* 42 (April 1971): 253-64.

Elder, P. "Women in Higher Education: Qualified Except for Sex." *NASPA Journal* 13, no. 3 (Fall 1975): 1-17.

Ferber, M. A., and J. W. Loeb. "Performance, Rewards and Perceptions of Sex Discrimination Among Male and Female Faculty." *American Journal of Sociology* 78, no. 4 (June 1973): 995-1002.

Fishel, A. "Organizational Positions of Title IX: Conflicting Perspectives on Sex Discrimination in Education." *Journal of Higher Education* 47, no. 1 (January/February 1976): 93-105.

Furniss, W. T., and P. A. Graham (eds.). *Women in Higher Education.* Washington, D.C.: American Council on Education, 1974.

Harris, A. S. "The Second Sex in Academe." *AAUP Bulletin* 56, no. 3 (September 1970): 283-95.

Goldstein, J. M. "Affirmative Action: Equal Employment Rights for Women in Academia." *Teachers College Record* 74 (February 1973): 395-422.

Hopkins, E. B. "Unemployed! An Academic Woman's Saga." *Change* 5, no. 10 (Winter 1973): 49-53.

Howe, F., et al. *Women and the Power to Change.* Carnegie Commission on Higher Education. New York: McGraw-Hill, 1975.

Johnson, G. E., and F. P. Stafford. "The Earning and Promotion of Women Faculty." *American Economic Review* 64, no. 6 (December 1974): 888-903.

LaSorte, M. A. "Academic Women's Salaries: Equal Pay for Equal Work?" *Journal of Higher Education* 42, no. 4 (April 1971): 265-78.

Liss, L. "Why Academic Women Do Not Revolt: Implications for Affirmative Action." *Sex Roles* 1, no. 3 (1975): 209-23.

Loeb, J., and M. Ferber. "Sex as Predictive of Salary and Status on a University Faculty." *Journal of Educational Measurement* 8, no. 4 (Winter 1971): 235-44.

Oltman, R. M. "Focus on Women in Academe, 1980." *Improving College and University Teaching* 20 (Winter 1972): 73-5.

Reagan, B. B., and B. J. Maynard. "Sex Discrimination in Universities: An Approach Through Internal Labor Market Analysis." *AAUP Bulletin* 60, no. 1 (Spring 1974): 13-21.

Rossi, A., and A. Calderwood (eds.). *Academic Women on the Move.* Beverly Hills, Calif.: Sage, 1973.

Sadker, D., and M. Sadker. "Nepotism: A Cause for Concern." *Phi Delta Kappan* 53 (Fall 1972): 376-7.

Sadler, B. "Women on the Campus and Collective Bargaining: It Doesn't Have to Hurt to Be a Woman in Labor," *Journal of the College and University Personnel Association* 25, no. 2 (April 1974): 82-9.

Schmeller, K. R. "Collective Bargaining and Women in Higher Education." *College and University Journal* 12, no. 3 (May 1973): 34-6.

Sigworth, H. "Legal Status of Antinepotism Regulations: State Universities." *AAUP Bulletin* 58, no. 1 (March 1972): 31-4.

Sinowitz, B. E. "College Faculty Women Fight Sex Bias." *Today's Education* 63, no. 1 (September 1974): 58-9.

Status of Women Faculty and Administrators in Higher Education Institutions, 1971-72. West Haven, Conn.: National Education Association, 1973.

X. MINORITY EDUCATORS—OTHERS

Johnson, S. O. "Minority Educators and Promotion: A Dilemma." *Educational Leadership* 37, no. 11 (April 1974): 633-4.

Mommsen, K. G. "Black Ph.D.s in the Academic Marketplace: Supply, Demand, and Price." *Journal of Higher Education* 45, no. 3 (May 1974): 253-67.

Rafky, D. M. "Black Professor and Academic Freedom." *Negro Educational Review* 22, no. 3 (July 1971): 170-82.

Rist, R. C. "Black Staff, Black Studies, and White Universities: A Study in Contradictions." *Journal of Higher Education* 41, no. 8 (November 1970): 618-29.

Index